ISLAMIC POLITICAL ETHICS

ETHIKON SERIES IN COMPARATIVE ETHICS

The Ethikon Series publishes studies on ethical issues of current importance. By bringing scholars representing a diversity of moral viewpoints into structured dialogue, the series aims to broaden the scope of ethical discourse and to identify commonalities and differences between alternative views.

TITLES IN THE SERIES

Brian Barry and Robert E. Goodin, eds.
Free Movement: Ethical Issues in the Transnational Migration of People and Money

Chris Brown, ed.
Political Restructuring in Europe: Ethical Perspectives

Terry Nardin, ed.
The Ethics of War and Peace: Religious and Secular Perspectives

David R. Mapel and Terry Nardin, eds.
International Society: Diverse Ethical Perspectives

David Miller and Sohail H. Hashmi, eds.
Boundaries and Justice: Diverse Ethical Perspectives

Simone Chambers and Will Kymlicka, eds.
Alternative Conceptions of Civil Society

Nancy L. Rosenblum and Robert Post, eds.
Civil Society and Government

Sohail H. Hashmi, ed.
Foreword by Jack Miles
Islamic Political Ethics: Civil Society, Pluralism, and Conflict

Richard Madsen and Tracy B. Strong, eds.
*The Many and the One:
Religious and Secular Perspectives on Ethical Pluralism in the Modern World*

Margaret Moore and Allen Buchanan, eds.
States, Nations, and Borders: The Ethics of Making Boundaries

ISLAMIC POLITICAL ETHICS

CIVIL SOCIETY, PLURALISM, AND CONFLICT

EDITED BY
Sohail H. Hashmi

WITH A FOREWORD BY
Jack Miles

PRINCETON UNIVERSITY PRESS   PRINCETON AND OXFORD

Copyright © 2002 by Princeton University Press
Published by Princeton University Press, 41 William Street,
Princeton, New Jersey 08540
In the United Kingdom: Princeton University Press, 3 Market Place,
Woodstock, Oxfordshire OX20 1SY
All Rights Reserved

Library of Congress Cataloging-in-Publication Data

Islamic political ethics: civil society, pluralism, and conflict / edited by
  Sohail H. Hashmi.
    p. cm.—(The Ethikon series in comparative ethics)
    Includes bibliographical references and index.
    ISBN 0-691-11309-2 (alk. paper)—ISBN 0-691-11310-6 (pbk. : alk. paper)
    1. Islam and state. 2. Political ethics. 3. Islamic ethics. 4. Civil society.
  5. Pluralism (Social sciences) 6. War—Religious aspects—Islam. I. Hashmi,
  Sohail H., 1962– II. Series.

  JC49 .I766 2002
  172—dc21   2002025293

British Library Cataloging-in-Publication Data is available

This book has been composed in Palatino

Printed on acid-free paper. ∞

www.pupress.princeton.edu

Printed in the United States of America

10 9 8 7 6 5 4 3 2 1

Contents

Foreword

Of Theology and Diplomacy

JACK MILES

WESTERN foreign ministers and secretaries of state may have to learn a little theology if the looming clash between embattled elements both in the West and in the Muslim *umma* is to yield to disengagement and peaceful coexistence, to say nothing of fruitful collaboration. If al-Qaʻida is a Muslim movement with military designs both on the umma itself and on the West, then it must be understood, in the first place, for what it is—namely, a deviant form of a major world religion and not simply a latter-day species of organized crime. To say this is not to dignify al-Qaʻida. It is rather to suggest that containing the threat to world peace that it poses may entail constructing and promoting a viable and authentically Muslim alternative to its fatally appealing political vision.

It is, then, no idle academic exercise that the thinkers whose work is collected here have in hand. The long-term practical importance of their work can scarcely be overstated. The West has been eager to see more democratic political systems emerge within the Muslim world but—for reasons rooted deep in Western history—slow to recognize that the task of creating such alternatives must involve Islam itself. Although President George W. Bush did well after the terrorist attacks of September 11, 2001, to declare that Osama bin Laden did not represent true Islam, the American State Department seems little interested in asking who does represent true Islam. This question—directly involving, as it does, the study of religion—is one that officially secular Western military and diplomatic institutions are designed never to ask, one that they rarely even notice they are not asking. This silence marks the knowledge gap that must be closed if peace is to be achieved, and the authors of this volume may well be a part of closing it.

At the end of World War I, as historian David Fromkin cogently demonstrates in *A Peace to End All Peace*, Britain and France vastly overestimated the importance of Arab nationalism and correspondingly underestimated the importance of Islam as an organizing principle in the polity they sought to construct on the ruins of the Turkish empire. In effect, the British and the French were psychologically incapable of dealing with the Middle East other than through leaders manufactured to resemble their passionately nationalist but only residually religious selves. They were at a loss when confronted with a culture whose real leaders were passionately religious and only nominally nationalist.

After 1956, when the United States became the dominant power in the Middle East, it made the same mistake—vastly overestimating, for example, Iranian nationalism as represented by the shah and correspondingly underestimating Muslim religion as represented by Ayatollah Khomeini. It was as if the United States had to find or invent someone like the shah to deal with because, well, how could a self-respecting secretary of state possibly do business with an ayatollah? What would they discuss? Theology?

Let me suggest that in the crisis we now face the answer to that question is "Yes, theology." In the search for an alternative conception of civil society that can bridge the gulf between the umma and the West, theology is quite properly an inescapable topic. In "Alternative Conceptions of Civil Society: A Reflective Islamic Approach"—to single out just one of the contributions to this volume—Hasan Hanafi states as his premise the belief "that similarities can be maintained and differences can be bridged through creative reinterpretation–or *ijtihad*—of the basic ethical sources of Islam." Although Western political leaders cannot, clearly, take the lead in this creative reinterpretation, they would be ill-advised to ignore it. On the contrary, they should follow it with keenest interest, for its success or failure will have everything to do with their own.

Reducing this ethical and, by extension, political ijtihad to mere *jihad* will not do. Just as militant Communism could not be militarily defeated in the last clash of civilizations, so militant Islam cannot be militarily defeated in this new one. Western containment and Communist peaceful coexistence emerged as twin strategies when both sides recognized that, in fact, neither side could win a definitive military victory. At the present juncture, unfortunately, no comparable recognition has yet taken place. The West still expects globalization backed by Western military ascendancy to encompass all, while at least a significant militant segment of the umma has not surrendered its older vision of a *dar al-Islam* containing all of mankind. Rather than a "twinnable," bilateral strategy analogous to containment/coexistence, we witness a pair of contending and deeply incoherent unilateralisms.

To speak, for the moment, only of American unilaterism, the American campaign against the Muslim nations that have harbored the agents of al-Qaʿida and kindred movements is incoherent inasmuch as every major Western nation has harbored them as well. Germany, France, Italy, Britain, Canada, and the United States itself may have harbored these agents more unwillingly and unwittingly than has, say, Egypt—but how witting or willing was Egypt to harbor Islamic Jihad, the alienated offshoot of the Muslim Brotherhood that assassinated President Anwar Sadat? To be sure, it is the Muslim umma as a whole that has harbored the murderous al-Qaʿida movement within it, but by that very token it is the Muslim umma as a whole that must somehow be persuaded to make its repudiation of al-Qaʿida's perverted vision of Islam more unmistakable, more persistent, and more emphatic. And that repudiation cannot be achieved by arms alone. It will not come, in other words, when or because al-Qaʿida has been bled dry in a dozen scattered international police actions but only when and because a living, breathing alternative to it has stepped into the light.

The development of such an alternative vision, however, will require not just the belated valorization of the kind of expertise so impressively on display in this volume. It will also require a major paradigm shift in Western diplomacy. If religion is mere happenstance ("I happen to be Christian," "I happen to be Muslim"), then it may be defined downward into political irrelevancy. Downward definition may have served the West well enough in overcoming Christianity's own hideous wars of religion. But the old method will not meet this new challenge, for it takes off the table just the topic that militant Islam finds most compelling. By the same token, the word *theology* must no longer be used as shorthand for "that-which-does-not-matter" or, worse, "that-which-gets-in-the-way." One can no more discuss Islam without discussing theology than one can discuss Communism without discussing ideology. Theology is the intellectual element in religion, and nothing at this moment could be more painfully obvious than that the West has ignored this element to its peril.

Western leaders, in sum, must find a way to untie their tongues on a topic of world-historical importance, and as they do so they must not overlook the allies who stand nearest to hand. In 1968, anthropologist Clifford Geertz wrote a book called *Islam Observed* in which he compared and contrasted what were then the western and eastern extremes of the House of Islam: Morocco and Indonesia. Since 1968, however, the western extreme has moved westward from Morocco to North America and, in fact, all the way to California. The contempt of radical Islamism for the acculturated Muslim communities of North America may be extreme. But in the years and decades ahead, why may it not be the voice of the increasingly large and prosperous Western Muslim communities—through thinkers like those gathered here—that resounds most loudly in the world umma? Rather than the threat within, the Muslims of the West must be seen as the ally within. They must not be demeaned as retrograde latecomers to globalization but embraced as the indispensable fellow architects of a world order that does not yet exist.

Muslims often, alas, have reason to fear other Muslims. The bloodiest international war of the latter half of the twentieth century, surpassing even the genocide in Rwanda, was the Iran-Iraq War of the 1980s. The peril to Muslim intellectuals, in particular, cannot be minimized. For American and other Western Muslims who dare to claim an international role, the personal risks may be as large as the intellectual challenge. But if they can rise to this historic challenge, the good news is that they will not be without allies elsewhere in the House of Islam. Is there a single Muslim nation in the world that aspires to the condition of Afghanistan under the Taliban? Is there not, instead, every reason to believe that a voice both authentically Western and authentically Muslim would find a wide Muslim audience? Time will tell, but the enemies of the West's enemy may yet prove to be the friends of its Muslim friends.

Meanwhile, if scholars like those gathered in this volume muster the necessary courage and intelligence, the question that must be asked is: Will they find correspondingly courageous or appropriately educated allies in Washington—allies for whom theology is not "theology"? To repeat, the Muslim communities of the West must be dignified with much more than the occasional courtesy invitation to the diplomatic dinner table. They must be not just cultivated as allies of convenience but heard and honored as teachers. They must be protected and supported both materially and spiritually as they take on the enormous challenge of raising from their own ranks the political and religious thinkers and leaders whose labors may yet save two worlds at once.

Preface

SOHAIL H. HASHMI

OVER THE PAST several years, the Ethikon Institute has organized a number of high-level dialogue conferences in which authoritative spokespersons for diverse ethical traditions have presented the views of their respective traditions on particular topics and specific questions of great contemporary importance. The conferences are designed to identify and explore the commonalities and differences among different moral outlooks, both religious and secular. The results of these dialogue events are published in the Ethikon Series in Comparative Ethics. By thus encouraging a systematic exchange of ideas both within and across moral traditions, Ethikon seeks to advance the prospects for cross-tradition consensus and to facilitate the accommodation of abiding differences.

The chapters in this book were originally written for publication in earlier volumes of the Ethikon Series alongside a variety of other perspectives. They have been assembled here to provide ready and convenient access for readers with a particular interest in the relation of Islamic political ethics to contemporary social concerns.

The attack upon the United States on September 11, 2001, has once again raised profoundly difficult questions relating to the understanding of Islam in the modern world. Osama bin Laden and his supporters have repeatedly sought justification for their operations on Islamic grounds. Their Muslim critics have vociferously denounced al-Qa'ida's terrorism as the work of extremists on the fringes of the Muslim community. Somewhere in the middle are large numbers of Muslims who may sympathize generally with Bin Laden's anti-imperialist rhetoric while shuddering at the extreme violence he is prepared to use in realizing his aims.

Most of the ten essays collected in this volume were written before the September 11 attacks. But they individually and collectively highlight issues that have been starkly illuminated by the recent events.

First, the essays show that one of the most dynamic aspects of the Islamic revival during the past two centuries has been the rethinking of Islamic political theory. Muslim peoples around the globe have gone in rapid succession from living in traditional empires or principalities, to colonial rule, to political independence in some fifty-six predominantly Muslim states. European imperialism introduced into the Muslim world a bewildering array of political ideas, such as nationalism, secularism, statism, socialism, democracy, constitutionalism, feminism, and human rights. Following World War II, the Muslim states were swept up, like most others in the third world, in the ideological struggle between capitalism and communism, both of which promised the fruits of modernization. The present reality in most Muslim countries, however, is economic stagnation, growing class differences, and pervasive governmental corruption under authoritarian regimes. Is it any wonder then that many Muslims would seek explanation, legitimation, even redemption in Islamic thought?

All of the essays in this volume argue for the abiding relevance of classical Islamic theory even as modern Muslims struggle to apply this heritage to new contexts. Prominent among these are the spread of human rights norms that challenge discrimination based on gender or religion, the division of the Muslim *umma* into nation-states, the emergence of civil society institutions within and among Muslim states, and the evolution of international laws on war and peace. Islamic political discourse often means a conversation by modern Muslim scholars with men living centuries ago who produced what are still considered authoritative understandings of the basic ethical sources, the Qur'an and *sunna* of the Prophet. Yet several of the authors point out that reform and renewal of Islamic thought has meant for many Muslims a respectful nod toward the leading lights of the early Islamic centuries, but an awareness of the need and a willingness to return themselves to the ethical sources. And this search for a modern Islamic political ethics has involved a truly diverse set of participants: traditional religious scholars (*'ulama*) as well as many with secular, Western education; women in growing numbers alongside men.

Which leads us to the second theme highlighted by these essays: This quest for understanding of novel situations in light of traditional values has inevitably produced myriad outcomes. In the dialectical evolution of ideas, attempts at synthesizing classical Islamic thought and modern Western ideas have yielded their own antitheses. And so the dialectic—and the controversies—continue. Western analyses of "political Islam" too often focus on merely one small part of the spectrum, the one that is the most vocal and arguably the most mobilized, namely, the fundamentalists or, as some would prefer, the Islamists. What these essays demonstrate clearly is that Islamism cannot be equated with fundamentalism, that it is truly a broad phenomenon, and that the rifts among Islamists are often as deep as those separating them from their non-Muslim interlocutors. The rifts sometimes lead to violent and very public clashes. But they are also frequently mediated privately by respectful dialogue, legal adjudication, and institution building.

Third, the essays evince the close interrelationship between domestic and international concerns. The struggle between state and nascent civil society that features so prominently in many Muslim countries is directly affected by the international climate, both among Muslim states and in the broader international community. Islamic movements often see themselves as transcending the national state model, which they dismiss as a foreign import while at the same time attempting to seize control of it. Likewise, issues of war and peace on the international level are determined by the struggle for justice, or the lack of checks provided by civil society upon repressive governments.

Finally, these essays point to the likelihood that the present turbulent phase of Islamic self-definition will not end anytime soon. And while Muslims must necessarily take the leading role in this process, it cannot be conducted entirely by Muslims. The world is too small a place for such monumental changes affecting some one billion people not to affect all people. Nor can Muslims in the twenty-first century expect to immunize themselves from outside political and ideological currents any more than they were able over the past two centuries. As long as Muslims are motivated to act on ideas, on the conviction that they have a moral obligation to right the wrongs of their societies, the definition of Islamic political ethics will, in a very real way, involve us all.

The trustees of the Ethikon Institute join with Philip Valera, president, and Carole Pateman, series editor, in thanking all who contributed to the development of this book. In addition to the authors and the original volume editors, special thanks are due to trustee Lea Ann King for suggesting this anthology, and to the Pew Charitable Trusts, the Ahmanson Foundation, Joan Palevsky, and the Doheny Foundation for their generous support of the various Ethikon dialogue projects from which these essays and other books emerged.

We are especially grateful to Jack Miles for his thoughtful foreword. Finally, we wish to express our thanks to Ian Malcolm and Maura Roessner of Princeton University Press for their valuable guidance and support.

Chapters 1 and 2 were first published in *Civil Society and Government*, ed. Nancy L. Rosenblum and Robert Post (Princeton: Princeton University Press, 2002), 284–316, 317–33.

Chapter 3 was first published in *Alternative Conceptions of Civil Society*, ed. Simone Chambers and Will Kymlicka (Princeton: Princeton University Press, 2002), 171–89.

Chapters 4 and 5 were first published in *Boundaries and Justice: Diverse Ethical Perspectives*, ed. David Miller and Sohail H. Hashmi (Princeton: Princeton University Press, 2001), 183–202, 203–12.

Chapters 6 and 7 will be published in *The Many and the One: Religious and Secular Perspectives on Ethical Pluralism in the Modern World*, ed. Richard Madsen and Tracy B. Strong (Princeton: Princeton University Press, forthcoming in Spring 2003).

Chapter 8 was first published in *International Society: Diverse Ethical Perspectives*, ed. David R. Mapel and Terry Nardin (Princeton: Princeton University Press, 1998), 215–36.

Chapters 9 and 10 were first published in *The Ethics of War and Peace: Religious and Secular Perspectives*, ed. Terry Nardin (Princeton: Princeton University Press, 1996), 128–45, 146–66.

Part I

STATE AND CIVIL SOCIETY

1

Civil Society and Government in Islam

JOHN KELSAY

A FEW COMMENTS on terms seem appropriate. Thus, *civil society* can mean many things. One way to summarize involves tying the term to a specific set of institutions or organizations that are held to "mediate" between private and public life. Churches and synagogues fit, as do labor unions, political parties, and such associations as the People for the American Way, the ACLU, the Rotary Clubs, and the National Organization for Women. For those influenced by Hegel, in particular, organizations like these are critical for the development of the type of people who can participate as full citizens in the political life of a modern state. They "mediate," in the sense that taking part in them helps people to develop loyalties beyond those of kinship. To put it another way, the importance of civil society is that it represents a crucial stage in the development of people who can deal with those who are different from themselves. And this is held to be crucial "practice" in anticipation of the more extensive experience of difference characteristic of the modern state.[1]

For others, influenced more by Anglo-American writers such as Locke, "civil society" seems largely identical with a certain kind of political or governmental regime: namely, constitutional democracy. Churches, synagogues, and the rest of the mediating institutions listed above are important in preserving a balance of power between those holding the reigns of government and ordinary citizens. To put it another way, strong mediating institutions help to keep society "civil." They give ordinary citizens a means to participate in government, as well as to check the power of more specifically governmental institutions, like the various departments that make up the federal bureaucracy. In so doing, they also help citizens to feel that they have had their say. The hope is that in allowing people to express themselves or in providing a balance to governmental power, the issues that (in noncivil societies) give rise to violence may be dealt with. Give people freedom, tolerate different points of view, allow a wide set of opportunities for participation in social life, and thereby limit the tendencies of government toward authoritarianism and of disenfranchised citizens toward sectarian strife—this is the basic idea of the Lockean tradition on civil society.[2]

In contemporary Islamic discussion, those who speak most about civil society do so in ways that resonate with aspects of both Hegelian and Lockean traditions. Yet there are important differences. Thus, President Khatami of Iran, the Egyptian sociologist Saad Eddin Ibrahim, and other Muslim intellectuals emphasize the importance of allowing certain institutions a degree of independence from state control. Free (that is, nonstate-controlled) newspapers and television stations, an independent business sector, and less carefully regulated political parties all receive attention; policies that allow an increased range for freedom of speech and association are said to be important because they will increase a sense of "ownership" or participation on the part of the public. This will improve the quality of life in Muslim societies, both in the Hegelian sense of educating people for citizenship and in the Lockean sense of limiting violence, both on the part of elites with authoritarian tendencies and on the part of people who feel compelled to resist tyranny. One notes, however, that the institutions spoken about are not precisely comparable to those in our earlier list. The political contexts of discussions of civil society in contemporary Western and Islamic societies are distinct. While there are shared characteristics—for example in the focus on opportunities for activities that are sub- or nongovernmental—the emphasis of Muslims seems to be on the creation of a sphere of citizen liberty. By comparison, Europeans and North Americans seem focused on citizen participation in specific organizations.[3]

Government, by contrast, seems a less controversial term. For both Western and Muslim analysts, the term indicates the state, with its power of command and control. As Max Weber put it, the modern state is defined as that entity which has a monopoly on the use of legitimate force within a given territory.[4] For purposes of this discussion, "force" extends beyond the power to employ arms or use violence, and includes the power to punish, to tax, and to regulate the life of citizens. Muslims, along with Europeans and North Americans, can identify with this sort of understanding, as well as with the part of Weber's definition that refers to legitimacy.

Just what constitutes legitimate government, by contrast, may be a controversial point. Western analysts presume the legitimacy of constitutional democracy. Muslim advocates of civil society do so as well. The latter, however, speak within a context where a term like *democracy* has a more complicated valence. Thus, Khatami, Ibrahim, and others must respond to those who see democracy as a recipe for the elevation of (purely) human desires and understandings, and who argue that a just society is one ruled according to the "limits set by God." Properly understood, many who argue in this way end up legitimating something like democratic (in the sense of representative) government, by means of the notion of *al-shura* (consultation).[5] There is thus room for discussion between advocates of constitutional democracy and those who speak of "Islamic government." At the same time, there are differences, most notably in the ways that the latter insist that the makeup of a consultative assembly (what a Western theorist would call a "representative assembly") as well as the process of selection (voting) must be such as to ensure that legislation is crafted in terms that satisfy the Islamic conscience. Consultation is not just a matter of the citizens of a state involved in give-and-take with respect to their various interests; it must have a moral component, which is secured by the notion that those making policy will consult sources of Islamic authority, as well as their fellow citizens.[6]

A Western advocate of constitutional democracy might well say in response that the rights of citizens rest on, and are somehow limited by, the "higher law" spoken of in Christian or natural law circles, or at least by the precedent of common law. Government in a constitutional democracy is thus not simply a matter of the whim of the majority, a fact that Khatami, among others, recognizes.[7] Nevertheless, it is worth recognizing again the distinctive contexts of Western and Islamic discussions of civil society, since they do rest on and call forth somewhat different terminology.

Thus, finally, *Islam*, which my comments on the relationship between Khatami, Ibrahim, and others already suggest, will be a controversial term. I do not say this lightly, for there are certain references that are, for purposes of this essay, more or less constitutive of any "Islamic" perspective on civil society and government. But the meaning or, perhaps better, the interpretation of those references with respect to this topic is clearly a matter of discussion; of this we must take note. Arguments among contemporary Muslims are often cast in terms of the positions of "reformists" (for example, Khatami and Ibrahim) and "revivalists" (like the critics of democracy mentioned above). Whether such terms are entirely apt is not our concern at the moment; the point is that "Islam" can be taken to indicate a wide variety of judgments about contemporary political practice. Similarly, the term is utilized to identify expressions of political thought that occur in widely disparate historic and geographic contexts. Thus, for example, the terms "Western" and "Islamic" are utilized above to identify two comparable, though distinctive, conversations about civil society and government. In connection with the examples of Khatami (Iran) and Ibrahim (Egypt), these terms serve a useful purpose, partic-

ularly as we try to understand some of their particular emphases. Just
how the ideas of these two figures relate to the conversations of Muslims in earlier periods or to the judgments of Muslims living in Europe and North America (and who thus might be considered as participants in the "Western" discussion of civil society) is not an easy
matter to adjudicate. And this is not even to mention questions about
the role of different schools of thought or modes of political conversation within Islam.[8] Each of these has its own integrity and, depending
on which group of Muslims one is talking about, might be considered
"primary."

    That said, there are certain sources and themes that are basic to any
presentation of Islamic political thought. I begin with an overview of
some of these, before proceeding to a discussion of specific issues
regarding civil society and government.

The Example of the Prophet

Our presentation of Islamic political thought can begin with the example of Muhammad, the Prophet of God.[9] Born circa 570 C.E., Muhammad came to adulthood in the context of a tribal society characterized by the politics of clan loyalty. His particular tribe, al-Quraysh,
enjoyed prominence in Mecca, one of the few urban areas in the Arabian peninsula. In the late-sixth century, Mecca (and thus, the Quraysh tribe) knew increased prosperity as a primary stop for caravans
transporting goods between the old cities of Syro-Palestine and the
Arabian Sea (and, from there, to India). With increased prosperity
came increased status, or at least the ambition for it; Mecca was the
site of an ancient shrine known as the Ka'ba, and the Quraysh sought
to use it, along with the attraction of trade, to achieve greater cooperation between the disparate tribes of the peninsula. The notion of a
hajj, or "pilgrimage," to the Ka'ba in honor of ancestral deities may
have been quite old. For Muhammad's story, however, it is important
only that the Quraysh seem to have persuaded at least some of the
tribes to observe an annual truce, four months during which there
was to be no fighting, with the correlative purpose of encouraging the
tribes to make the pilgrimage. There, they would trade—primarily
commercial goods, or so we presume, but also (and rather naturally)
in the sorts of things that encourage people to think cooperatively.
The pilgrimage months seem to have become a kind of large commercial and cultural festival, with the Quraysh as sponsors and hosts. For
the Quraysh, at least, it seems appropriate to consider the observance
as an expression of pan-tribal or, if one likes, of Arab consciousness.

There are stories about Muhammad from this period, which are told in pious biography as a way of showing that he was chosen by God all along, prepared for the great work he was to do. Those are worth telling, however, only in the light of what happened during the first third of the seventh century. According to tradition, in the year 610, Muhammad understood himself as called to prophecy. Within a few years, he gathered a small band of followers among the residents of Mecca, and gained enough attention that some of the more prominent members of Quraysh sought to counter the new movement, using economic boycotts, acts of torture, and other forms of persecution. Eventually, in the series of events Muslims call the *hijra*, or "migration," Muhammad moved his community to Medina, a city some distance to the north. From this new location, the Prophet led the Muslims in a campaign by which he sought to unite the various Arab tribes, including Quraysh, into a new social entity—an *umma*—which would not only express, but would carry on his sense of mission. By the time of his death in 632, Muhammad's campaign, which included what we would call diplomatic and military initiatives as well as preaching, succeeded so thoroughly that tradition has him proclaim that "Arabia is solidly for Islam." As the reader is to understand, all the peninsula, and thus all the tribes residing there, were now united under the banner of Islam.

There are important issues for historical-critical understanding of this "founding" narrative. Those are, however, not the point in the current context. Rather, the interesting point to note is the way the Prophet's career encompasses both religious and political leadership. In an oft-repeated phrase, Muslims speak of religion and politics (Arabic *din wa dunya*) as "twins." While the phrase shows the influence of other, surrounding cultures (for example, the Byzantine and Sassanid), many Muslims have also thought of it in connection with Muhammad's life.[10] The Prophet called human beings to faith by means of "beautiful preaching."[11] He also pursued the cause of Islam by means of statecraft, including warfare. Why the Prophet practiced both religion and statecraft is an important question. Some, noting that traditional accounts stress that the latter only begins with the migration to Medina, argue that politics, in particular warfare, is a secondary and derivative aspect of Muhammad's ministry. He becomes a statesman, in other words, under duress, as indicated in the words of Qur'an 22:39–40:

> To those against whom war is made, permission is given to fight, because they are oppressed. Truly, God is most powerful in their cause. Those who have been expelled from their homes in defiance of right, without cause

except that they say "God is our Lord." If God did not check one set of
people by means of another, then monasteries, churches, synagogues, and
mosques in which the name of God is often commemorated would be
pulled down. God will help those who help God. Truly God is full of
strength, exalted in might.

According to the oldest extant biography of the Prophet, these verses,
revealed at the time of the hijra, constitute the first time Muhammad
was given an order to fight.[12] And thus some, as indicated, take it that
politics is something Muhammad was forced to. The military and
diplomatic initiatives of Medina are tactics to which the Prophet had
to resort in order to provide security for his fledgling and oppressed
community.

Other interpreters, while agreeing that resort to war was a kind of
last resort for the Prophet, argue that it was nevertheless a means to
what he had in mind all along. In other words, preaching in Mecca
and warfare in Medina were both politically oriented activities. While
no one should make the mistake of believing that the submission
achieved by means of statecraft is equivalent to faith (so this line of
thinking goes), it is an important way of spreading the influence
of Islam or, to speak in terms of the Qur'an, to "make God's cause
succeed."

Thus, if Muhammad's example supports the notion that religion
and politics are twins, it does not negate the space between the two.
To put it another way, one may speak here of a prominent example of
what I shall be calling throughout the *complementarity thesis*—namely,
the idea that religion and politics or, more properly, religious and political institutions play complementary roles in the pursuit of human
welfare. Complementarity does not indicate identity, however. Indeed, it sets up a certain set of tensions, as the human beings engaged
with each type of institution attempt to carry out their assigned tasks.
Just where are the limits of religious authority? Of political? These are
questions to which I shall return.

For now, one should simply note the example of the Prophet as
religious leader and statesman. In the end, Muhammad built a community that challenged the system of clan loyalty characteristic of
pre-Islamic Arabia. The solidarity of the umma would lie not in the
blood loyalties of kinship, but in the members' consciousness that
they were, before all else, Muslims—people characterized by submission to the one true God. As the Qur'an has it,

> O believers! Have regard for God, with true piety, and do not die except as
> Muslims. Hold together, by the rope of God; do not be divided. Remember
> God's favor to you, how you were enemies, but God put love between your

hearts. By God's graciousness, you became brothers. You were on the brink of destruction, when God rescued you. Even so the signs of God are clear for you, that you should be rightly guided. From you, let there come a community, calling to the good, commanding what is plainly right, forbidding what is plainly wrong. These are the ones who will find happiness. Don't be like those who are divided, or differ after receiving clear signs. Theirs is a dreadful punishment.

On the day that some faces are made bright, while others will be cast down, and the downcast are asked "Did you act as ingrates, after faith came to you? Taste the punishment for ingratitude."

Those whose faces are made bright receive God's mercy, and enjoy it forever.

These are signs from God, brought to you in the cause of truth. God does not will harm to any rational being.

To God belongs everything in the heavens and the earth; and their works return to God. You are a good community, called out from humankind. You command the good; you forbid the evil. You trust in God. (3:102–10)

Classical Islam

The community established by Muhammad soon became a force to reckon with. Following the Prophet's death, the Muslims became a conquering army, making Islam the dominant political reality throughout Egypt, Syro-Palestine, Iraq, and Iran by 661.[13] And this was only the beginning. As the center of the empire moved, first to Damascus, where the Umayyads held sway from 680 to the 740s, then to Baghdad, where the Abbasid caliphs ruled for nearly five centuries, Islam became the established religion of an imperial state of world significance.[14]

In this setting, Muslims developed types of political practice that may be regarded as "classical," in the sense of establishing precedents that carry a continuing weight. For our interests, the most important of these precedents have to do with working out a version of the complementary relation of religion and politics that establishes a relative independence on the part of two sets of institutions. The one, standing for the independence of religious practice, was constituted by a class of religious specialists known as 'ulama (knowers). Recognized, as the name implies, for their expertise in the interpretation of certain agreed-upon sources (in particular, the Qur'an, but also of ahadith, "reports" of the example of the Prophet), these specialists carried the power to "bind and loose" with respect to the Islamic legitimacy of rulers, government policies, and the answer to such questions as Who is a true Muslim? Their power, which was intrinsically moral, rested in their knowledge—not in their political expertise or their military capacity. Through the associated institutions of the *masjid* (mosque, place of communal gathering), the *madrasa* (religious school), and eventually the *jami'a* (university), the 'ulama established a kind of sphere of influence, politically relevant but not quite "governmental," that limited the power of government officials. *To my mind, this sphere represents the closest analogy in classical Islam to "civil society."* It is aimed, that is, at providing and protecting an institutional setting for citizen expression regarding social and political, as well as religious, affairs. This setting is not identical with that of "government," though it can have an impact on policy, and is thus of interest to government officials. It acts as a kind of protection for the expression of dissent, in a manner reminiscent of the Lockean tradition; at the same time, it helps citizens move out of the sphere of familial relations and establish a set of broader loyalties, as in the Hegelian tradition.

"Government" is correspondingly represented by officials involved in a second set of institutions, the foremost of which was the *khilafat* (caliphate). By this term, which carries the meaning of "successor," rulers of the Muslim empire established continuity with the example of the Prophet. And, in the manner of rulers throughout the ancient world, those who exercised power in Islam often employed the trappings of religion. The holders of the caliphate, in other words, sometimes led prayers at the great mosques of Damascus or Baghdad. They, or their representatives, might preach from the pulpit of the mosque. They gave financial support to those 'ulama who pleased them and withheld it from those who did not. But when it came to the presumption of legitimacy in knowing the sources of Islam, the caliphs, whether Umayyad or Abbasid (or, in later periods, Ottomans, Safavids, or Mughals), simply could not compete with the 'ulama. The role of the caliph, as "commander of the faithful," was to preserve and protect the security of the Islamic state. It was his duty to defend and, if possible, to extend the borders of Islam; to maintain the peace of the empire; and to collect taxes and administer the worldly affairs of state in a just manner. Through such governmental institutions as the army, the courts, and the bureaucracy associated with a courtly culture, the caliphs carried on the traditions of Islamic statecraft (they hoped) with the blessings of the 'ulama.

To illustrate something of the way this worked, consider the example of Abbasid policy under the great al-Ma'mun, who held power from 809 to 833.[15] The Abbasids came to power in the 740s, as the result of an uprising against the Umayyad dynasty. One feature of the

Abbasid triumph had been their ability to marshal support from a number of pious groups. Abbasid propaganda included promises to rule "by the book of God" (the Qur'an). Numerous groups, most of which featured prominently one or more persons with the religious expertise of the ʿulama, responded to these promises. Perhaps inevitably, most of the groups in question were disappointed to find that whatever the Abbasid propagandists meant by government "by the book of God," it did not precisely correspond to the understanding of their featured ʿulama.

Correspondingly, Abbasid rulers always worried about the tendencies toward sectarianism within their religious support. Al-Maʾmun, who seems to have been a pious and learned ruler, sought in several ways to deal with this. In 817, for example, he floated publicly the suggestion that ʿAli al-Rida, a leader in Shiʿi circles, might rule as successor to al-Maʾmun.[16] The experiment came to nothing when al-Rida died the following year.

Most notably, however, al-Maʾmun decided to regulate the teaching of the ʿulama. In the 820s, following the doctrine of certain Muʿtazili scholars prominent in his court, the caliph declared that all ʿulama should give answer to a question about the nature of the Qur'an— was it created or not? The answer al-Maʾmun wanted was "created."

The precise theological import of this question need not concern us at the moment; for our purposes, al-Maʾmun's "test" or "inquisition" is an important experiment in the relationship of religious and political institutions in Islam. Extant sources tell us that most of the ʿulama yielded to al-Maʾmun's pressure, affirming that the Qur'an was indeed created. The most outstanding exception was Ahmad ibn Hanbal, a scholar particularly noted for his knowledge of reports of the Prophet's example, and thus a fine example of the basis of the authority of the ʿulama. Ahmad, we are told, was noteworthy for his insistence on financial independence from the caliph's court. He would not take governmental stipends, and criticized scholars who did. He also, in the instance at hand, became notable for his insistence that al-Maʾmun's test went beyond the rights of a Muslim ruler. From all one can tell, Ahmad probably believed the Qur'an was uncreated. But his public response to the inquisitors seems simply to have been that they had no right to ask the question. The Prophet had never inquired of anyone about the nature of the Qur'an; there was no *hadith* concerning it. Thus, the nature of the Qur'an was a matter on which the Muslim conscience should be regarded as free.

Now, Ahmad was known as one who stressed respect for government; as I shall indicate below, the general tendency of classical Islam was against revolution, even in the case of an unjust ruler. In a manner consistent with this, his resistance to the inquisition was purely moral. Ahmad gave answers when asked; he accepted imprisonment; finally, he submitted to a public beating. When this led to popular unrest, the architects of the inquisition ceased; Ahmad was eventually released and, in an ironic twist, one of al-Ma'mun's successors (al-Mutawakkil, ruled 847–61) reversed his predecessor's policies and tried to secure Ahmad ibn Hanbal's public support. From what we know, it appears the scholar, quite old by this time, refused to give his support or even to take a stipend from the court, eventually dying in poverty.

Ahmad's example is particularly outstanding in terms of a scholar maintaining a certain independence for the religious in relation to the political. But the principle holds. In classical Islam, as in the example of the Prophet, religion and politics are to complement one another. To exist in complementary relation, however, does not suggest identity. And, particularly once Islam became identified with a large, diverse imperial state, it was rather natural that there be a kind of unpredictability about the relationship of the guardians of the message and the guardians of the borders of the territory of Islam. To restate the judgment above: to my mind, the ʿulama, with their associated institutions of mosque, school, and university, present the closest classical analogue to civil society. In thinking of an Islamic perspective on civil society and government, then, we should think about the relations between ʿulama and khilafat.

Modern Islam

As one moves to more contemporary examples, the first thing to be noted is the falling away of the imperial state. Following the demise of the Abbasid caliphate in 1258, Islamic political power was divided between three great dynasties: the Ottomans, who from Istanbul ruled over south-central Europe, the Middle East, and North Africa; the Safavids (followed by the Qajars), who ruled in Iran; and the Mughals, who held sway in the Indian subcontinent (inclusive of what we call Pakistan, Bangladesh, most of India, and parts of Afghanistan). By the end of the First World War, only the Ottomans survived; within five years after the war, they too were gone.[17]

The abolition of the Ottoman caliphate created something of a crisis for Muslim political thought.[18] Some used the opportunity to wonder whether Islam, as a religious tradition, needed the institution of khilafat at all. The Egyptian ʿAli ʿAbd al-Raziq, for example, presented a fascinating argument about religion and politics in Islam, focusing

on the uniqueness of the authority exercised by the Prophet. Muhammad, 'Abd al-Raziq argued, did not so much "combine" the roles
of prophet and statesman as he exercised fully the role of prophet.
Muhammad's prophetic authority did not so much combine or complement his statecraft as subsume it. Politics, or better, government, is
natural to human beings, who need social order to survive. Religion
is something more, something beyond politics. Only a prophet can
exercise political *and* religious authority. The danger of the classical
institution of khilafat, with its religious trappings, was always that it
would exceed its proper boundaries, as the example of al-Ma'mun
shows. Better to let religion (with the 'ulama) be religion, and government be government, in whatever form.[19]

'Abd al-Raziq was too radical for most. And thus, contemporary
Islamic political thought continues to reach for a complementary relation between religion and government, 'ulama and khilafat, with the
latter now understood to include constitutional regimes, elected par-
liaments, an independent judiciary, and the like. The 'ulama, with
their power to bind and loose, still provide an entree into civil society
in Muslim societies; they represent the dynamic, associational power
of religion, and understand themselves as dedicated to the preservation of an Islam that cannot be simply identified with any existing
governmental regime. Even the insistent calls of revivalists for Islamic
government are often best understood in this light. The idea of the
late Ayatollah Khomeini, for example, seems to have been that the
record of modern Iranian governments was so dominated by attempts to usurp the proper authority of the 'ulama that the religious
specialists would have to take a place within government in order to
protect the independence of Islam. In the attempt to maintain complementarity, Khomeini and other revivalists "fudge" the civil society/
government relation one way, in order to limit the power of over-
weaning government.[20]

In modern settings, of course, the 'ulama cannot be identified simply as the whole of civil society. We do have to deal with the concerns
of reformers like President Khatami and Saad Eddin Ibrahim. Despite
Khatami's strong identification with the 'ulama, calls for strengthening the independence of the press and, more generally, for greater
freedom of association and speech might be understood as a way of
creating an independent sphere for a new class of people, who judge
that their interests and their understanding of Islam are not entirely
represented by either existing governments or by the 'ulama. Particularly in Iran, a relatively well-educated, highly motivated business
and professional class, inclusive of many women as well as men, appears to be reaching for a sphere in which liberty is regulated by

neither centralized political nor religious authorities. What this will yield is impossible to predict. One can only note that with respect to this class of people, the relationship of civil society and government in Islam seems an open question.

I now turn to specific issues in the civil society/government relationship.

Boundaries

Islam's emphasis on the complementarity of religion and politics creates a number of possibilities for the relationship between the religious community and state authorities; or more generally, between civil society and government. 'Ulama and khilafat share in a common task, to make God's cause succeed, or to bring about justice in the earth.

I have already suggested that such complementarity does not rule out distinctions in roles; neither should it obscure the fact of recognizable boundaries between the religious community and the state. In particular instances, such boundaries were and are well noted. The state thus has the task of regulating behavior with respect to military and police force; the religious community, with its scholars operating through the associated institutions of mosque and school, has the task of rendering normative judgments about the state's fulfillment of this task. The state, to take another case, has the task of collecting taxes and distributing funds. The religious community passes judgment as to which taxes can be collected and as to whether funds are distributed in accord with Islamic values.

An important test case of such boundaries lies in the duties Muslims are said to have toward their rulers. The following are examples of standard ahadith on the duty to obey the caliph.[21]

> Abu Huraira reported God's messenger as saying, "He who obeys me has obeyed God and he who disobeys me has disobeyed God; he who obeys the commander has obeyed me and he who disobeys the commander has disobeyed me. The imam is only a shield behind whom fighting is engaged in and by whom protection is sought; so if he commands piety and acts justly he will have a reward for that, but if he holds another view he will on that account be guilty."
>
> Ibn Umar reported God's messenger as saying, "Hearing and obeying are the duty of a Muslim both regarding what he likes and what he dislikes, as long as he is not commanded to perform an act of disobedience to God, in which case he must neither hear nor obey."
>
> Ibn Abbas reported God's messenger as saying, "If anyone sees in his

commander what he dislikes he should show patience, for no one separates from the community and dies without dying like those of pre-Islamic times."

Auf b. Malik al-Ashja'i reported God's messenger as saying, "Your best imams are those whom you like and who like you, on whom you invoke blessings and who invoke blessings on you; and your worst imams are those whom you hate and who hate you, whom you curse and who curse you." They asked God's messenger whether in that event they should not depose them, but he replied, "No, as long as they observe the prayer among you; no, as long as they observe the prayer among you. If anyone has a governor whom he sees doing anything which is an act of disobedience to God, he must disapprove of the disobedience to God which he commits, but must never withdraw from obedience."

The list goes on. Clearly, the idea is that political authority is important to the welfare of the religious community, and is to be respected. One might even say that the duty to respect goes in the direction of forbidding more extreme forms of resistance, as, for example, in the case of revolution or an attempt to depose existing authority. But there is, just as clearly, a delimitation on the authority of rulers. They are primarily "a shield behind whom fighting is engaged in and protection is sought." They are to be obeyed, though one must disapprove of any actions or policies that fall short of God's design. And indeed, further ahadith recommend disobedience and attempts to correct political authority when its departure from God's purpose is severe enough. Thus,

An-Nawwas b. Sam'an reported God's messenger as saying, "A creature is not to be obeyed when it involves disobedience to the Creator."

[Abu Sa'id] reported God's messenger as saying, "The most excellent jihad is when one speaks a true word in the presence of a tyrannical ruler."[22]

Now, it is clear, as previously indicated, that the tendency of classical Islamic political thought presents a picture of rule by one person (some ahadith, in fact, stress that rule should reside in one person, and that if a second presents himself as a candidate, one of the two should be killed!) and of a religious community that considers itself as obligated to respect the "powers that be," at least in the sense that one rarely finds texts that would support a right to armed revolt. In al-Mawardi and other writers, one finds the saying that "a thousand years of tyranny are better than one night of anarchy"; obviously, there was a great worry about the harmful potential of revolutionary activity.[23]

Such a picture should not suggest, however, that opposition was impossible, or that the distinction of roles for the religious and political arms of society is collapsed. Nor can the emphasis on rule by one person (or, more realistically, by a courtly culture having one person standing as the symbol of power) be understood as "Islamic," in any simple sense, given the predominance of imperial models in the world of the sixth through the twelfth centuries. In a more contemporary setting, we find different patterns of political thought emerging, partly as a result of the collapse of the imperial state. For example, the constitutions both of the Islamic Republic of Iran and of Pakistan stipulate the requirement of an elected legislature. The legislature or "consultative assembly" is understood to fulfill the requirement that leadership should be a matter of consultation—in some sense, in both cases, this consultation is understood to include all those living within the boundaries of the state, although the process is decisively weighted toward Muslims. The constitution of the Islamic Republic of Iran understands itself to establish a set of checks and balances between the religious community and political leaders. While its emphasis on the role of religious leaders in supervising elections, legislation, and ultimately all matters of public policy suggests that the balance of power is thrown toward the religious, it is clear from the history of revolutionary Iran that the intent of the framers (in particular, the late Ayatollah Khomeini) was to safeguard the independence of the religious community, and to limit what was understood to be over-reaching by the late shah of Iran or, more generally, by the political leaders of most states. The religious leadership, which is represented first in the person of the "supreme leader" (a religious scholar chosen for excellence in knowledge of Islamic sources, for piety, and for the ability to practice justice), has ultimate oversight in all matters of policy. Together with the supreme leader, a council of guardians, made up of a dozen religious specialists (half chosen by the supreme leader and half by the consultative assembly), effectively carries out the role envisioned in classical thinking for the ʿulama (the power to bind and loose). A president elected by popular vote is able to appoint ministers and, with them, to run the day-to-day affairs of the state, given the supervision of the religious leaders. Constitutionally, at least, the balance of powers is protected by provisions for a free press and other communications or information media, by the delineation of certain sectors of the economy as "public" (owned by the state), "cooperative" (mixed public/private ownership), and "private" (particularly in the area of agriculture), and by the stipulation that everyone, including the supreme leader, is understood to stand in equal relationship before the law. Boundaries are drawn between civil society and government, with the common limitation being the law recognized as the standard for all normative discourse, political or otherwise:

All civil, penal, financial, economic, administrative, cultural, military, political, and other laws and regulations must be based on Islamic criteria. This principle applies absolutely and generally to all articles of the Constitution as well as to all other laws and regulations, and the religious scholars of the Guardian Council are judges in this matter. (Article 4)[24]

Needs

For the classical period, the relations outlined above indicate the general ways in which civil society and government "need" each other. Roughly, the ʿulama lend legitimacy to the caliphate; the caliphate employs legitimate force to protect the independent practice of Islam. Even the duty of the caliphate to call on the people and to carry out the duty of jihad on the "frontiers" of Islamic territory can be seen in this light. The notion of the extension and protection of the borders of the imperial territory known as the territory of Islam should be seen as part of a program to extend and protect the influence of Islamic values in the world, and thus "to make God's cause succeed." The task of the government, working in support of the ʿulama, was to extend the realm within which Islam's influence as the "state religion" could be established. The task of the ʿulama, working with the support of the government, was to spread the message of Islam through "beautiful preaching" or, more prosaically, to convert the hearts of the conquered to Islam. Each institution needs the other; thus the complementarity of civil society and government.

With the demise of imperial Islam, the principle of complementarity is extended, as indicated above, more and more in the direction of participatory democracy: extended—but not negated. Thus, the constitution of the Islamic Republic continues to see all as united by the notion of God's law.

> In the Islamic Republic of Iran, the commanding of the good and the forbidding of the evil is a universal and reciprocal duty that must be fulfilled by the people with respect to one another, by the government with respect to the people, and by the people with respect to the government. The conditions, limits, and nature of this duty will be specified by law. (Article 8)

The government, as specified in Article 3, is to direct "all its resources" toward, among other things, "the creation of a favorable environment for the growth of moral virtues based on faith and piety and the struggle against all forms of vice and corruption." One notices, of course, that the government is not said to be responsible to secure such growth—that is a matter outside its competence, as more generally one should say about faith. But the provision of an environment where faith can take root—this is language typical of the complementary relationship envisioned in classical sources.

The government also, however, must direct "all its resources" to such goals as "raising the level of public awareness in all areas, through the proper use of the press, mass media, and other means." In connection with Article 175, which stipulates that the power to appoint and dismiss the head of the state radio and television network belongs to the supreme leader, one would be justified in reading "proper use" as opening the door to censorship. It is interesting, however, that the grammar of the article makes possible more than one reading on such a key point; thus one reads that the "freedom of expression and dissemination of thoughts in the Radio and Television of the Islamic Republic of Iran must be guaranteed in keeping with the Islamic criteria and the best interests of the country." Is it that freedom of expression and dissemination of thoughts are goods so important to the well-being of the republic that they are thought to be worthy of guaranteed protection, based on Islamic values? Or is it that these are to be guaranteed, insofar as their exercise is in keeping with (that is, within the bounds of) Islamic criteria and the good of the country? If the former, we have an important contemporary expression of the value of an aspect of civil society to the exercise of good government and a recognition of the importance of an independent news media. If the latter, we have a notion that allows civil society to be collapsed or delimited, in the interests of good or effective government.

Liabilities

From Michael Walzer and others, one gathers that the associations covered by civil society, resting as they do on loyalties more delimited and more intense than those inspired by the state, pose a kind of sectarian problem. Government, by contrast, poses a threat to civil society, in that its monopoly on the use of legitimate force gives it a means to regulate, and even to eliminate, associations it deems threatening.[25]

One can understand, with slight alterations, much of the Islamic perspective on liabilities in the civil society/government relationship through Walzer's terms. The imperial version of complementarity between civil society and government, as we have seen, supposed that representatives of the former, in particular the ʿulama, might give Islamic legitimacy to those filling the latter's function. Given the limits on this legitimacy, however ("A creature is not to be obeyed when it involves disobedience to the Creator" and "The most excellent jihad is when one speaks a true word in the presence of a tyrannical ruler"), one might expect the recognition of legitimacy to be contentious. The possibilities for such contention are multiplied when one considers the nature of religious authority in Islam. The ʿulama, that is, are specialists who are recognized, carrying a kind of "certification" from one of several persons or institutions whose standing is undisputed. And those who cannot themselves gain such certification—which is to say, practically speaking, nearly everyone—are supposed to attach themselves to an individual specialist or, more generally, to a recognized "school" or "way" of interpreting Islamic sources with which publicly recognized specialists are attached.

But there is nothing—that is, in the way of Islamic norms themselves—that keeps one from changing allegiance, from adhering to the judgments of one authority for a time, then changing to follow another. Indeed, on some counts, adult Muslims are allowed to take stock of the judgments of all the recognized "ways," and then to choose the judgment that pleases them. The potential for slippage in the civil society/government relation is clear, I think. In effect, the lack of a full-blown ecclesiastical structure, with its own canon law and methods of punishment, allows a great deal of autonomy in the practice of religion. One could not, on classical Muslim standards, publicly criticize certain fundamentals of religion (could not, for example, speak of the Qurʾan as a fabrication). One could, however, manage to find a religious scholar and a kind of subcommunity interested in criticizing the courtly culture and, with it, scholars representing establishment Islam. Judging from the preoccupation of Muslim scholars with the delineation of sects and stories of conflicts between the followers of very great ʿulama and the courtly culture, one would have to say that many Muslims did exactly that.

We will return to some specific instances of conflict, and to the great attempt of Muslim jurists to craft rules to bring such conflict under the rule of Islam, below. For now, however, it is important to notice that from the governmental point of view, the liability of civil society lies precisely in the notion that religious specialists own the power of binding and loosing. As indicated above, this indicates that the ʿulama have the power to withhold or withdraw legitimacy, as well as to give it. And the lack of a formal regulatory structure, which in one way leaves the ʿulama open to government domination, at the same time inhibits the government's ability to regulate civil society. Al-Maʾmun's infamous inquisition, discussed above, may be interpreted as one ruler's attempt to address this problem.

From the side of civil society, the great fear seems to be that governments will overreach. Correspondingly, the ʿulama of Islam express interest in limiting government's sphere of influence. Thus, in a "creed" attributed to al-Maʾmun's famous interlocutor, Ahmad ibn Hanbal, we read that

> [t]o fight in the jihad, as commanded by rulers, is a valid obligation, whether the rulers act with justice or not. . . . The Friday worship, the Two Feasts, and the Pilgrimage are observed according to the declarations of the rulers, even if they are not upright. . . . Taxes are to be paid to the commanders, whether they deal justly or not. . . . Those to whom God has entrusted your affairs are to be followed . . . and not opposed by your sword. . . . To keep aloof in civil strife is an old custom whose observance is obligatory.[26]

Taking this statement piece by piece, one finds affirmed the basic notion that the duties of government include military action in the interests of the umma; provision for public acts of worship; the collection and administration of taxes; and, in general, affairs important for public order. What is missing, and importantly so, is the notion that the caliph is a religious authority, able to regulate or trump others on matters of interpreting sacred texts. In effect, the question of the nature of the Qurʾan could be said to be a matter of conscience, which the caliph has no right to regulate.

As the story of Ahmad, or really of al-Maʾmun's doctrinal test, indicates, the liability of government (that is, from the standpoint of civil society) is its monopoly on legitimate force. Ahmad's understanding of the complementary roles played by religious and political authority is that the latter is not to be opposed by the sword. In effect, the right of arms belongs to government. The strength or duty of each side in the complementary relation is, correspondingly, a threat that it poses to the other.

Similarly, this is true in more contemporary settings. Reading the speeches of Ayatollah Khomeini from the 1960s, one cannot help noticing how often he criticizes the shah of Iran for failing to exercise his constitutional duties to protect the "Islamic people of Iran." The shah is said to pursue private interests, rather than the common good. He is said to undermine the independence of the religious leaders, and thus of Islam. In effect, he is accused of violating the "compact" between religious and political authority, and thus of a kind of default with respect to the complementary relationship between the two.[27]

This kind of criticism is characteristic of much modern Islamic political writing. What is interesting to think about is what complementarity means in a constitutional democracy. The shah, for example, characterized certain changes in policy as giving greater rights in citizenship to minority groups—for example, the Baha'i, who by all accounts have suffered greatly under the regime of the Islamic republic. By securing the welfare of the people and safeguarding the independence of Islam, must one think of Muslims first? This leads to considerations of groups and individuals, and of citizenship in an Islamic polity.

Groups and Individuals

A.K.S. Lambton, among others, argues that the "individual and the state . . . are broadly at one in their moral purpose, and so the conception of the individual is not prominent, nor the conception of rights. Islam does not in fact recognize the legal personality of the individual in which his rights are secured to him and vested in him by law. The state or the government is both expected and able to exercise a very considerable degree of coercion. . . . In Islam the antithesis between the individual and the state or the government is not recognized, and no need is therefore felt to reconcile and abolish this antithesis."[28] Reading these sentences, one supposes that much hangs on phrases like "not prominent," "very considerable degree," and "antithesis between the individual and state." It certainly seems true that Islamic thinkers do not picture individuals as solitary, or as preexisting society in an apolitical "natural" state, à la the Rousseau of *Emile*, and perhaps even of *The Social Contract*. Nor does the existence of the state require explanation, as in some Christian thinkers' suggestion that without the Fall, there would be no state, or at least no coercive power. So far as I can tell, the notion of a power regulating or ordering social life is simply assumed in Islam. God deals, as indicated above, with peoples or nations; each has a prophet or prophets, who come to remind them, in their personal and collective identities, of the truth which is represented by the phrase *al-islam*.

God deals with peoples; but it is ultimately the individual members of each people who are judged, and sent either to eternal damnation or to Paradise, on a "day about which there is no doubt, when each soul will be paid out what it has earned, and there will be no injustice" (3:25b). Given such an emphasis on persons and their responsibility, it is not strange, then, to find ample evidence that runs counter to Lambton's statements. Thus, in his *Bidayat al-mujtahid*, Ibn Rushd argues that every person has rights to life, to liberty, and to property.[29] These are not to be violated, unless one acts in ways that mitigate or sacrifice one's claim—for example, by fighting in an un-

just cause. The law of property recognizes the right of personal or
individual ownership, as does the law of contracts, which is in large
part a set of rulings concerning the ways ownership may be transferred, for example, by sale.[30] And finally, one must consider the law
of personal status, which to a great extent could also be termed "family" law. It was, in fact, in this regard—that is, the attempt to order
human relations in terms of marriage and divorce, the recognition of
children, and rights to inheritance—that the state allowed the most
latitude for religious scholars. The denizens of courtly culture, that
is, tended toward the view that the great matters of policy, such as
treaties, wars, and taxes, were "their" concern, while regulating ordinary life was a safe preoccupation for the ʿulama. Judging from the
responsa of the scholars on issues "great" as well as "small," one
should say that the scholars did not share this delimited view of their
power. The relative freedom they enjoyed in the realm of personal
or family law, however, did give room for a great deal of practical
experience.

As such, government's role with respect to family life seems largely
to have been "backing up" the religious leaders. Thus, in the division
of tasks characteristic of the complementary relation I have been describing, the jurists understood family life, contracts, and the like, as
"their" sphere. Their judgments on these matters form the great bulk
of what Muslims call "the branches of comprehension" or "applied
religious norms." Thus, in the texts of the ʿulama, we find descriptions of marriage, or nikah, as a "contract for the legalization of intercourse and the procreation of children."[31] It is important here, as in
commercial settings, to know just what establishes a contract; in general, the "essential requirements are offer and acceptance."[32] Provided
these take place before the required number of witnesses and that
there are no grounds for a claim of incompetence, offer and acceptance establish a contract by which intercourse becomes valid. If incompetence can be established or if it can be shown that one or both
parties did not give consent (for example, in the case of minors married by the agreement of their parents), the contract may be regarded
as invalid, or in the latter case, one would better say that it may be
repudiated. And, in general, it is inappropriate to speak of the Islamic
law regarding contracts like marriage without noting that the judgments pertaining to divorce allow for its dissolution.

Family life, commerce, property holding are all in the sphere of
civil society, by long-standing tradition in Islam. This leads to a concern about the possibilities for oppression within civil society, and to
questions about a possible role for governments in regulating or
transforming civil society. Thus, the classical judgments on marriage

follow a pattern that distinguishes between the rights and obligations
of men and women, as is well known. A Muslim man may be married to as many as four women at any given time. A Muslim woman,
by contrast, may be married to only one man at any given time. Similarly, most judgments indicate that a Muslim man may be married to
a non-Muslim woman. A Muslim woman, however, may be married
only to a Muslim man. And, regarding divorce, the weight of tradition favors a form that gives the husband the power of initiating the
action. While there are forms of divorce recognized by the tradition in
which the woman's power to initiate or request divorce is important,
these seem to have been less emphasized; indeed, the most prominent
of these, the form called *khul'*, is so called because the desire to separate comes from the wife—but in legal terms, the divorce is by common consent, and thus implies that the husband has agreed to her
request. Much more difficult is the notion that a woman could seek to
end a marriage, on her own or without the consent of her husband.[33]

Such judgments regarding marriage and divorce are only a small
part of the set of practices approved by Islamic scholars, which appear to run counter to the Qur'an's dictum "Those who do righteousness, male or female, and have faith, will be among those entering the
garden and no harm will come to them," or "to men is allotted what
they earn, and to women is allotted what they earn."[34] That such practices are, in large part, authorized by the Qur'an itself only compli-
cates the issue. As noted, some argue that this is a point at which
an enlightened government ought to intervene in civil society; that,
in effect, government has a valid interest in instituting an egalitar-
ian regime with respect to gender relations, whatever the weight of
tradition.

In response, it should be said that Muslims often have a different
"take" on the traditional precepts than do many who are "on the
outside looking in." Thus, for example, Ziba Mir-Hosseini's very interesting study of debates among Iranian 'ulama over the proper understanding of Islamic judgments pertaining to gender makes clear
that many Muslim scholars, reformers and traditionalists alike, see
the distinctions drawn between men and women in matters of marriage, divorce, and inheritance law as reflecting certain presuppositions about social and economic practice.[35] Thus, the fact that women
receive a share of a testee's estate less than that of men, or that the
amount of "blood money" required to pay a tort to the family of a
deceased victim of deliberate or accidental death is less in the case of
a female than of a male victim, is said by Mir-Hosseini's scholar infor-
mants to reflect the social fact that men generally carry greater responsibilities for earning. Families losing a male member may thus be

considered to have a greater need. As Mir-Hosseini points out in the give and take of her interviews, it may be argued that this kind of social background is no longer to be presumed in contemporary Iran. The scholars are often willing to admit this, many of them quite evidently struggling for a language that will allow them to move toward a more consistent egalitarianism of the type envisioned in the Qurʾanic verses quoted above.

In Mir-Hosseini's own reflections, one finds expressed the dilemma of those who wonder whether governments should intervene to push reforms in gender relations; that is, reform from above is almost always depicted as anti-Islam or as a plot hatched by a West still unwilling to give up colonial aims. Thus, the shah's attempts to reform Islamic laws in ways suggestive of gender equality have been discredited, and it is the ʿulama who, according to Mir-Hosseini, hold the key to new models of gender relations. In some sense, this is unsurprising. If family law has been the sphere of the ʿulama for centuries, one would hardly expect to find them willing to relinquish it to governments; similarly with commercial law. The ʿulama have seen themselves, with some validity, as the guardians of freedom, struggling with an overweening government. The question now is whether some groups of citizens will think it necessary to organize in ways constructed so as to limit an overweening ʿulama. Thus, Mir-Hosseini remarks on the remarkable presence of women in Iranian professional life, and notes that there is now an institution dedicated to educating women in the traditional manner of the ʿulama. She wonders where this can go, and so may we.

Citizenship

With respect to citizenship, classical judgment, by and large, reflected the pattern evidenced in the famous "Medina Constitution," or agreement between the Prophet and the various groups living in the city. The Muslims and those who "followed them and joined them and labored with them . . . are one community to the exclusion of others."[36] The Jews of Medina are said to constitute a distinct community with their own religion. They are tolerated or, more literally, "protected" by the Muslims, in the sense that they are free to follow their own sacred texts and laws, within limits indicated by the security needs of the Muslims. They are not to run their own foreign policy, for example. Nor are they to engage in public criticism of the Prophet or to attempt to persuade Muslims to drop their allegiance to Muhammad. Over centuries, the pattern of imperial Islam was governed by this model. Thus, *ahl al-dhimma*, the "protected" peoples, paid tribute to the Islamic government in exchange for the right of limited freedom. Christians, for example, were allowed to govern their own affairs in family and commercial law, provided these created no conflict with Muslims. They were allowed to worship, so long as their public displays did not disturb the peace of Islam.[37]

What Christians and others were not is full citizens in the sense of participants in the enterprise of Islamic government. As we move into the modern period, we do better, in fact, to think of them as recognized minorities. Thus, once notions of representative government appear, we find such groups receiving a certain delimited place in the political process. The constitution of the Islamic Republic of Iran, for example, sets aside one seat in the Consultative Assembly for each of the recognized religious minorities present in the republic. Similar patterns hold in Egypt, where Coptic Christians receive a set portion of representation.

Among other things, it is important to note the persistence of a religious dimension in understandings of citizenship. And it is important that in terms of certain aspects of citizenship, the disabilities for women present in family law seem to be overcome. After some initial opposition from religious scholars, there is now no question about women's right to vote in contemporary Iran—it is established in the constitution and in practice. Similarly, women may hold office in the legislature, though it should be noted that, in the complicated procedure by which candidates are approved to run for president, none of the women applying for certification has been approved for the ballot.

Conflict

The religious nature of citizenship, and thus of participation in an Islamic state, shows up in a fascinating set of rules developed by classical scholars for dealing with a variety of intrastate conflicts. *Ahkam al-bughat* are "judgments about rebels," specifically, Muslims who take up arms against an established caliph. These are different from *ahkam ahl al-dhimma*, "judgments about the protected communities," which attempt to guide caliphal policy in cases where religious minorities violate the terms under which they are tolerated. And both are distinguished from the rules for fighting against *al-murtadd* (Muslims who "turn" and are thus apostates), as well as those for dealing with criminal bands ("highwaymen," as most translators have it). Rules pertaining to rebels, in particular, illustrate the attempt of the ʿulama to create a protected space for religious practice; as I have been arguing, this is the classical Islamic analogue to civil society. The rules specify the characteristics of a legitimate rebel group, as opposed to a group of apostates or thieves; correspondingly, there are strict limits on the response of government.[38]

We have already seen that classical Islam viewed rebellion with suspicion. The ahadith cited above are only a few of the reports suggesting the problematic nature of taking up arms against an established government. The ʿulama feared the propensity of zealots to put considerations of purity above the welfare of the community as a whole; they also feared that, whatever the intention of rebels, harm would come to many innocent people. Thus they favored quiet resistance, conscientious refusal to obey unjust commands, or the speaking of a well-placed warning over outright revolt. Better a thousand years of tyranny than one night of anarchy—that summarizes the scholars' general view; one hardly needs to say further that it establishes an anti-revolutionary tone.

Nevertheless, governments are prone to overreach, and the Muslim caliphate provided numerous examples of this. Given this, the ʿulama recognized the import of at least some room for more boisterous forms of resistance. In recognition of the independence of civil society, they drew up a description of the characteristics of legitimate activist groups. Generally speaking, there are three such characteristics: *al-khuruj*, *al-taʾwil*, and *al-shawka*. The first, which draws on the Arabic for "exiting" or "secession," indicates that the group resists an established regime, employing means beyond speech or "merely" expressive activity. "Rebels" must, as a group, clearly violate the laws or policies of the regime.

The second characteristic, al-taʾwil, indicates that the rebels provide public justification for their action. Further, in its ordinary sense, al-taʾwil (interpretation) implies that this justification is offered in terms of recognized Islamic sources. The point is that the rebels provide a demonstration that they are Muslims. They are not apostates, meaning people who have turned from Islam and are rejecting its authority. Nor are they Jews or Christians, whose taʾwil might be expressed in terms that challenge the honor of Islam. The rebels are Muslims—an important way of drawing the lines between legitimate expressions of civil society, and illegitimate activities.

The third characteristic, al-shawka, or "strength," indicates that the rebels must have a following or that the group must be of a certain size. What exactly this entails is a matter of disagreement. Some scholars say ten, others forty, others more. The point is that the rebellion is not "private"—say, the activity of an extended family disenchanted with the government. To be classified as a rebel group, there must be a demonstration of support from the Muslim community.

Provided a group demonstrates the required characteristics, governmental response is limited in important ways. A caliph responding to a rebel group is not allowed to deal with its members as criminals. He must follow the directive of the Qur'an.

> If two parties of believers fall to fighting, then make peace between them. And if one party of them does wrong to the other, fight the one that does wrong until it returns to the way of God; then, if it returns, make peace between them with justice, and act equitably. Lo! God loves those who act equitably. The believers are brothers: so make peace between your brothers and observe your duty to God, that you may receive mercy.[39]

Reconciliation, rather than punishment, is the goal in responding to rebels. Further, the caliph must exercise extreme care in resorting to armed force against a rebel group. His policy should be set by following the example of 'Ali, son-in-law of Muhammad, viewed as the fourth caliph by most Muslims.

> [A contemporary of 'Ali said:] I entered the Mosque of Kufa through the Kinda gates where I met five men cursing [the caliph]. One of them, covered with a burnus [hooded cloak], said: "I have made a covenant with God that I shall kill him." Whereupon, I kept close while his companions dispersed, and I took him to 'Ali and said: "I heard this man saying that he has made a covenant with God that he will kill you." "Bring him nearer," said ['Ali] and added: "woe to you, who are you?" "I am Sawwar al-Manquri," replied the man. "Let him go," said 'Ali. Thereupon, I said: "Shall I let him go, though he made a covenant with God to kill you?" "Shall I kill him even though he has not killed me?" replied 'Ali. "He has cursed you," [I said]. "You should then curse him or leave him," said 'Ali.
>
> It has been related . . . that, while 'Ali was once making a sermon on Friday, [some] Kharijis, from one side of the Mosque, pronounced the formula: "Judgment belongs to none save God." "A word of Truth to which is given a false meaning," said 'Ali [and he added]: "we shall not prohibit you from entering our mosques to mention God's name; we shall not deny you [your share of public funds], so long as you join hands with us; nor shall we fight you until you attack us."
>
> It has also been related . . . that 'Ali said in the Battle of the Camel: "Whoever flees shall not be chased, no prisoner of war shall be killed, no wounded in battle shall be dispatched, no enslavement shall be allowed, and no property shall be confiscated."[40]

By comparison with the rules governing armed conflict with non-Muslims, these examples restrict the caliph considerably. In all, the message is that the government is responding to Muslim groups, who are to be accorded a kind of legitimacy. Formally recognized as "rebels," they must be treated in ways that will foster reconciliation. Or, in terms of the civil society/government relation, one might say they are to be treated in ways that recognize that there are limits on the caliph's right, with respect to the conscience of the Muslim community. Whatever liabilities result, whatever fears the caliph has of the sectarian possibilities implicit in a relatively independent religious sector, the government's response to Muslim rebel groups must be crafted so as to recognize and respect the limits on the claims of khilafat as the successor to the Prophet. The caliph's duties are (primarily) political. The ʿulama safeguard a relatively independent religious sector, within the general model of the complementarity of civil society and government.

In contemporary Islamic societies, it might be argued that the status of rebel groups is the most contentious point in the relationship between civil society and government. In settings where, despite constitutional provisions for elections, an independent judiciary, and the like, many citizens consider that their ability to speak and associate freely or to express their conscientious judgments is unfairly restricted, the tendency to form activist, even revolutionary groups whose identity is in some way "Islamic" is very strong. In Egypt, for example, a member of the group of activists accused of conspiracy in the assassination of President Anwar Sadat provided a public justification for such acts in a much-discussed treatise called *The Neglected Duty*.[41] The argument of the treatise was that political leaders who claim to be Muslims but whose policies are not consonant with Islam are apostates or traitors to the Islamic community. Following longstanding tradition, the author said that such people are deserving of death. In the absence of a "real" Islamic government willing to carry out such a sentence, the duty of punishing people who commit crimes against Islam devolves upon the community as a whole. The author's group, one of many bearing the name "Islamic Jihad," simply stood in for the Muslim community against the traitor, Sadat.

The ensuing trial of members of Islamic Jihad featured, among other things, arguments by defense attorneys to the effect that the accused were, in the technical sense of classical Islam, "rebels." In particular, the claim was that the imposition of the death penalty would be wrong and, according to Article 2 of the Egyptian Constitution, illegal. As Khaled Abou El Fadl puts it, "The military tribunal ignored this argument in passing the death sentence on certain defendants."[42]

Certainly activities like assassination go beyond the scope of what is ordinarily considered "civil society." Groups like Islamic Jihad are

in one sense outside the scope of that term, as they involve themselves in a kind of ongoing armed conflict with existing political
power. The focus on their military or paramilitary activities often
leads observers to miss, however, a number of other aspects of such
groups. The "duties" the members see government neglecting have to
do with the efficient provision of social services, health care, and basic
education, especially for growing numbers of urban poor, numbers
created by government policies that unsettle traditional rural patterns
of life (for example, policies that promote agribusiness). Groups like
Islamic Jihad ordinarily serve multiple purposes, mediating not only
between governments and families, but between families and survival. Governments count these groups as liabilities, because their af-
finity for violence threatens public order, and their public use of Islamic slogans undermines the legitimacy of an established regime. At
the same time, governments and, even more, the urban poor need
such groups to counter some of the effects of poverty.[43] Currently, the
approach to this set of tensions between civil society and government
in Muslim societies moves back and forth between several options.
One approach attempts to broaden the scope of political participation
by allowing activist groups to play an official role—for example, by
allowing Islamic groups to function as political parties, who field candidates in elections, bargain for members of their group to hold certain cabinet offices, and in general take part in parliamentary politics.
Such parties receive a portion of public funds for patronage purposes,
and put them to use by providing social services to the public, or at
least to some portion of the public. In return, activist groups lay down
their arms, or at least curtail their paramilitary activities. The long-
standing part played by the Muslim Brethren in Egyptian politics provides an illustration of this approach.

Difficulties arise, however, in cases where the parties formed by
activist groups secure a broad enough following that they threaten to
change established patterns of power distribution. In the case of Algeria, where Islamic parties actually won an electoral victory in the
early 1990s, those elites used to exercising authority were simply unwilling to transfer power. A military regime was put in place, the
election results canceled, and the resulting civil war has yet to play
itself out.

If inclusion is one approach, and nullification (as in Algeria) a second, yet a third option is presented by revolutionary Iran. There, opposition to the shah reached such heights during the 1970s that a
coalition of ʿulama and reform-minded business and political leaders
rallied public support in a successful revolution in 1978–79. The resulting Islamic Republic, the constitution of which has been men-

tioned in passing at several points in this essay, is an attempt to safeguard the independence of the ʿulama as guardians of Islamic values.
In this attempt, it is arguable that the notion of a relatively independent governmental sphere is violated; it is also arguable that the complementarity of civil society and government swings so far in the direction of the ʿulama that their role as guardians of an independent
civil sector is undone. Recent elections, in which large numbers of
young, relatively well-educated voters expressed their desire for a
greater sphere of personal liberty, might be taken to suggest that the
ʿulama, or at least those most directly identified with the governing
apparatus of the Islamic Republic, are coming to be seen as tyrants in
their own right; people who, in the name of protecting Islam, set
themselves the role of so regulating the practice of members of the
Islamic community that they endanger the freedom of conscience to
which every Muslim has a right.

Conclusions

Throughout this discussion, I have suggested that the complementarity thesis—that is, that religion and politics play distinct, though
mutually supportive, roles in the life of a Muslim society—suggests
one way to develop an Islamic perspective on the civil society/gov-
ernment relation. Particularly in the classical model of Islamic society,
whereby a class of scholars, the ʿulama, have authority as interpreters
of Islamic values; and a corresponding class of rulers, advisers, military, and bureacrats have authority under the umbrella of khilafat to
secure the peace of Islamic society, I have suggested that one might
view the ʿulama/khilafat relation as an analogy to that between civil
society and government. I have suggested that throughout the history
of Islam, inclusive of more recent developments in the Islamic Republic of Iran and in other Muslim-majority societies, the complementarity thesis holds. Thus, "civil society" becomes a discussion of the
ways that Muslims have understood that social life should be organized, so as to protect the relative independence of Islamic values
from the authoritarian tendencies of governments. In turn, "government" comes to stand for the set of institutions whose legitimate monopoly on armed force within a given territory must be carried out in
ways that respect the relative independence of the religious sphere.
    Three points seem to follow.
    First, there is a way in which the analogy I have suggested (whereby
ʿulama/khilafat stands for civil society/government) might be characterized as uneasy, or even inept. If civil society means, as in the more

contemporary versions of the Lockean tradition, that one must think in terms of the ways a society like the United States legitimates a thorough-going regime of liberty in religious and, more generally, civil matters, then the concept does not fit neatly with most of Islamic political thinking. Complementarity, in the Islamic setting, has meant and continues to imply some sort of established status for Islam. Governments carry out their political duties with the presumption that they are Islamically legitimate. Leaders give at least lip service to the notion that they form policies based on consultation with the ʿulama. Rights of citizenship are set with religious distinctions in mind; distinctions of gender, insofar as those are thought of as having a basis in authoritative Islamic texts, are also part of the public regime of Islamic societies. A fully developed civil society, in the sense that many analysts presume, has not been, and is not at this time, an aspect of most Islamic political thinking.

Second (however), one must note that complementarity, as a model for the civil society/government relation, provides an indefinite norm. In general, it establishes certain limits on institutions. In the Islamic case, the tradition has been especially to stress the limits on government, with respect to the threat that its officials will overreach their mandate and encroach on the sphere of religious values. If one thinks positively, one might say that complementarity sets civil society and government in a relation of creative tension. Governments will always be worried, given the loose structure of religious authority in Islam, about the sectarian potential of religion. Correlatively, they will always be tempted to regulate religion, to foreclose or delimit the independence of the ʿulama, and to regulate the conscience of Muslims. The ʿulama will always be tempted by the prospect of religious purity. They will be critical of government, particularly insofar as they perceive that the realities of political life often involve officials in activities that leave them with dirty hands. The loose structure of religious authority in Islam will also create problems for the ʿulama. Since every Muslim has the right to read the Qurʾan and ahadith, and to interpret them for him/herself, the idea of a special class of experts rests on somewhat tenuous grounds. As a practical matter, most Muslims have identified themselves with the ʿulama of a particular school. They have, and will continue to, defer to the consensus of these ʿulama. Every Muslim has the right to interpret for him/herself, however; that much is shown, even in the traditional allowance for an adult male Muslim to examine the judgments of ʿulama from a variety of schools on a particular question, and to follow whichever school he likes best. This loose structure has relevance for our discussion of civil society and government in yet another way, as well—for it points to the potential for new judgments. The discussion of Iranian ʿulama concerning traditional judgments about gender is one example of the tendency built into the religious structure of Islam. One consults the sources of Islam; one should be informed by the precedent of earlier generations of interpreters. But new contexts require new judgments. The idea that the thesis of complementarity somehow forecloses reform within Islam should be avoided.[44]

Finally, I want to revisit a question raised earlier in this essay, regarding the place of a professional and business class in Muslim societies. The recent elections in Iran, the results of which clearly favor President Khatami's calls for a greater independence of "civil society," may be analyzed as the expression of desires on the part of such a class for a certain independence, not only from the overreaching of governments like that of the shah, but from the overreaching of certain ʿulama. The business and professional classes of Muslim societies are not themselves religious specialists (at least most are not). Nor are they politicians or government bureaucrats. They are *citizens*, most of them "lay" Muslims, interested in the building of a society in which freedom and justice are respected values. Khatami's speeches and writings articulate a view, which many business and professional types would share, that in the history of Islam the ʿulama have been the protectors of liberty, over against authoritarian, not to say despotic, governments. As Khatami has warned his fellow scholars, however, those who utilize their position as guardians of Islamic values in ways that deny the hopes of citizens for freedom and justice (for example, by closing newspapers and television stations associated with opposition parties) run the risk of undoing this history. The ʿulama, in short, begin to look like the government officials they previously despised.

When Khatami speaks about the importance of civil society, he means to call for a way of organizing an Islamic state that increases freedom for this business and professional class. He does not emphasize so much the role of American-style voluntary associations like the Rotary Clubs or the National Organization for Women. Nor does he imply a society in which religious identity becomes a matter of indifference with respect to citizenship. Khatami means to preserve an Islamic identify for Iran and, by extension, for other Islamic states; this means the complementarity thesis, with its supposition of some sort of Islamic religious establishment, is presumed. By civil society, Khatami does mean a greater role for ordinary citizens in discussions of the policies of an Islamic state. Whether his call will be successful and what it will mean for Islamic political thought are matters on which only time will pronounce a verdict. That a greater role for lay Muslims in Islamic societies would have an impact on the Islamic perspective on civil society and government seems, however, beyond question.

Notes

1. See the expositions in Shlomo Avineri, *Hegel's Theory of the Modern State* (Cambridge: Cambridge University Press, 1972); and Michael O. Hardimon, *Hegel's Social Philosophy: The Project of Reconciliation* (Cambridge: Cambridge University Press, 1994), in addition to Hegel's own *Philosophy of Right*, trans. (with notes) T. M. Knox (New York: Oxford University Press, 1967).

2. Cf. John Locke, *Treatise of Civil Government and A Letter Concerning Toleration*, ed. by Charles L. Sherman (New York: Appleton-Century-Crofts, 1937); also Adam B. Seligman, *The Idea of Civil Society* (Princeton: Princeton University Press, 1995).

3. Cf. Mohammed Khatami, *Islam, Liberty, and Development* (Binghamton, N.Y.: Global Publications, 1999). A second volume, *Hope and Challenge: The Iranian President Speaks* (Binghamton, N.Y.: Global Publications, 1998) contains some of the same material. Saad Eddin Ibrahim's work is well represented in "Civil Society and Prospects for Democratization in the Arab World," in *Civil Society in the Middle East*, ed. Augustus Richard Norton (Leiden: E. J. Brill, 1995), 1:27–54. The entire collection of essays in Norton's volume is useful, though they are more social scientific and less philosophically oriented than the present essay.

4. Max Weber, "Politics as a Vocation," in *From Max Weber*, trans. and ed. H. Gerth and C. Wright Mills (New York: Oxford University Press, 1946), 78. Despite Weber's reference to the "modern" state in this oft-quoted remark, the description stands generally for the type of institutions that may be classed as "government" in the present essay.

5. With respect to Arabic terms: In this essay, I follow the practice of the *International Journal of Middle East Studies*, and have thus omitted most diacritical markings in the transliteration. The exceptions are ʿayn (signaled by ʿ) and hamza (signaled by ʾ). In addition, I shall use italics for only the first use of a term.

6. Hamid Enayat, *Modern Islamic Political Thought* (Austin: University of Texas Press, 1982) provides an excellent survey of Muslim discussions of democracy, among other issues.

7. Khatami, *Islam, Liberty, and Development*.

8. With respect to "schools of thought," one must at least take note of the great division between Sunni and Shiʿi Islam. In surveys of Islam, the former is usually said to be the marker of identity preferred by some 85 to 90 percent of Muslims; the latter would then be preferred by 10 or 15 percent. It is difficult to establish such percentages with precision, but most analysts would agree with the implication that Sunni Islam is "majoritarian," and Shiʿi Islam a

minority expression within the tradition. Most would also then agree with a gloss on the figures indicating that, in reality, the terms Sunni and Shi'i are broad "umbrella" terms; each school contains multiple groups.

Many texts suggest that the division between Sunni and Shi'i begins almost immediately following the death of the Prophet in 632, and involves a dispute over whether or not the Prophet designated his son-in-law, 'Ali ibn Abi Talib, to succeed him as the ruler of the Islamic community. As things turned out, an older companion of the Prophet, Abu Bakr, in fact served as the first caliph or successor to the Prophet, and 'Ali did not serve in that capacity until the year 656.

Whatever the historical case for the claim of such an early appearance of the two schools (and one must note that, in contemporary Sunni-Shi'i polemics, the dispute over the proper understanding of these early events is very prominent), the terms Sunni and Shi'i gradually came, over several centuries, to identify two schools within Islam, each with its characteristic ways of talking about politics, theology, and piety. With respect to politics, in particular, the Shi'i groups were and are distinguished by their emphasis on the rule of a righteous *imam*, or "leader," who is the "proof" of God's justice on earth. There is one, and only one, such imam on earth at any particular time. That person is designated by God to lead; the imam is characterized not only by piety and learning, in the ordinary sense of the terms, but by special insight into the sources of Islam and by the quality of sinlessness. Politically speaking, right authority or legitimate government exists only when the imam of the age is in charge of the affairs of the Islamic community. Sunni Islam, by contrast, is usually presented as a tradition in which consultation and consensus establish legitimate government.

The importance of this difference, in terms of perceptions of the ultimate purposes of politics, is very great, as it also may be for certain issues in political ethics, for example, the justification and limitation of war. For the issue before us, however, the import seems surprisingly small. This is so, to a great extent, because the largest Shi'i subgroup, the Twelver or Imami Shi'a, holds that the Imam of the Age has been absent, in a state of occultation, since 873 or 874. He will appear at a time of God's designation, and will then establish justice and equity. In the meantime, the Shi'i religious leaders are charged with preserving the integrity of Islamic practice in relation to an established government. They thus occupy a place in Islamic political thought very similar to that of the Sunni scholars (see below). That being the case, I shall move freely between Sunni and Shi'i examples as my argument proceeds, and will not be concerned with the distinctions between the two schools. For more on the Shi'i tradition, I refer the reader to two works by Abdulaziz Sachedina: *Islamic Messianism* (Albany: State University of New York Press, 1981); and *The Just Ruler in Shi'ite Islam* (New York: Oxford University Press, 1988).

With reference to "modes" of political conversation, I have in mind the distinction A.K.S. Lambton drew between legal, philosophical, and "literary" styles in her *State and Government in Medieval Islam* (Oxford: Oxford University Press, 1988).

9. The next few paragraphs contain nothing that would be considered "controversial." Readers may supplement my brief comments by turning to a standard biogaphical study like that of W. M. Watt, *Muhammad: Prophet and Statesman* (London: Oxford University Press, 1961). A more recent study, less biographical but covering much of the same material, is F. E. Peters's *Muhammad and the Origins of Islam* (Albany: State University of New York Press, 1994). Both of necessity draw heavily from pious sources, in particular the biography by Ibn Ishaq (d. 767), which is available as *The Life of Muhammad*, trans. A. Guillaume (New York: Oxford University Press, 1955).

10. For more on the relation between Byzantine, Sassanid, and Muslim notions of statecraft, see Fred M. Donner, "The Sources of Islamic Conceptions of War," in *Just War and Jihad: Historical and Theoretical Perspectives on War and Peace in Western and Islamic Traditions*, ed. John Kelsay and James Turner Johnson (Westport, Conn.: Greenwood Press, 1991), 31–70.

11. Qur'an 16:25. Throughout this essay, I make use of the translation of Yusuf 'Ali, though I have sometimes altered the translation according to my own sense of the Arabic text.

12. The oldest extant biography is that of Ibn Ishaq (see n. 9).

13. Cf. Fred M. Donner, *The Early Islamic Conquests* (Princeton: Princeton University Press, 1981) for a chronology of the spread of Islamic power, as well as a survey and critique of the literature on the "reasons for" the Muslim push out of Arabia.

14. For details and a penetrating analysis, nothing surpasses Marshall G. S. Hodgson, *The Venture of Islam*, vol. 1 (Chicago: University of Chicago Press, 1974).

15. For the next few paragraphs, see John Kelsay, "Divine Commands and Social Order," *Annual of the Society of Christian Ethics* (1990), 63–80, and literature cited there.

16. According to Shi'i tradition, 'Ali al-Rida was the eighth imam, in the line beginning with 'Ali ibn Abi Talib.

17. In general, see Marshall G. S. Hodgson's *Venture*, vols. 2 and 3.

18. Here, see Enayat, *Modern Islamic Political Thought*; also, Albert Hourani, *Arabic Thought in the Liberal Age, 1798–1939* (Cambridge: Cambridge University Press, 1984).

19. 'Ali 'Abd al-Raziq's book on "Islam and the Basis of Government" (*Al-Islam wa usul al-hukm*, published in Cairo in 1925) is excerpted (trans. Joseph Massad) in *Liberal Islam: A Sourcebook*, ed. Charles Kurzman (New York: Oxford University Press, 1998), 29–36, among other places.

20. Cf. the collection of Khomeini's speeches and writings published as *Islam and Revolution*, trans. Hamid Algar (Berkeley, Calif.: Mizan Press, 1981). Cf. also Farhang Rajaee, *Islamic Values and Worldview* (Lanham, Md.: University Press of America, 1983); R. Mottahedeh, *The Mantle of the Prophet* (New York: Simon and Schuster, 1985). My own exploration of Khomeini's thought is "Spirituality and Social Struggle: Islam and the West," published in *What Kind of God? Essays in Honor of Richard L. Rubenstein*, ed. Betty Rogers Rubenstein and Michael Berenbaum (Lanham, Md.: University Press of America, 1995).

21. The following reports are cited from the compendium Muslims know as *Mishkat al-Masabih*, trans. James Robson, 4 vols. (Lahore: Sh. M. Ashraf, 1963–64). *Mishkat* collects representative ahadith on various issues (for example, political obligation) from each of the six collections regarded as authoritative by Sunni Muslims.

22. Ibid.

23. Al-Mawardi (d. 1058) is the author of one of the most authoritative classical treatises on the caliphate. See the translation by Asadullah Yate, *Al-Ahkam as-Sultaniyyah: The Laws of Islamic Governance* (London: Ta-Ha Publishers, 1996).

24. Here and elsewhere, I quote from the official English version, available online at *http://www.iranonline.com*. Article numbers will simply be noted in the text.

25. M. Walzer, "The Concept of Civil Society," in *Toward a Global Civil Society*, ed. Michael Walzer (Providence, R.I.: Bergahn Books, 1995), 7–28.

26. As in W. Montgomery Watt, *The Formative Period of Islamic Thought* (Edinburgh: Edinburgh University Press, 1973), 293.

27. Khomeini, *Islam and Revolution*.

28. Lambton, *State and Government in Medieval Islam*, xv.

29. As in the "chapter on *jihad*," translated in R. Peters, *Jihad in Mediaeval and Modern Islam* (Leiden: E. J. Brill, 1977).

30. Cf., among others, Joseph Schacht, *An Introduction to Islamic Law* (Oxford: Clarendon Press, 1964); N. J. Coulson, *A History of Islamic Law* (Edinburgh: Edinburgh University Press, 1964); Asaf A. A. Fyzee, *Outlines of Muhammadan Law*, 4th ed. (Oxford: Oxford University Press, 1974).

31. Fyzee, *Outlines*, 90.

32. Ibid., 91.

33. It should be noted that it is possible for a provision to be placed in the original contract of marriage, by which a woman's right to initiate divorce is stipulated. This is considered binding in Islamic law. For a discussion of this provision, see Ziba Mir-Hosseini, *Islam and Gender: The Religious Debate in Contemporary Iran* (Princeton: Princeton University Press, 1999).

34. 4:124, 4:32.

35. Mir-Hosseini, *Islam and Gender*.

36. Ibn Ishaq, *Life of Muhammad*, 651.

37. Cf. Ronald L. Nettler, "Dhimmi," in *The Oxford Encyclopedia of the Modern Islamic World*, ed. John L. Esposito (New York: Oxford University Press, 1995), 1:374.

38. For more extended analysis, cf. John Kelsay, *Islam and War: A Study in Comparative Ethics* (Louisville, Ky.: Westminster/John Knox Press), 77–110; and also Khaled Abou El Fadl, "*Ahkam al-Bughat*: Irregular Warfare and the Law of Rebellion in Islam," in *Cross, Crescent, and Sword: The Justification and Limitation of War in Western and Islamic Tradition*, ed. James Turner Johnson and John Kelsay (Westport, Conn.: Greenwood Press, 1990), 149–78. My understanding of this material is largely due to Abou El Fadl's incisive presentation.

39. 49:9–10.

40. From Muhammad ibn al-Hasan al-Shaybani, *The Islamic Law of Nations: Shaybani's Siyar*, trans. M. Khadduri (Baltimore: Johns Hopkins University Press, 1966), sec. 1372.

41. Trans. Johannes J. G. Jansen (New York: Macmillan, 1986). Jansen provides an introduction, and also translates a number of Egyptian responses to the document. I analyze the argument at some length in *Islam and War*.

42. Abou El Fadl, *"Akham al-Bughat,"* 168.

43. Cf. analyses presented in the five volumes produced by the Fundamentalisms Project, directed by Martin Marty and R. Scott Appleby (Chicago: University of Chicago Press, 1991–93).

44. This is the place to refer the reader to several works by Muslim intellectuals who advance proposals about the relationship between religion and politics in Islam that suggest a wider sphere for religious liberty. Such a widening of scope for liberty suggests a model of civil society more like that characteristic of the Lockean tradition, in particular. See, among others, Abdulaziz Sachedina, "Freedom of Conscience and Religion in the Qur'an," in *Human Rights and the Conflict of Cultures*, ed. David Little, John Kelsay, and Abdulaziz Sachedina (Columbia: University of South Carolina Press, 1988), 53–90; Abdullahi an-Na'im, *Toward an Islamic Reformation* (Syracuse, N.Y.: Syracuse University Press, 1990); and Khaled Abou El Fadl, *And God Knows the Soldiers: The Authoritative and Authoritarian in Islamic Discourses* (Washington, D.C.: University Press of America, 2001).

2

Perspectives on Islam and Civil Society

FARHAD KAZEMI

Context: Civil Society and Islamic Politics

Civil society has become an important issue in Islamic politics in recent years and a central topic of discourse for scholars, policy makers, and other observers. Its renewed relevance is a reflection of a set of two relatively recent international and domestic developments. On the international side, these developments included the collapse of the Soviet Union, the end of the Cold War, the initial movement toward democratization in several parts of the world, and what appeared to be major progress toward resolving the Arab-Israeli conflict. The external environment seemed to be moving away from a preoccupation with festering international and regional conflicts and, hence, allowing for greater attention to important issues of governance at home.

On the domestic front, the collective impact of internal dynamics in the Islamic world (particularly the Middle East) created significant pressures on the traditional relationship between the state and society in the region. These developments included rapid urbanization; dramatic increases in literacy, especially among females; regular and major movement of population within the region and abroad; increased use of different forms of electronic communication; and other similar factors. The changed environment ushered in more forceful demands for accountability and the rule of law for an ever-expanding segment of the population. The theme of civil society in many ways emerged as a vehicle (especially among the intelligentsia) for expressing the demands for greater freedom for the people and less oppression by the ubiquitous arms of the state.

Civil society as a theme of governance and as a reflection of state-society relations, however, was contentious from the beginning. The thrust of the debate concerned the relevance of the concept to non-Western societies and particularly its applicability to Islam. Some have argued that civil society "does not translate into Islamic terms."[1] It is often argued that civil society developed as an essentially modern phenomenon in the West, while much of the theoretical elements of Islam have premodern roots. The applicability is, therefore, problematic. Others, including the author, have argued that the concept is eminently applicable to Islamic politics.[2] The premodern features, though occasionally problematic, are not insurmountable barriers. The real task is more one of ascertaining the extent of civil society's presence and its level of autonomy from the state.[3]

The contending views have resulted in a large number of meetings, conferences, and publications in the Middle East and elsewhere. Two other developments brought additional public attention to the topic. The first was Huntington's article, "The Clash of Civilizations?" with its contention that liberal democracy is not compatible with the religious traditions of Islam.[4] This article has received an inordinate amount of attention (both positive and negative) among the Muslim activists on all sides. The second critical development was the enshrinement of civil society (and the corollary themes of pluralism and respect for the rule of law) in the successful presidential campaign of the relatively moderate Iranian candidate, Muhammad Khatami, in 1997.[5] These sharply opposing conceptions further fueled the debate in the Islamic world about the congruence of Islam, civil society, and democracy. The political context for an analysis of Islam and civil society is, therefore, quite clear.

Civil Society

I use the concept of civil society in the classical Western model and contend that it has a direct relevance to Islam and Islamic politics. Following Walzer's usage, I maintain that "the words 'civil society' name the space of uncoerced human association and also the set of relations networks—formed for the sake of family, faith, interest, and ideology—that fill this space."[6] This separation of the state from civil society does not eliminate the state's critical role. The state "lays down laws" that provide the framework for and limits of action. Beyond these constraints, "the actions of individuals and collectivities are freely chosen."[7] The idea of civil society, then, to use Shils's words, is "a part of society which has a life of its own, which is distinctly different from the state, and which is largely in autonomy from it. . . . It lies short of the state."[8]

Several components must be present for civil society to exist. In addition to the space separating the individual from the state, civil society encompasses two other principal components: (a) the existence of a complex of autonomous institutions and (b) the prevalence of "civility" in the social order and in relations among individuals. The network of autonomous institutions—family, groups, tribes, guilds, unions, clubs, associations, parties—provides the buffer between the individual and the state and allows for the development of a participant society.[9] These institutions permit individuals to express their attitudes, views, and orientations. They allow for participation in civil life.

Civil society, however, is not just a mélange of different groups and associations. As Norton points out, "it also refers to a quality—civility—without which the milieu consists of feuding factions, cliques, and cabals. Civility implies tolerance, the willingness of individuals to accept disparate political views and social attitudes; sometimes to accept the profoundly important idea that there is no right answer."[10] Civility implies not only tolerance of the other, but also "attachment to the institutions which constitute civil society."[11]

To sum up, then, civil society implies the existence of associations autonomous from the state and of individuals tolerant of others and accepting of institutions of civic order. These are institutions that allow for the development of democracy and citizenship in various spheres of life. Among these are institutions of market economy, competing political parties, independent judiciary, free press, and a host of voluntary associations.[12] Ultimately and as Michael Walzer has indicated, "only a democratic state can create a democratic civil society; only a democratic civil society can sustain a democratic state. The civility that makes democratic politics possible can only be learned in the associational networks; the roughly equal and widely dispersed capabilities that sustain the networks have to be fostered by the democratic state."[13]

Critical Issues

As a respondent to John Kelsay's discussion of civil society and Islam in the preceding chapter, I have selected a few broad issues of special and continuing relevance. These issues can be subsumed under two general categories of needs and boundaries, and groups and individuals. I will then use the example of Islamists, who play an important role in the debate on Islam and civil society, to illustrate the problematique of group conflict and citizenship rights from this perspective. In order not to repeat Kelsay's discussion I will review the topics in a more general fashion.

Needs and Boundaries

In the Islamic worldview, a vibrant society needs the state in order to allow for full participation in public life. It is the state that provides protection, maintains legal order, and safeguards rights of individuals and groups. Traditionally Islam has been preoccupied with order and overwhelmingly fearful of chaos (*fitna*). The assumption, then, is that a properly functioning civil society has a basic need for the existence of the state. As Kelsay points out, "the idea is that political authority is important to the welfare of the religious community, and is to be respected."[14] By the same token, a believing Muslim citizen is also expected to be an activist for the faith and involved in civic matters. Mutual need and dependency of state and society is eminently recognized in Islam.

There are several classical Islamic concepts that have traditionally facilitated the state-society relationship. These include the need for the ruler to consult with the elders of the community (*shura*), adherence to the consensus within the community (*ijma'*) on relevant legal issues, some degree of allowance for independent inquiry (*ijtihad*), and fidelity to the pact between rulers and the ruled (*bay'a*). The meaning and relative importance of these concepts have been conditioned by historical and sectarian specificities. On the whole, however, they have had some degree of continued relevance to state-society relationships.

Moreover, Islam has also developed the general notion of a just ruler. A just ruler is one who first and foremost upholds the Islamic law (*shari'a*), which for all practical purposes functions as the constitution of the Islamic state. In addition, the ruler is expected to defend the community, collect taxes, supervise the conduct of war, consult with leaders of the community, and administer judicial and executive regulations. There are no clear-cut provisions for dismissing a ruler who violates these norms. In fact, concern with order is so strong that classical jurists had even rationalized tyrannical rule at times and judged it to be superior to chaos and social and political disorder. However, such a view has not ever stopped the not-so-infrequent overthrows of political leaders and dynasties or the onset of upheavals, riots, and revolutions. There has not often been a conjunction of theory and practice in this matter.

The complexity and diversity of Islamic civilization, and its multiple cultural and political poles, do not allow for simple generalization on any one issue. There is, however, an enduring pattern in the state-society relationship in the more modern and contemporary period that requires some attention. This concerns persistence of authoritarianism in the Islamic world. Why is it that the Islamic world is generally behind other regions in the democratization process and in limiting authoritarian state power?

Authoritarianism

Authoritarianism has been an enduring and common feature of much of the Islamic world and Middle Eastern political systems for some time.[15] Despite the large variety of regime types that the Muslim world has experienced (monarchical, socialist, secular nationalist, Islamist, mobilizational, military junta, and others), authoritarian rule has persisted. Since authoritarianism depends largely on the use of tacit or explicit coercion to secure popular compliance, it also raises questions about the political legitimacy of the regimes and the region's long-term political stability.

What, then, is the problem? Let me start by stating that I reject the purely cultural or essentialist explanations for the persistence of authoritarianism. Although it is quite accurate, for example, to point to patrimonialism and clientelism as critical forces in Islamic politics, it is more accurate to view these as symptoms rather than causes of authoritarianism. Religious explanations, likewise, also fall short for at least two reasons. First, Islam, like all other great religions, embodies elements that can be used instrumentally for both authoritarian or democratic purposes. There is no necessary incompatibility between Islam and democracy. Second, as the not-too-distant elections in secular Turkey, Bangladesh, Pakistan, and other places have shown, open contestation for political office can take place in an Islamic society with Islamic political parties participating fully and responsibly in the electoral system. Moreover, although many regimes in the region have explicit references to Islam in their constitutions, most of the regimes are in fact secular. The source of authoritarianism, therefore, must be found in areas other than simply the religion.

A far better explanation for the persistence of authoritarianism and exclusionary political systems may be found in other realms. There are a number of political and economic factors that have sustained authoritarian control in the Islamic world in general, and in the Middle East in particular. In this regard, the role of the state has been especially problematic. Broadly speaking, the region's states have dominated the economy, manipulated sociocultural diversity to fragment the opposition, used repression to stifle dissent, and promoted different ideological formulas to rationalize nondemocratic regimes.[16] These features are in turn nurtured by both the internal and external environments. Internally, the so-called rentier states—that is, allocation states dependent on either oil or security rents for their revenues—have cultivated governmental nonaccountability and have promoted autonomy of the state from society.[17] Even when pressured by fiscal crises, as in the post–Gulf War era, rentier states of the Middle East have so far been able to adjust and, at least for now, maintain the old patterns of governance. For a variety of reasons, these fiscal crises have not yet played the same role in helping open the political systems as debt crises did for Argentina and Brazil.

The emergence of the rentier state in the Middle East, then, has had a detrimental effect on both economic development and political liberalization. Its economic impact can be seen in the state's dependency on rents, extracted primarily from oil, as its essential source of revenues. This has in turn discouraged the emergence of an independent bourgeoisie that can engage the state in economic give-and-take. The state has in effect attempted to satisfy the population at large through provision of a host of services and economic activities paid through income received from rents. As long as rent is available, the state will respond only to those concerns of the population which it finds necessary for maintaining its power and position. Moreover, the rentier state's often extensive economic programs tend to engage the bourgeoisie fully and reward it economically in projects conceived and funded by the state. Hence, the bourgeoisie's fortunes come to center on the state and its defined economic goals. It becomes a dependent bourgeoisie unable and unwilling to engage the state in delineation of rights, responsibilities, and obligations.

The rentier state has the additional problem of becoming increasingly autonomous from the society. It can use the income from rent to enlist compliance and to pursue goals not necessarily in the best interests of society. Since most of the state's revenues are not extracted from the population, the corollary sense of obligation and responsiveness to the society does not necessarily develop. Rentier states find themselves increasingly reluctant to liberalize their political systems. As Luciani indicates, the oil rent becomes "a factor perpetuating authoritarian government."[18] This stands in sharp contrast to what Luciani calls "production states," where income is derived primarily "through taxation of domestic economic activity."[19] In Luciani's view, taxation and the widening of the state's fiscal base are essential inducements for democratization. He further posits that a state facing fiscal crisis and forced to resort to increased taxation will create demands from within the society for accountability and democratic institutions.

To sum up, then, authoritarianism in the Islamic world is a phenomenon that is intimately tied with the process of state formation and the form of economic and political control that the states have established over the population. These have allowed the state to extend the boundaries of its control over civil society and to try to enforce one-way dependency. These actions of the state have been and are being challenged in much of the Islamic world. The slow but clear emergence of a more vibrant civil society as a counterweight to state domination is simply one of the more positive developments in the region. If ultimately successful, it will bring in a more balanced relationship between the state and society and help pave the path of reform, accountability, and probable democratization.

Groups and Individuals

Islam is, in many respects, a highly communitarian religion. Although individual rights are recognized and the sanctity of the private realm acknowledged, the thrust of Islamic civilization has been essentially group emphasis, not individual rights. Society is categorized into groups of people with legally differentiated rights. The broadest two categories juxtapose the two largest groupings known as the "abode of peace" (*dar al-Islam*) and the "abode of war" (*dar al-harb*). The abode of peace encompasses all those Muslims who make up the Islamic community (*umma*) and are subject to the rules and regulations of the Islamic state. Those in the abode of war are further subcategorized into the "people of the book" and idolaters. The people of the book are adherents of monotheistic religions who may become citizens of the Islamic state should their territory be absorbed into *dar al-Islam*. Broadly speaking, they are given certain second-class citizenship rights and are expected to pay specified taxes and uphold their expected duties. Idolaters are all others outside the boundaries and jurisdiction of Islam.

This pattern of categorization of people with different citizenship rights and duties extends even to the Islamic community. For example, minors or those with mental disabilities have different rights. Both Islamic criminal and civil codes (personal status laws) make clear differentiation along gender lines in favor of males. Moreover, any Muslim—individual or group—who denies the finality of the prophet Muhammad's message or rejects Islam for another religious community is viewed to be an apostate. The individual risks not only the loss of civil and political rights but is also subject (at least theoretically) to capital punishment.

There are also certain groups in the Islamic world that have come to acquire privileged positions in the community. Descendants of the Prophet are often treated as one such group. This inchoate privilege is institutionalized in Shiʻi Islam in the form of special taxation on the faithful for the benefit of the prophet Muhammad's descendants. Moreover, and in spite of Islam's prophecy to what can be called "priesthood of all believers," the clerics have assumed a privileged position in the social order. Their importance has varied according to time, space, and sectarian fissures in Islam. For example, and due to particular historical and doctrinal developments, the clerics have assumed a far greater institutional importance among the Shiʻis (especially the numerically dominant group of Twelver Shiʻism) than among the majority Sunnis.

In spite of these divisions and differences, the overriding group identity in Islam is with the community (umma). Islamic history has frequently taken account of this sense of solidarity and group identity irrespective of time and space. Although the actual operational relevance of group solidarity is subject to dispute, it does serve as a psychological bond that crosses boundaries and historical periods and brings Muslims together under the banner of God's unity (*tawhid*).

Norms and Group Exclusion

It is perhaps appropriate to raise the issue of group exclusion more systematically in the Islamic world. The key question is whether civility and the acceptance of the other is any less prevalent in Islamic traditions than in other great monotheistic religions. The charge here would be that in the Islamic world, norms of exclusion, whatever their origins, are more common than in other regions of the world and are applied more regularly to keep the out-groups at bay. This observation takes into account differences between two principal classes of norms, universalistic norms and norms of difference and exclusion. As Hardin has argued, universalistic norms apply to essentially all members of society, while norms of difference basically benefit a well-defined subgroup in the social order. The force of universalistic norms is their indifferent application. Norms of exclusion, however, are not universally applied; they work to differentiate among ethnic, religious, social class, gender, or other groupings. These norms can succeed depending on their level of support, cost of deviation, and the availability of enforceable sanctions.[20]

In the Muslim world, as in all societies and regions, both universalistic and exclusionary norms operate. What makes the Islamic case different may be the significant role of the state and some social groups in defining and enforcing a set of exclusionary norms. The problem is further exacerbated when norms of exclusion are derived from universalistic religious criteria. In other words, this amounts to invoking a universal norm but particularizing it—that is, applying it to one group only. Such exclusionary postures can benefit only a well-defined in-group and will exclude others. Similar observations can be made about norms of difference that are based on ethnicity, gender, and nationality. All of these serve to exclude the other on the basis of preconceived and unchanging norms.

As alluring as this explanation may be, it has some problems. Can one confidently say that norms of exclusion are more common in the Muslim world than, say, in sub-Saharan Africa, Latin America, or Central Europe? I doubt that norms of exclusion are more prevalent in the Islamic world than in other regions. Clearly, the recent history of conflicts and warfare in the Muslim areas, especially the Middle East, has increased the saliency of exclusionary norms because of anger, perceptions of injustice, and the like. It is also true that certain groups, particularly those with fundamentalist religious orientations, use universalistic norms to exclude the other. But this does not amount to any kind of conclusion asserting that norms of exclusion are more common among the Muslims.

We can, however, say that any analysis of the politics of inclusion in the Islamic world must also take into account the role of values and other cultural artifacts that have become part of the Middle East over time. Some of these are positive and conducive to inclusive politics; some are not. Clearly, when an extremist Islamist group claims that it alone knows the truth, and that you either join them or risk excommunication, then there is a serious problem. This issue is also relevant to extremist groups elsewhere in the Middle East, whatever their religious orientation may be. An immediate and serious consequence of such exclusionary attitudes is to raise legitimate fear among religious minorities and women. Rather than promoting ecumenism, these views perpetuate particularism and deny a proper place for pluralism in politics and social affairs.

I do not deny the relevance of these factors and their bearing on people's attitudes and views. What I am concerned with, however, has less to do with deeply seated views of individuals and groups and more with their behavior in the political arena. And it is in the political arena, in the context of the rule of law, where the inclusion is most applicable to the Muslim world.

Group Conflict and Citizenship Rights: The Islamists

The pressing problem of inclusion-exclusion is particularly relevant to Islamists and their vision of an Islamic polity based on the shari'a and religious norms. Historically, the revivalist movements in Islam have generally concerned themselves with two broad themes of reform (*islah*) and renewal (*tajdid*).[21] Their interest has been to reform the existing social order, since it has strayed from the Straight Path, in order to once again renew Islam in public life. Although the form of relationship between renewal and reform has varied from one group of Islamists to another, all groups have dealt with this problem in one manner or another.

An inherent element in the concern with reform and renewal is the reintroduction of some form of traditionalism in the discourse of the Islamists.[22] As Sivan explains, "Islamic Resurgence is to be explained to a large extent by the durability of what one may dub the Islamic 'traditional bedrock', i.e. the persistence through constant adaptation of classical Islam as *living tradition*."[23] Traditionalism requires adoption of certain basic authentic Islamic views and practices borrowed from the past. These include their views on (1) sovereignty and social contract, (2) religious minorities, (3) gender, and (4) lay intellectuals. Although the precise differences among the Islamists on these issues are not always clear, there remain important variations among them on the direct relevance and applicability of these views to the political system. Since the impact of the differential application of these views is potentially profound, it behooves us to underline points of convergence and divergence, as well as several problem areas in the Islamists' use of these norms.

Sovereignty and Social Contract

All Islamist groups maintain that sovereignty belongs to God. It is sacrilegious to hold a contrary opinion. It is the supremacy of tawhid (God's unity) as the essential doctrine that defines an Islamist. The Rousseauian idea of social contract with its explicit acceptance of people's sovereignty has no place among the diehard Islamists. It is, however, possible to move beyond the debate on God's sovereignty and allow for the human agency to have extensive, if not complete, control over the organization of political life, including the legislative domain.[24] Islamic history is a rich depository of precisely this practical form of freedom to legislate in a vast array of fields for the interest of the polity.

It is also possible to conceive of the time-honored concept of bayʿa (allegiance to the ruler) as a way to legitimize on theological grounds a form of contract between the ruler and the ruled. In its essential meaning, this is clearly not social contract. In its implementation, however, it can codify and underscore the existence of certain rights and responsibilities for both the rulers and the polity. It can also give rise to a sense of entitlement that is critical for holding regimes responsible and accountable to the citizenry.[25] It is perhaps not too far-fetched to think that the more modern notion of pacts between regimes and their adversaries is not unrelated to this practice. Pacts are predicated on agreements, rights, obligations, and entitlement. As Tilly has shown, rights of citizenship have historically developed in Europe as part of bargains in the course of long struggles with the invasive state.[26] Rights do not emerge on the scene overnight. They have to be acquired and then preserved against all odds.

The durability of basic rights is largely dependent on their collective enforcement by the state and its citizens. Hence, the definition of citizenship becomes highly poignant—a murky and problematic area for many Islamists. Again as Tilly says, "citizenship rights belong in principle (if not always in practice) to everyone who qualifies as a full-fledged member of a given state; membership in the category suffices to qualify a person for enforceable claims."[27]

Religious Minorities

Islamists' views of citizenship, and who is entitled to it, have different gradations and important differences. There are those Islamists (e.g., Islamic Jihad, Takfir waʾl-Hijra) whose view of citizenship is highly exclusionary. Even monotheistic religious minorities are basically denied such rights except as they are granted to them by virtue of benevolence of the Islamists in power. This form of exclusion also extends to the Muslims, rulers and otherwise, who do not fully share the Islamists' view on the organization of the polity.

Introduction of the concept of *jahiliyya* (ignorance) by Sayyid Qutb and some of his followers to modern Egypt is in essence a rejection of the existing society and its particular conception of rights and obligations. Jahiliyya has traditionally been used to refer to Arabia before the rise of Islam. The Prophet eliminated jahiliyya through the force of monotheistic Islam. The term itself was used exclusively for this era until the Pakistani Islamist Abu al-Aʿla Mawdudi applied it in his writings to the modern period. In Qutb's further application, places such as modern Egypt are reincarnations of pre-Islamic Arabia in their ignorance of divine design and religious norms. As Qutb states emphatically, the jahiliyya society is Godless, subject to its own rules and regulations, and it rejects the central place of divinity in human affairs. The Muslim vanguards should fight this corrupt society until it is overthrown.[28] This is a decisive call to action on behalf of a rigid and exclusionist Islamic state.

Other Islamist groups have also made explicit denunciations of broadly defined non-Islamic groups. In his analysis of some of the Egyptian Islamists and their rejection of the Western culture and ideas, Gilles Kepel refers to a broad set of rejected categories, the Four Horsemen of the Apocalypse. They are Jewry, the Crusade, communism, and secularism.[29] Those who adhere to these groups or their ideas are, then, denied citizenship rights in this particular form of an Islamic state. These Islamists do not make a distinction between Judaism and Zionism, collapsing them into one rejected category. The Crusade refers essentially to the Egyptian Copts, whom they denounce for their attributed links with the Western culture. Clearly, neither communism nor secularism can have any place in these Islamists' rigid conception of the universe. After all, communists are Godless and secularists reject the paramount role of religion in Muslims' political life. They must all be eliminated.

This extreme rejectionist stand is in contrast to many other Islamists who not only have a more liberal conception of citizenship but also extend it to at least some religious minorities. The example of the Islamic Republic of Iran is of interest here. In conformity to the traditional Islamic treatment of monotheistic religious minorities, certain citizenship rights are granted to the Christians, Jews, and Zoroastrians. These include freedom to enact religious ceremonies, religious education, and personal status matters such as marriage, divorce, and inheritance. Although it can be argued justifiably that there is an element of second-class citizenship that defines these rights, it is nevertheless clear that some formal rights have been granted to these religious minorities. The problem is most severe, however, when another religious minority, the Baha'is, is concerned. The refusal to recognize this significant group as a religious minority, and their arbitrary designation of it as a political group, has resulted in the regime's systematic persecution of the Baha'is. In other words, citizenship rights have been denied to the Baha'is because of certain aspects of their doctrinal belief that the theocratic state finds fundamentally unacceptable.[30]

The case of the Coptic Christians of Egypt is also illustrative. Copts and Muslims have lived side by side in Egypt for centuries. Coptic and Muslim traditions have shaped Egypt's culture, and while each community has sustained its unique rites and institutions, there is little to distinguish an individual Christian from a Muslim. Comprising less than 10 percent of the country's population, the Copts have admittedly been circumspect in their practice of religion. A leading Coptic personality, Makram Obeid, once said that we are all Muslims culturally. This was repeated by Adel Hussein, a leading pro-Islamist politician, who noted: "in Egypt, all people are Muslims. Some pray in churches, others in mosques."[31] In recent years, however, the Copts and Christian institutions in Egypt have come under steady attack by Islamic militants. More disturbing, arguably, is the fact that recent Egyptian governments have not generally encouraged Coptic representation in state offices. For instance, none of Egypt's twenty-six governors is Christian.

The right to religious freedom is a serious issue with implications that extend beyond the Islamists. Many Islamic countries do not fully appreciate the meaning of this fundamental right. This problem is evident in the 1990 Cairo Declaration on Human Rights in Islam, issued by the Organization of the Islamic Conference, which includes all Muslim countries. Endorsed by Saudi Arabia, Iran, and other Islamic countries, the Declaration (as Mayer points out accurately) falls short of international human rights standards in not designating freedom of religion as "a fundamental and nonderogable right."[32] This failure is potentially detrimental not only to all non-Muslim citizens, but also to those who dissent from the officially imposed constructs of Islam. As Mayer points out,

> The failure to provide for religious freedom also has serious practical implications for Muslims, given the number of Muslim dissenters from officially-imposed constructs of Islam and members of local minority sects who have been mistreated, charged with apostasy from Islam, or subjected to pressures or threats to compel them to abjure nonconforming belief.[33]

The important point here for our purposes is to put the Islamists' view on freedom of religion and religious minorities in proper contextual perspective. Clearly, many militant Islamist groups have negative perceptions of both religious minorities and secularists. This perception is nurtured, however, in a larger environment where even the moderate pro-Western regimes do not fully appreciate the fundamental right of religious freedom. This does not, of course, excuse either the Islamists or the moderate regimes. It only underlines a significant problem that needs to be addressed on a larger scale.

Gender

Another problem area with special application to the Islamists is the issue of equality of women and gender rights and relations. The difficulty here stems from two related sources: first is the essentially dis-criminatory nature of Islamic personal status laws and the criminal code when applied to women. Second, there is a prevalence of certain fixed attitudes and views, learned through the socialization experi-ence, about women and gender roles.[34] The combination of these two factors places women in a highly disadvantageous position in the Is-lamists' universe.

All Islamists emphasize the role of family and its critical impor-tance as the backbone of a moral and ethical society. Women are praised as the carriers of virtue and as the key agents of socialization for children. Family values, and women's essential role in their propa-gation, are recognized and given special praise in the discourse of all Islamists. Nevertheless, and in spite of the recognition given to women, Islamic personal status laws discriminate against women in the areas of inheritance, divorce, and marriage rights. A woman's inheritance from her parents is half that of a male sibling's. Despite certain re-strictions, a man can divorce a spouse rather freely, while a woman's rights to do so is substantially more restrictive. Men can engage in polygamy; women cannot. In Twelver Shi'i Islam, marriage based on a temporary contract (mut'a) for a specified time is allowed.[35] Al-though women also partake of temporary marriage, restrictions on them are more stringent. Islamic criminal code based on the concept of talion is dependent on witnesses' testimonies. Testimony of a woman is valued as half of a man's. Additionally, testimonies of women alone, irrespective of their numbers and validity, are not sufficient to convict a murderer. In all cases, a male witness is required for validation.

Closely tied in with legal restrictions are the Islamists' attempts to segregate women in public space. The moral imperative that dictates such a view may be hard to fathom but it is advanced by the Islamists as a justification for enforced separateness. The public space applica-ble to this form of separateness includes public transportation, all levels of education, even parts of the workplace. The separateness is further reinforced through application of female veiling and the im-position of penalties for its nonobservance. While voluntary veiling is also done for economic reasons by women, and at times as an act of protest, the relevant issue to the Islamists is state-imposed involun-tary veiling.

Lay Intellectuals

The intellectuals as a broad category (many of whom are secularists) comprise another potential problem area for the Islamists. Although there are many traditional intellectuals who may not feel necessarily constrained by the Islamists' vision, most intellectuals feel otherwise. Their often individualist and nonconformist postures can create problems, especially if they are accompanied by avowed secularist attitudes. Many recent examples of intolerant attitudes toward intellectuals abound in places such as Egypt, Iran, Sudan, and elsewhere. The intellectual's propensity to secularism is fundamentally not acceptable to hardline Islamists.

The one hopeful area of mutual acceptance between practicing Muslims and those with secularist orientation is the progressive evolution of Islamic modernism, with its growing acceptance of separate realms for religion and the state. In other words, a religious society does not necessarily require an Islamic state to dictate its course and direction. There have already been some important and influential beginnings in this domain by those who find Islam, popular sovereignty, and democracy compatible. Noted Islamic modernist thinkers of the present Middle East—the likes of Hasan Hanafi, Muhammad Shahrur, and Abdol-Karim Soroush—have already advanced the idea that it is necessary to reorient critical Islamic themes in light of the developments of modern society. Since these thinkers and their followers remain faithful to the essential precepts of Islam, their potential impact can be significant. More importantly, since Islam has never been a static civilization, and has had a rich tradition of modernism, a successful fusion of Islam and modernity can remove the hostile cultural edge from the interaction of the Islamic world with the West.

Conclusion

I have stressed that the concept of inclusion can be a serious problem with most Islamists' *weltanschauung*. I have further argued that citizenship disenfranchisement falls most heavily on religious minorities, women, and lay intellectuals. However, I also observe that there are significant ranges of opinions and views among Islamists on fundamental issues of governance. These differences apply even to the operation of such critical concepts as sovereignty, legitimacy, human rights, and the rights of women and religious minorities. More importantly, the problem of exclusion and authoritarianism needs to be put in its proper perspective by comparing it with the record of secularist and authoritarian regimes. Unfortunately, the regimes' record is not all that promising.

There is no simple solution for the foreseeable future, and the Islamists are here to stay. In my view, it is important for us to note their demonstrated differences, recognize those potentially positive views that promote social justice and fair redistribution of wealth, and acknowledge attempts that make human agency dominant while at the same time pay respect to God's sovereignty. All this said, we must also be prepared to expose and denounce exclusionary practices of radical fundamentalists.

As far as the broader theme of Islam and civil society is concerned, it is clear that it has become an important subject of debate and discussion in the Islamic world. The practical applicability of this discourse on issues of governance, civility, and pluralism remain unclear. Islamic politics in the next millennium, however, points to a real ray of hope in the potential impact of its youth. If real change (with greater inclusivity and accountability) does come about in Islamic politics, it will be because of pressures from the youth. Two other factors also support the youth's demands for change and inclusive politics. The first has to do with women, especially the younger generation. Women will become increasingly a force for change and openness. The other will be the vibrancy of civil society and associational life in the region. Although states in the Middle East and other parts of the Islamic world have traditionally tried to control and thwart the development of autonomous civil society, associational life and "social capital" remain important assets in the Middle East. These three interrelated forces are potentially the harbingers of change. They help cement the growing differentiation between the spheres of religion and the state—a differentiation that can only promote the development of civil society. They have the ability to influence, but not dictate, the course of Islamic politics in the direction of accountability, civility, and pluralism.

Notes

Passages have been excerpted from the following published articles (all cited in full in the endnotes that follow): Farhad Kazemi and Augustus Richard Norton, "Civil Society, Political Reform, and Authoritarianism"; Farhad Kazemi, "The Inclusion Imperative"; Farhad Kazemi and Augustus Richard Norton, "Political Challenges to Middle Eastern Governments in the Twenty-First Century."

1. Şerif Mardin, "Civil Society and Islam," in *Civil Society: Theory, History, Comparison*, ed. John A. Hall (Cambridge: Polity Press, 1995), 279.

2. See, for example, the "Civil Society in the Middle East" project at New York University as reflected in the following publications: Augustus Richard Norton, ed., *Civil Society in the Middle East*, 2 vols. (Leiden: Brill, 1995–96); Jillian Schwedler, ed., *Toward Civil Society in the Middle East: A Primer* (Boulder,

Colo.: Lynne Rienner, 1995); Farhad Kazemi, guest ed. "Special Issue on Civil Society in Iran," *Iran Nameh* 13, no. 4 (Fall 1995), and 14, no. 1 (Winter 1996).

3. See John Kelsay, "Civil Society and Government in Islam," in this volume.

4. Samuel Huntington, "The Clash of Civilizations?" *Foreign Affairs* 72 (Summer 1993): 22–49.

5. Said Amir Arjomand, "Civil Society and the Rule of Law in the Constitutional Politics of Iran under Khatami," *Social Research* 67 (Summer 2000): 283–301.

6. Michael Walzer, "The Idea of Civil Society," *Dissent* (Spring 1991): 293. For further discussion see Jean L. Cohen and Andrew Arato, *Civil Society and Political Theory* (Cambridge: MIT Press, 1994); Adam Seligman, *The Idea of Civil Society* (Princeton: Princeton University Press, 1992); John Hall, ed., *Civil Society: Theory, History, Comparison* (Cambridge, UK: Polity Press, 1995). See also the definitions in Norton, *Civil Society in the Middle East.*

7. Edward Shils, "The Virtue of Civil Society," *Government and Opposition* 26 (Winter 1991): 4.

8. Ibid.

9. Augustus Richard Norton, "The Future of Civil Society in the Middle East," *Middle East Journal* 47 (Spring 1993): 211. See also Bryan Turner, "Orientalism and the Problem of Civil Society in Islam," in *Orientalism, Islam, and Islamists,* ed. Asaf Hussain, Robert Olson, and Jamil Qureishi (Brattleboro, Vt.: Amana Books, 1984), 27.

10. Norton, "Future of Civil Society," 214. See Michael Walzer, *On Toleration* (New Haven: Yale University Press, 1998); David Heyd, ed., *Toleration: An Elusive Virtue* (Princeton: Princeton University Press, 1996).

11. Shils, "The Virtue of Civil Society," 11.

12. Ibid., 9–10.

13. Walzer, "The Idea of Civil Society," 302. See also Robert Putnam, *Making Democracy Work: Civic Traditions in Modern Italy* (Princeton: Princeton University Press, 1993).

14. Kelsay, "Civil Society and Government in Islam," chap. 1 above, under "Boundaries."

15. See Farhad Kazemi and Augustus Richard Norton, "Civil Society, Political Reform, and Authoritarianism in the Middle East: A Response," *Contention* 5 (1996): 107–19.

16. Jill Crystal, "Authoritarianism and Its Adversaries in the Arab World," *World Politics* 46 (1994): 262–89.

17. See Giacomo Luciani, "Allocation vs. Production States: A Theoretical Framework," in *The Rentier State,* ed. Hazem Beblawi and Giacomo Luciani (London: Croom Helm, 1987).

18. Giacomo Luciani, "The Oil Rent, the Fiscal Crisis of the State, and Democratization," in *Democracy Without Democrats: The Renewal of Politics in the Muslim World,* ed. Ghassan Salamé (London: I. B. Tauris, 1994), 131.

19. Luciani, "The Oil Rent," 131. See also Luciani, "Allocation vs. Production States." For a somewhat different view, see Yasuyuki Matsunaga, "L'état

rentier est-il refractaire à la démocratie?" *Critique Internationale* 8 (July 2000): 46–58.

20. Russell Hardin, *One for All: The Logic of Group Conflict* (Princeton: Princeton University Press, 1995); Farhad Kazemi, "The Inclusion Imperative," *Middle East Studies Association Bulletin* 30 (1996): 147–53.

21. John Voll, "Renewal and Reform in Islamic History: *Tajdid* and *Islah*," in *Voices of Islamic Resurgence*, ed. John Esposito (New York: Oxford University Press, 1983), 32–47. See Farhad Kazemi and Augustus Richard Norton, "Political Challenges to Middle Eastern Governments in the Twenty-first Century," in *New Frontiers in Middle East Security*, ed. Lenore Martin (New York: St. Martin's Press, 1998), 79–104.

22. Ali Banuazizi, "Social Psychological Approaches to Political Development," in *Understanding Political Development*, ed. Myron Weiner and Samuel Huntington (Boston: Little, Brown, 1987), 287; and see Said Amir Arjomand, "Traditionalism in Twentieth-Century Iran," in *From Nationalism to Revolutionary Islam* (London: Macmillan, 1984), 195–232.

23. Emanuel Sivan, "The Islamic Resurgence: Civil Society Strikes Back," *Journal of Contemporary History* 25 (May–June 1990): 357.

24. Ahmad S. Moussali, "Modern Islamic Fundamentalist Discourses on Civil Society, Pluralism, and Democracy," in Norton, *Civil Society in the Middle East*, 1:70–119. See also Roxanne Euben, *Enemy in the Mirror: Islamic Fundamentalism and the Limits of Modern Rationalism* (Princeton: Princeton University Press, 1999), 49–92.

25. Amartya Sen, *Poverty and Famines: An Essay on Entitlement and Deprivation* (Oxford: Clarendon Press, 1981), cited in Charles Tilly, "Where Do Rights Come From?" (paper presented for the Vilhelm Aubert Memorial Symposium, University of Oslo, August 1990), 1.

26. Tilly, "Where Do Rights Come From?" 2.

27. Ibid.

28. Sayyid Qutb, *Milestones* (Indianapolis: American Trust Publications, 1990).

29. Gilles Kepel, *The Prophet and the Pharaoh: Muslim Extremism in Egypt* (London: Al Saqi Books, 1985).

30. See Firuz Kazemzadeh, "The Baha'is in Iran: Twenty Years of Repression," *Social Research* 67 (Summer 2000): 537–58.

31. Interview with Adel Hussein, Cairo, July 11, 1995.

32. Ann Mayer, "Universal versus Islamic Human Rights: A Clash of Cultures or a Clash with a Construct?" *Michigan Journal of International Law* 15 (1994): 334.

33. Ibid.

34. For further elaboration, see Farhad Kazemi, "Gender, Islam and Politics," *Social Research* 67 (Summer 2000): 453–74.

35. Shahla Haeri, *Law of Desire: Temporary Marriage in Shi'i Islam* (Syracuse, N.Y.: Syracuse University Press, 1989).

3

Alternative Conceptions of Civil Society

A REFLECTIVE ISLAMIC APPROACH

HASAN HANAFI

CONTEMPORARY MUSLIMS articulate a number of alternative conceptions of civil society. First, there are some who reject the very idea of civil society as alien to Islam, a concept coming from the West: secular, antireligious, and aiming at Westernizing Muslim societies. This is the radical fundamentalist position. Second, there are some who affirm the concept of civil society as a universal concept, a global ideal irrespective of its Western origins. They accept it as a model, a norm of practice, and an ideal in lifestyle for individuals and societies. In this view, Islamic tradition becomes an archaic expression of bygone values reflective of their own peculiar historical conditions. This is the other radical position—the secular, Westernized alternative. Third, there are some who argue for the possibility of developing the ingredients of classical Islam to reflect modern social needs. They argue that similarities can be maintained and differences can be bridged through creative reinterpretation—or *ijtihad*—of the basic ethical sources of Islam. This final position is the reformist or modernist alternative.

These three broadly defined alternative conceptions of civil society are not merely theoretical constructs. We can find each position reflected in the spectrum of Muslim political societies; in practice, civil society is not one uniform type in the Muslim world. It varies from Lebanon to Afghanistan. In Lebanon today, civil society is reemerging after having been ripped apart by a decade of civil war. It exists because of the relatively equal power between society and state. Lebanon is unified in the public space by the general allegiance to the civil law, in spite of some balancing of power between different religious groups required by its multiethnic and multireligious composition. Still present are some illiberal vestiges of the old Lebanon: a Christian head of state, a Sunni prime minister, a Shi'i house speaker. Nevertheless, the civil war minimized the weight of sectarianism and maximized the feeling of citizenship, which was reinforced by the resistance to the Israeli occupation in the south.

On the other extreme, Afghanistan under the Taliban offered a strict application of Islamic law, especially in family law and the penal code, the two obsessions of religious conservatism. The same practice in a more sophisticated way exists in Saudi Arabia and Sudan under the banner of applying Islamic law (*shari'a*), using religion as a camouflage for patriarchal society and for military dictatorship. Human rights in this type of state are routinely violated and human rights organizations are even banned.

The third practice is a middle course, which is more common in the rest of the Arab and Muslim world, in states such as Morocco, Tunisia, Libya, Egypt, Syria, Jordan, Kuwait, the United Arab Emirates, and Oman, where we find a balance between civil society and the dictates of medieval Islamic law. In the public sphere, the rules of civil society are maintained: citizenship, equality of all in front of the law, the constitution, freedom of expression, democracy, pluralism, and the like. In the private sphere, such as family law, the shari'a is maintained since it is one of the sources of civil law.

It is clear from the above list of states following the middle course that civil society in its fullest sense is still far from realized in most of the Muslim world.[1] But the fact that democracy and respect for human rights are still the exception rather than the norm in the Muslim world does not reflect in my view the validity of either of the two extreme conceptions of civil society that I outlined above. Indeed, I believe that while the concept of civil society may be of Western origin, most of its key features may be found in Islamic ethical theory, and these features are slowly being realized in cultural contexts as different as the Moroccan and the Malaysian. Indeed, as I will argue in this chapter, the development of the third approach to civil society—the reformist, modernist approach—is the only viable one for pluralistic Muslim societies, whether they are African, Asian, or European. An Islamic state is not one that advocates only the application of the penal code or the observance of external rituals, but the state that implements the spirit or intent of the law (*maqasid al-shari'a*). A state that pursues this spirit may not replicate all the institutions associated with Western civil society, but it will foster and protect many of the values that underlie it.[2]

Ingredients

The concept of civil society is a Western concept, coined in the seventeenth century by the English political philosopher Thomas Hobbes as an alternative to kingdom and church. The human being is neither a subject of a king nor a believer in a church. He is a citizen of a state, where everybody is equal to everybody, where all citizens are governed by the same law embedded in the constitution. Hegel in his *Philosophy of Right* considered civil society as a step toward the state. The original concept held more political than economic connotations: equal citizenship, social contract, equality in front of the law, a constitution, and freedom and democracy. That liberal concept of civil society was the foundation for liberal economics, and found expression in the rise of capitalism, free enterprise, and private property.

Civil society is not a panacea for the age-old problem of balancing the powers of the state, the society, and the individual. When it does exist, however, it provides a certain balance between the power of the ruler and the power of the people, between power from the top and power from the bottom, between the government and the opposition, which allows state and society to coexist without falling into the extremes of authoritarian rule or popular revolt.

Islamic culture historically has shared this concern for limiting the power of political authorities by diffusing it among a number of formal and informal institutions. If civil society means a system of checks and balances that prevent a preponderance of power residing in either the state or societal institutions, then Islamic theory from the earliest period demonstrates similar concerns. However, indigenous concepts of civil society from within Islamic culture are more innocent concepts, value free and without a hidden agenda. They are more consistent and less opposed than the ingredients of civil society projected from Western culture onto Islamic societies in a misguided attempt to replicate the Western model. The key Islamic ingredients for civil society require less oppositional tension between institutions because in Islam there are no kings or popes, no kingdoms and no churches. Instead we begin with the following salient concepts.

The first is the *umma*, which means a nation without boundaries, a community of believers. Islam views all human beings to be ontologically members of the same family, the same umma. And today, even though humankind is fractured into different moral communities (*umam*), Islam upholds the essential similarities that link all human beings with mutual obligations of respect and decent behavior.

All Muslims everywhere are members of the Islamic umma, this ideal community irrespective of geography. And yet Islam acknowledges that human identities are never monolithic, but varied and sometimes cross-cutting. So even though Islam posits the moral primacy of membership in the single community of Muslim believers, it also accepts the reality of other societies and nations, sometimes existing within the Muslim umma and at other times including non-Muslims as well.

Groups that may or may not connote a religious basis include *qabila*, or tribe; *ta'ifa*, which means an intimate group dedicated to a cause; *milla*, which means a religious community or sect; and *nas*, which could mean either a group of people or the whole human race. All refer to different sizes of human groups.

Related concepts refer to place or abode, such as *madina*, a town or city; *qariya*, a village; and *wadi*, a populated valley or low-lying area. The important point about these terms is that they refer to inhabitants, not just to place.

Another set of concepts refers to specifically religious groups apart from the Muslim community. The most important such concept is that of *ahl al-kitab*, or "people of the book," namely Jews and Christians who share with Muslims the revelation of Abraham. The word *ahl* suggests a common family or parenthood. Jews, Nazarenes, and Sabeans all form communities of believers equal to Muslims. They are groups for positive action and common cause.

Some categories refer to social classes, such as rich and poor, the deprived, and the homeless. Others relate to political categories, such as princes and other wielders of power; to religious authorities, such as priests and rabbis; to gender categories, such as male and female. Finally, there are a number of concepts related to the core institution of the family, which establish the rights and duties connecting fathers, mothers, sons, daughters, parents, neighbors, and friends.

The above list may read as an agglomeration of unrelated terms. In fact, the concepts and the groupings outlined above are intrinsically related to one another because they combine to form an integrated whole that is Islam's conception of human society. Islam certainly puts primacy on the rights and obligations incumbent upon Muslims as members of the same religious community. But it does not renounce the possibility of the affiliation of Muslims to nonreligious identities and groups, nor does it obviate the rights and obligations that emerge from such membership. A Muslim man, for example, may marry a woman from the ahl al-kitab, thereby becoming a member of a non-Muslim extended family, with all the attendant privileges and duties such an alliance entails. Similarly, a Muslim ruler who contracts with non-Muslim communities residing within the Islamic state incurs obligations toward these communities while retaining the prerogatives of sovereignty.

In short, Islamic theory and practice sustain a number of legitimate human groupings existing between the state and the individual. These groupings are endowed with their own sphere of autonomy free from government intrusion, which made Islamic societies historically far less monolithic and undifferentiated than some Western stereotypes of a theocratic society allow.

Islamic theory also provides a number of institutions that serve to operationalize the concept of civil society. Medieval theorists posited a tension between the wielder of power (variously termed the *imam*, the *khalifa*, or the *sultan*) and the ʿ*ulama*, namely the intellectuals and legal scholars who were most familiar with the shariʿa. The latter are the guarantors of the shariʿa's proper interpretation. They are in theory independent from political authority, thus maintaining the system of checks and balances in society—similar to the role of the mass media in modern societies.

The judges are also independent from the political authority. They judge according to the law, which is just as binding on the ruler as it is on a common person. The high judge, similar to the supreme court, is appointed by the ruler, but he cannot be removed by him. In case the ruler does not abide by the law, the high judge can lead a revolution against him.[3]

Islamic theory provides for a number of other subsidiary institutions that bridge the executive power of the imam and the judicial authority of the ʿulama. One key concept is that of *hisba*, which means the supervision of the application of the law in society, especially in the marketplace, against treachery, mishandling, monopoly, usury, exaggerated profits, and the like. The person performing this function (*muhtasib*) serves as the eye of the law on both state and society.

Furthermore, there is the *diwan al-mazalim*, which served in ways analogous to both a small claims court as well as a court of popular appeal. The mazalim court was a tribunal to which every Muslim could go and complain against any form of injustice done to him directly by the ruler or the ruler's agent. It allowed a direct appeal to the highest institutions of the state when the institutions of either the state or society failed to defend a common person's legal rights.

Awqaf, or religious endowments similar to scientific, literary, and academic foundations for the development of art and science, are another key autonomous institution in medieval Islamic societies. Individuals could endow awqaf so that scholarships, schools, universities, and publications were all supported by the institution without government interference. Likewise, mystical orders (the Sufi *tariqas*) were able to recruit members and form religious autonomous societies that existed largely independently from state control and played extremely important mediating roles between families or tribes and the state in which they lived.

All of these institutions played roles analogous to those of institutions we today identify with civil society. Of course, the relative weight and independence of all these institutions varied according to time and location. What is important to emphasize is that Islamic theory contains within it the idea of an integrated politico-religious community, but with power dispersed among its constituent elements. As modern Muslim states began to emerge in the early twentieth century, it is no surprise that one of the first targets of their secular, nationalist state-building enterprise was traditional Islamic institutions. The Egyptian state placed awqaf under the control of a government ministry at the beginning of the Egyptian revolution. It is directed now in the spirit of doing business and making profit. Similarly, the Sufi tariqas were among the first social institutions to be affected (and dissolved) when Mustafa Kemal Ataturk began his nationalist project in Turkey. And yet despite all attempts to co-opt or crush them, Sufi orders remain a very important autonomous force in such Muslim societies as Morocco, Sudan, Turkey, Eastern Europe, and Central Asia.

Society

The Islamic ideal of the umma is grounded in the concept of unity. The unity of God (*tawhid*) reflects itself in the unity of the umma. The unity of God is not a simple, closed dogma or a reified abstraction, but a whole worldview that affects the individual, society, and history. The individual is one, which means that his powers and energies are one. His internal powers of cognition, feeling, and thinking are one. His thoughts should express what he feels, and what he feels can be rationally demonstrated. Hypocrisy is to think something without feeling it. Fear is to feel something without thinking on it.

Man's external powers of action are also one. His words should be related to his acts; what he says, he should do, and what he does, he should say. Incapacity is to say something without doing it. Automation is to do something without saying it. The unity between the inside world—feeling and thinking—and the external world—saying and doing—makes the human personality one, free of fear, double-talk, double-face; it creates a free individual. To believe is to attest. To declare is to testify. This is the meaning and the significance of *shahada*, the first pillar of Islam, the solemn declaration that there are no other gods except the only God, the Omniscient, Omnipresent, and Omnipotent.

All human beings are equal before this Universal Principal, equal in

birth and death, equal in life and worth. There is no human geneal-
ogy stemming out of royal families, of caste systems, or of social
classes. All human beings are the sons and daughters of Adam and
Eve. Every human being has a body and a soul, a reason to distinguish good from evil, and a free will to choose the good, not the evil.
They are all created from one soul.

Society is a unity of equal individuals. No distinction exists between human beings according to color, language, tribe, or state. All
societies, peoples, tribes, classes, and the like, are also equals. They all
have the same rights and the same duties. The right to differ is a legal
right. Diversity of language, social customs, and manners is part of
people's rights. All ought to be treated according to the same international law without any double standard in practice. Peaceful coexistence between peoples is guaranteed by treaties of nonaggression and
mutual respect. There is no elected people or chosen tribe or best
umma except through the good deed and ethical standards. Election
is offered to all, to every individual, according to perfection acquired
through ethical performance.[4]

To realize this principle of equality in society, Islam enshrines the
notion of the brotherhood of all believers. Given the natural differences among individuals in aptitudes and talents, which yield different incomes and generate social classes, brotherhood intervenes to
bring back equality to its early stand. Those who have give to those
who have not. Those who have more give to those who have less.
This is not the conventional idea of charity or altruism on the part of
the rich toward the poor. In Islamic society, the poor have a vested
right in the wealth of the rich, not only through *zakat*, the tax on
surplus wealth that is another pillar of the faith, but also through
other measures to be taken by the ruler, such as nationalization of
public services and confiscation of exploitative monopolized means of
production. Public goods, such as water, salt, and mineral resources
lying deep below the surface—including oil—cannot be claimed as
private property because they touch the lives of all members of society. Even so-called private property is only a deposit or a trust
granted conditionally, because absolute ownership can be properly
assigned only to the Creator. Property is granted to the individual to
use, not to misuse; to invest, not to accumulate; to spend, not to withhold and hoard.

Faith in the unity of God and the unity of His Creation helps to
unify Islamic societies, despite their great social, cultural, and economic diversity. While Islamic civil society is differentiated and contains many organizations and subgroups, it forms a coherent society
by virtue of a shared commitment to faith and brotherhood. One
senses this unity immediately while traveling in Muslim countries,

whether it is in Mauretania or Turkey or Malaysia. The universal umma ideal may have little political significance today, but it is alive at the ethical and spiritual level, which unites individuals into a greater whole transcending their own often unrepresentative states. And it does have obvious importance within specific countries, where Islamic values of community pressure elites toward certain policies or even fuel popular resistance to corrupt regimes.[5]

But what is the status of non-Muslim groups? Are they excluded from Islamic conceptions of civil society? On the contrary, Islam has a long tradition of recognizing and accommodating non-Muslim communities. Indeed, the tradition originates from the earliest period of Islam's existence as a coherent society in Medina. In this society, established by the prophet Muhammad, Jews and Christians were granted a status that placed them on equal terms with the Muslims. Every community was accorded autonomy in language, costumes, manners, laws, and the like, within the larger community. The Islamic umma is not composed exclusively of Muslims, but it is a confederal umma composed of many communities bound together by a treaty of nonbelligerence and mutual respect. The millet system practiced by the Ottoman Empire into the twentieth century was de jure an Islamic system. This system acknowledged the right of each religious community to live within the confederated umma and exercise self-rule in many areas of communal life, while it prevented modern ethnic and religious cleansing.[6]

Today, this concept of Jews and Christians as *dhimmi* has acquired in public opinion a derogatory meaning, that of second-class citizenship. However, the etymological sense of this term is moral commitment. *Ahl al-dhimma* means those with whom a moral commitment is made to protect and defend them against all forms of injustices and aggression, as allies and brothers. In the old law, they have to pay an extra tax (*jizya*) in return for defense and protection, since they are exempted from military service. They have their own courts, and they are judged according to their own law. They have their own customs and manners, their languages, and their cults. But as members of the larger Islamic society, they have their claims to the social welfare provided by the state. They are entitled like all other members of the community to all the rights and privileges of the citizens on an equal basis: education, work, public services, and so forth.

Unfortunately, this earlier Islamic tradition of religious tolerance and inclusiveness is now under threat. In modern times and within contemporary nation-states many false images of the old law have been circulating that view Jews and Christians as second-class citizens, living in isolation from the broader Muslim population and yet subject to Islamic law, especially the penal code. This view is especially current in fundamentalist circles.

These false images need some clarification. The old law was conceived when religious identity was equated to political identity. Now national identity is taking over. All citizens of a nation are equal before the law by virtue of their citizenship and irrespective of their religious affiliations. In the past, Jews and Christians often preferred to take their own disputes to Muslim courts rather than to their proper courts because Islamic law is an objective law based on the idea of impartial justice. The actual civil code in much of the Muslim world today is based on secular, mainly European sources. The exception to this generalization remains family law, but this area is also under revision to cope with modern circumstances. Jews, Christians, and Muslims are equal in front of the civil law and the constitution. The fact that many otherwise secular states declare Islam to be the state religion, and that the head of state must be Muslim, does not mean there are any practical distinctions between ordinary Muslims and non-Muslims. In societies that are overwhelmingly Muslim in numerical terms, it is only natural that the population would want some acknowledgment of the role of Islamic values in their national life. Moreover, given the Muslim majority, it is likely that the head of state would be a Muslim. However, these positive expressions of Islamic values as undergirding national politics should not negatively affect the equality of all citizens before the law and the right of all citizens to participate and contribute to national life. Islamic values applied properly in politics promote not a communal culture favoring the Muslim population, but a pluralistic, "national" culture to which Muslims and non-Muslims belong.

In addition, the penal code in Islam—which fundamentalists are so eager to impose upon Muslims and non-Muslims—ought to be applied only to Muslims. Jews and Christians are liable under their own laws. Indeed, the severest penalties of the Islamic penal code are rarely applied even to the Muslims. The severity of some punishments is a motivation for the judge and for society as a whole to look for the causes of crimes in order to ameliorate them, to mitigate the chances for the crimes at their roots. The moral purport of Islamic punishments is not so much to punish the crime a posteriori but to prevent it a priori.

Thus, Islamic theory in its general outline does not view Jews, Christians, and others as necessarily or typically second-class citizens within Islamic societies. Indeed, non-Muslims are assured a remarkable degree of communal autonomy aimed at preventing their independent identities and cultures from being overwhelmed by the Muslim majority. In their communal life, they are autonomous from state regulation so long as they acknowledge the sovereignty of the Islamic state and the predominance of Islamic law as the regulatory mechanism across communities. At the same time, they are essential components of the broader, what may be termed quasi-federal, "national" structures. In other words, the Islamic conception embraces a number of limited civil societies with the hope that each will promote the greater civil society of all.

The generally positive picture presented thus far must of course be tempered with some caveats. Certainly, there have been some Muslim scholars who have argued for inequality of treatment and there have been some Muslim rulers who oppressed non-Muslim minorities within their realms. In some countries of the Muslim world today, religion is used to legitimize a political regime that lacks democratic legitimation. Religion is here only a cover for dictatorship. The sectarian clashes occurring in the Muslim world from time to time are not really due to sectarianism but to backward societies that suffer from marginalization of large numbers of people. The clashes are everywhere between poor and rich, between the state and the workers, between the government and the opposition, between the secularists and the fundamentalists. Since the state lacks legitimacy, democratic institutions, and legal opposition parties, apparently sectarian clashes are in reality driven by the economic-political struggle to seize the state, or at least to show its vulnerability and to destabilize the oppressive regimes. These are most often at root political clashes between the disenfranchised and the elites, not religious clashes between the Muslim majority and non-Muslim minorities arising out of a desire to exclude or marginalize non-Muslims because of their faith.

But we should end this section by emphasizing that there are numerous examples where Islamic conceptions of a peaceful, cooperative, pluralistic society are being realized. To cite but one example, Coptic Christians in Egypt (about 10 percent of the population) are equal citizens. They are very active in the political, social, and economic life of the country. They have their own schools, communal institutions, and intellectual presence. They are ministers in the government, generals in the army, and several rank among the eminent leaders of the Egyptian national movement in recent history. The positive facts throughout Islamic history are much more numerous than the negative incidents.[7]

Values

Individual human beings cannot live alone. They are drawn naturally toward social solidarity. The importance of civil society derives from the need to balance the desires and needs of the individual with the will and needs of society. Where civil society is present, an individual is a part of the body, joined to other members to form an organic whole, as the medieval philosopher al-Farabi describes in his virtuous city.

In Islam, civil society protects the rights of its members by anchoring these rights in a conception of universally binding duties or obligations that resemble Western conceptions of natural law. Within an Islamic framework, the ultimate author of these laws is God, but there is a long tradition in Islamic philosophy which argues that natural law is an objective law that human reason can discern. I shall pursue this line of thinking in outlining what I consider the principal values promoted by this law, which in turn foster civil society. Each of the values discussed below may be said to exist in a cyclical relationship with civil society, reinforcing it and being reinforced by it.

The first value must be the protection of life against all threats bringing death. Life is an absolute value. Genocide, assassination, murder, and even capital punishment are against life as an absolute value. God gives life and God takes it. As the Qur'an says in affirmation of biblical scripture, Whoever kills one person is as if he killed all mankind. But the commandment to preserve life—found in all moral systems—contains both positive as well as negative implications. It is not enough simply to abstain from killing; one cannot stand by passively while thousands, sometimes millions die even though society has the means to save them. The struggle against hunger, drought, disease, malnutrition, starvation, and nakedness is a struggle for human survival and welfare. It is a struggle intimately connected with the struggle for responsive and effective government and a tolerant, responsive society.

Reason is another absolute value, which translates into the right to know against withholding information for commercial monopoly and maximizing power. Ignorance and illiteracy are against the function of reason. Maleducation, misinformation through commercial or government propaganda, and blind imitation are all forms of anti-reason. Through reason man can prove that God exists, the world is created, and the soul is immortal. Reason is the very foundation of faith. Reason is not only deductive but also inductive. It deduces the causes of human behavior from the textual sources as it induces them from human actions. Reason is also the glue that binds individuals into a whole. If reason is not the common standard between human beings in communicating and understanding, the will to power takes over. Might will be substituted for right. Islam opens all avenues toward the promotion of reason and blocks all paths toward anti-reason.

Open scientific and spiritual inquiry is one of the hallmarks of classical Islamic civilization. The consumption of alcohol, on the other hand, is prohibited because drunkenness is against reason.

The defense of human honor and dignity is another of the pillars of civil society. Human honor includes all the principles stipulated in the Universal Declaration of Human Rights, including freedom of speech, belief, and movement; the right to privacy; and the respect of the human body against nakedness and torture. Human dignity is not confined to the individual, but applies also to whole communities, requiring for its realization the right for autodetermination and self-rule, the right for independence and respect.

Last comes the preservation of wealth against usurpation, pollution, or waste as the material basis for life. Wealth here does not mean only individual earnings, but national wealth as well, which must be safeguarded against corruption, profligate spending, negligence, and speculation. It has to be spent for development. Public servants including the ruler himself have to set a high example of honesty and integrity.

Private property is one of the Western individualistic human rights that may be incompatible with the communitarian concept of human rights in Islam. It was included in the Universal Declaration of Human Rights in 1948 because of opposition to the socialist regimes emerging after the Second World War and in the context of the cold war. Yet I would question whether it ought to be ranked among essential human rights. It is not, I would suggest, on the same level as the right to live, to survive, to believe, to think, to express, to work, to move, to choose, and to self-rule. Accordingly, in Islamic ethics the right to private property is decidedly lower in importance than the duty to ensure social justice. We noted earlier the positive mechanisms that Islam instituted for the distribution of wealth, including a tax on surplus wealth (zakat) that is collected by the state. In addition, in case of misuse, monopolization, or exploitation, the political authority has the right to confiscate and to nationalize this private property to become a public one.

But the social justice aims of Islamic ethics are not confined to state action. Indeed, the state is merely an agent of Muslim society in the realization of distributive justice goals. It is the society that bears the obligation to promote these values within itself, even if the state does not or cannot do so. We see how this obligation is taken up by society in many Muslim countries today, where myriad nongovernmental organizations, such as mosques, Sufi orders, and charitable organizations, perform social welfare tasks in the name of Islam while the state remains oblivious to its population's problems. This is where

Islamic civil society is most active and most visible, though these manifestations of civil society receive scant attention among Western students.

All of the values discussed above are values shared—in varying degrees of emphasis—by all cultures. This convergence alone permits us to generalize the concept of civil society (adjusted according to many confluents) and to avoid taking the Western concept as a yardstick according to which all other concepts stemming out of other cultures are judged. The only difference among cultures is in scope and practice. Many in the West suggest that reason, truth, and honor are relative concepts, changing from one society to another. If life and wealth are absolute values, they are applicable within the geographical borders of the West, not outside them. In Islam the objective values of "natural" law are absolute and universal. They do not change from one society to another, nor are they to be applied in one area not in another. These values, according to the Islamic approach, must be rooted in social consciousness, and they must be implemented foremost by society. If these values are not upheld by civil society, then they can hardly be expected to be enforced by the state.

Responsibility

Many individuals and institutions are responsible for the good management of civil society and the promotion of its values: the individual, the family, the state, and nongovernmental institutions. They are inseparable given the importance and the commitment of all to the common cause.

The individual is responsible for himself as well as for others. He cannot shirk his social responsibilties, because Islam enjoins upon all believers ordering the right and preventing the wrong (al-amr bi'l-ma'ruf wa al-nahy 'an al-munkar). A simple and wise counsel is: "Religion is the advice." Some conditions attend to the fulfillment of this responsibility. The advice should be dispensed when it may be best received. Thus, the person advising should consider the mood, the readiness, and so forth, of the person being admonished. The advice has to be in private, not in public, so that the advised should not be blamed publicly. No harm should result out of advising. It is better to accept a smaller harm before advising than to cause a bigger one after. Advising is not criticism from one individual to another, but mutual action for a common cause. It is not a personal matter but a collective work, a reminder for the common good and public welfare.

The family has a large role in maintaining the rights and the duties of individuals in civil society. The family is a microcosm of the larger society, and thus a harmonious family serves a crucial educational function in preparing its members to participate in a harmonious and well-balanced society.

The state is not an oppressive institution but a guarantor of human rights and responsibilities. Political power is wielded by representatives freely chosen by the people, as suggested by the old expression *ahl al-hall wa'l-'aqd* (literally, "those who loosen and bind"), namely, those who speak on behalf of the people. Political power is based on a contract between the ruler and the representatives of the people. The people must obey the chosen ruler as long as he is applying the law. If not, the first remedy is to admonish the errant ruler through public statements in mosques, schools, centers of learning, and even in the markets. If the ruler is still recalcitrant, disobeying the law, he has to be brought to court. If the high judge sentences him to obey the law and the ruler still disobeys, he becomes in contempt of the law and is no longer worthy of obedience. Now and then a revolt against him becomes the last resort and is directed by the *ahl al-hall wa'l-'aqd*. The unjust ruler cannot be obeyed.

Finally, nongovernmental organizations have an eminent role in assuming major responsibilities in the civil society. They are the neighbors, the relatives, the friends, and the comrades of work without institutional forms. Others are more institutional, such as workers' and students' unions, bar associations, press corps, literary and academic societies, university clubs, religious associations for public services such as burial, wedding, health care, social security, tutorship, and the like. They are quicker and more efficient than the state apparatus in dealing with national disasters such as earthquakes or floods. Mosques play extremely prominent social roles. They are not only houses of worship but community centers offering public services. Social annexes to the larger community mosques are more populated than the mosques themselves. Religion and society are intertwined. Helping the needy has more value than praying in the mosque.

Freedoms and Risks

As stated earlier, civil society is not a panacea for all the problems of state and society. If civil society is present and functioning properly, it fosters a distribution of power in the polity and a balance among the constituent elements of society. That balance allows group autonomy while preserving a wide scope for individual freedom. Nevertheless, maintaining the balance is always a precarious enterprise, and within an Islamic framework the following risks are particularly relevant.

If the state is strong and the power of the ruler becomes absolute, the whole system risks sliding toward theocracy because theoretically the purpose of the state is to apply divine law. The ruler, in order to consolidate his power, gain legitimacy, and tame the opposition, pretends that he is the representative of God on earth, the follower of the Prophet, the guarantor of the application of the law, the right interpreter of religion, and the guardian of public morality and public welfare. He is the custodian of law and order. Any opposition to his power is tantamount to a revolt against God. In this perverted approach, God chooses the ruler, not the people. He nominates him, not the community. Carried to extremes, this ruler sometimes claims that he is even mentioned in the religious text, if not by name, then at least by description; if not explicitly, then at least implicitly.

We find many examples of this theocratic authoritarianism in Islamic history. In this case, there is no difference between Sunnis and Shi'is. Even now many regimes, such as Morocco and Saudi Arabia, are based on religion as a legitimizing device. The rulers in these countries are considered to be following the model of the Prophet, or even to be descended from the Prophet's family. Any protest against them is treated as a violation of the shari'a.

Of course, the balance may tilt the other way, toward the strengthening of societal elements in the face of the loss of state power. This risk is particularly relevant to the Islamic case because of the strongly communitarian bent of Islamic social ethics. An individual's freedom and welfare may be just as jeopardized—perhaps even more so—by a society or smaller social groups convinced of their divine mission as they are by a state with similar ideological convictions.

One subset of Muslim society has historically been particularly vulnerable to overbearing societal pressures: women. Islamic family law is frequently mentioned as violating some values in modern civil society through its sanctioning of polygamy and discrimination against women in divorce, inheritance, witnessing, leadership, and the like. All of these legal limitations can be seen in their historical perspective. The purpose of Islamic laws relating specifically to women was to change gradually the gender situation in Arabia without setback, with the maximum of success and the minimum of loss. Before Islam, polygamy was unlimited, not to mention the taking of concubines and captives of war. In order to abolish this custom, Islam made it limited to four wives *in exceptional cases*, paving the way to monogamy, which conforms to human nature, physically and emotionally. The exceptional cases are sterility or some other physical handicap, or when the number of females exceeds the number of males, such as following war. Moreover, many restrictions have been put in the old law, such as separate apartments for each wife, the requirement of the first wife's permission, financial capacity, and so forth. All of these restrictions promote monogamy as the Islamic ideal.

Before Islam, women did not have the right of inheritance from their parents' property. On the contrary, women were inherited. Islam gave a woman a half share in order to change the status quo in a society where a female baby was buried alive for fear of shame. The share must be seen in the context of the shareholder's position, namely, as a member of a family. When the woman marries with a half share to a husband with a full share, the outcome is one and one-half shares in the new family. These minimum share requirements notwithstanding, during their lives either parent can distribute their wealth equally among their children regardless of gender, as many pious Muslims do.

Before Islam, women had no legal status. They were not recognized as autonomous persons. They could not buy and sell, witness, or participate in the political process. Islam made a woman a half witness for the same reason as in inheritance, to change her status gradually. In practice, the testimony of an educated woman was preferred to that of an uneducated man.

Women cannot be the head of state in the old law, since the head of the state is also the head of the army, which requires fatigue and hard work unsuitable for pregnant women. Veiling is an old custom in certain parts of Arabia. A simple head cover protects male and female alike from the heat of the desert. All limitations on women in Islam can be so conceived, in their historical perspective, as a gradual social change to be followed by other steps, since history does not stop.

Indeed, many Muslim states have realized that the dictates of the medieval Islamic law must be revised in light of the changed conditions and needs of twentieth-century Muslim societies. Family law has been the last area of the shari'a to be enforced, and wherever reform has been attempted, it has always been met with great controversy. Nevertheless, serious legal changes have been implemented in most Muslim countries that dramatically broaden women's rights and move them toward greater equality with men.

But it is one thing for the state to legislate women's rights and another thing for women to realize these rights. As numerous human rights organizations have documented, Muslim women lag significantly behind Muslim men in many states in key indicators of material and emotional well-being, such as infant mortality, literacy, life expectancy, age at marriage, and jobs. The problem stems often from government indifference toward enforcement of rights enshrined in constitutions and statutes. But an even greater obstacle is societal re-

sistance to change in an area that so many view as an essential aspect
of their tradition and faith. Women's status for many traditional Muslims falls into that broad area of privacy that their understanding of
Islam throws around the family. Within the confines of the family, the
state may not intrude. And for most Muslim societies that are heavily
rooted in patriarchy, even those rights that the medieval law guaran-
tees women are frequently flouted in the name of social mores and
tradition. In this area, the protected, private space occupied by the
family, which all civil society rightly fosters, can become an oppressive well of custom and convention.[8]

Conclusion: Reflections on the Prospects for Islamic
Civil Society

There are some risks to civil society stemming from Muslim societies
that are related not to Islamic conceptions of civil society per se, but
to the historical moment Muslim societies are living nowadays, a moment that can be characterized as conservatism dominating the Muslim world for over a millennium. Muslim societies in the first four
centuries were pluralistic societies with many philosophical, theological, mystical, and legal trends. No single school of thought equated
itself with Islam. In the fifth Islamic century, the great thinker al-
Ghazali launched a conservative revolution that stifled this pluralism
and transformed Islamic culture and society according to an absolute
and state-enforced doctrine: Ash'arism in theology and Shafi'ism in
law. All other schools of thought were marginalized, criticized, or
anathematized.

Over the last century reformers have tried to revitalize Islamic pluralism again. These efforts have been threatened over the past fifty
years or so as secular military revolutions erupted or new traditional
kingdoms were institutionalized. Conservatism and unilateralism generated dogmatism and fanaticism that spread in the mass media and
in the educational system from the smallest schools up to the university campuses. Muslim societies, which the reformers in the last century wanted to liberalize, and which the military regimes in this century wanted to revolutionize, persisted in their traditional culture.
Both efforts failed because the reformers had Western enlightenment
as a model, which tended toward Westernization and thus alienation
of the masses from the elites.[9] The military, on the other hand, was
interested merely in the infrastructure, not in the superstructure.

The failure of both modernist Islam and secular nationalism has in
recent decades played into the hands of the fundamentalists. "Authen-

tic" Islam according to these groups is equated with traditional conservatism, and this narrow interpretation is used as a whip against all liberals who continue the work of the reformers of the last century. Since Islamic movements were not legalized as legitimate elements of civil society and indeed have been suppressed by states, they tried to control the mass media, labor unions, professional associations, and to infiltrate other NGOs.

Elements that are not allowed to compete for popular support within civil society will inevitably become as averse to the values of civil society as those who suppress them. It is hardly surprising therefore that fundamentalist groups employ the traditional accusation of anathema, false innovation, and heresy against artists, thinkers, writers, professors—all methods to obstruct any alternative interpretation of Islam. They wage their battles in the mass media to sway public opinion. Sometimes they go to court to sue their opponents in the name of hisba, that is, in the name of the "public good." Sometimes conservative judges rule for them and declare the thinker accused to be an apostate who should suffer penalties including divorce from his wife because a Muslim woman cannot be legally married to an apostate. Such a ruling actually occurred in the famous case of Nasr Hamid Abu Zaid, a professor of literature at Cairo University, because of his studies in the Qur'an and Islamic law.

But acts of intimidation often do not stop with media campaigns or lawsuits. Zealous and ignorant followers of these conservative groups are willing even to murder the declared apostates or "enemies" of Islam, as they did successfully in the case of the journalist Faraj Fouda or unsuccessfully in the case of the Nobel laureate Naguib Mahfouz.

The zealots' call for an Islamic state means essentially the application of the penal code and the replacement of secular elites with religious men like themselves. Once this occurs, religion and politics will be united, they claim. Indeed, religion in Islam is a political system, an economic theory, and a social structure. But this does not mean the imposition by the state on society of any one interpretation of Islam. It means only that Islamic values cannot be divorced from the business of the state, and the foremost values are the free election of the political power, the defense of common interests and public welfare, and the maintenance of a social order exempt from huge differences between classes.

The struggle between fundamentalism and secularism to the point of civil war as in Algeria would completely destroy civil society. In both cases, whether religious groups take power or the secular state survives, human freedom is violated. The oppression is the same, in the name of the army or in the name of Islamic opposition. The major risk for the future is that Muslim societies will be offered only the fundamentalist/secularist alternatives. Unless Muslim advocates of a middle course resume the serious task of developing and implementing pluralistic and representative conceptions of state and society from within the Islamic tradition, Islam will offer no alternative conception of civil society.

As I have argued throughout this essay, such an alternative is possible. In constructing this alternative Islam can learn from the West, and the West can learn from Islam. Traditional Islamic culture may be based on the idea of duties rather than on the idea of rights (duties of man and rights of God), while modern Western culture is essentially based on the idea of rights rather than duties (rights of man and maybe duties of God). In both cultures, there is a certain imbalance between rights and duties. Muslim societies may have duties without rights while Western societies may have rights without responsibilities. Islam needs a universal declaration of human rights beside the traditional Islamic declaration of human duties. The West needs also a universal declaration of human duties to complete the Universal Declaration of Human Rights.

Pessimism in the short run leads to optimism in the long run. Islamic culture is still strongly bound to conservatism inherited over a millennium. Reformism is a recent phenomenon dating only to the last century. Modernism may have a better chance in the future, as Muslim consciousness achieves a more equal historical presence of both traditionalism and modernism so that a healthy dialogue between the two major schools results. In this progress, the lead must be taken by Muslim intellectuals and modernist scholars practicing ijtihad, creatively linking ageless concepts of a just and virtuous society with modern ideals of civil society. As the Islamic aphorism says, The scholars are the heirs of the prophets.

Further Reading

Leonard Binder. *Islamic Liberalism: A Critique of Development Ideologies.* Chicago: University of Chicago Press, 1988.
John L. Esposito and John O. Voll. *Islam and Democracy.* New York: Oxford University Press, 1996.
Albert Hourani. *Arabic Thought in the Liberal Age, 1789–1939.* Cambridge: Cambridge University Press, 1983.
Charles Kurzman, ed. *Liberal Islam: A Sourcebook.* New York: Oxford University Press, 1998.
Abdullahi Ahmed an-Naim, *Toward an Islamic Reformation: Civil Liberties, Hu-*

man *Rights, and International Law.* Syracuse, N.Y.: Syracuse University Press, 1990.

Augustus Richard Norton, ed. *Civil Society in the Middle East.* Leiden: E. J. Brill, 1995–96.

Jillian Schwedler. Introduction to *Toward Civil Society in the Middle East? A Primer*, ed. Jillian Schwedler. Boulder, Colo.: Lynne Rienner, 1995.

Notes

1. A survey of the prospects for civil society in different Muslim states is available in Augustus Richard Norton, ed., *Civil Society in the Middle East* (Leiden: E. J. Brill, 1995–96).

2. Many of the ideas presented in this essay are elaborated in Hasan Hanafi, *Al-Din wa'l-thaqafa wa'l-siyasa fi'l-watan al-'Arabi* (Cairo: Dar Qiba, 1998).

3. For succinct treatments of Islamic political theory, see H.A.R. Gibb, "Constitutional Organization," in *Law in the Middle East*, ed. Majid Khadduri and Herbert J. Liebesny (Washington, D.C.: Middle East Institute, 1955), 3–27; and Ann K. S. Lambton, *State and Government in Medieval Islam* (Oxford: Oxford University Press, 1981).

4. The Qur'an is very clear on this point: "Those who believe, the Jews, the Christians, and the Sabaeans—whosoever believe in God and the Last Day and do good deeds, they shall have their reward from their Lord, shall have nothing to fear, nor shall they come to grief" (2:62; see also 2:111–12, 4:124–25, 5:69, 18:30, 21:94). "But God is free of all wants, and it is you [Muslims] who are needy. If you turn back [from the path of Islam] He will substitute in your place another people. Then they would not be like you!" (47:38).

5. On modern understandings of *umma*, see Abdullah al-Ahsan, *Ummah or Nation? Identity Crisis in Contemporary Muslim Society* (Leicester, U.K.: Islamic Foundation, 1992).

6. Leading studies of the status of non-Muslims in Islamic societies include: Antoine Fattal, *Le statut légal de non-musulmans dans le pays d'Islam* (Beirut: Imprimerie Catholique, 1958); A. S. Tritton, *The Caliphs and Their Non-Muslim Subjects* (London: Frank Cass and Co., 1970); Bat Ye'or, *The Dhimmi: Jews and Christians under Islam* (London: Associated University Presses, 1985).

7. For a more developed argument regarding the place of non-Muslims in Islamic society, see Hasan Hanafi, *Religious Dialogue and Revolution: Essays on Judaism, Christianity, and Islam* (Cairo: Anglo-Egyptian Bookshop, 1977).

8. Three particularly useful discussions of the status of women in Islamic morality and law are: John Esposito, *Women in Muslim Family Law* (Syracuse, N.Y.: Syracuse University Press, 1982); Leila Ahmed, *Women and Gender in Islam: Historical Roots of a Modern Debate* (New Haven: Yale University Press, 1992); and Amina Wadud, *Qur'an and Woman: Rereading the Sacred Text from a Woman's Perspective*, 2nd ed. (New York: Oxford University Press, 1999).

9. A penetrating critique of the modernist agenda is available in Fazlur Rahman, *Islam and Modernity: Transformation of an Intellectual Tradition* (Chicago: University of Chicago Press, 1982).

Part II

BOUNDARIES AND DISTRIBUTIVE JUSTICE

4

Islamic Perspectives on Territorial Boundaries and Autonomy

M. RAQUIBUZ ZAMAN

AT THIS TIME in history, when the world is divided into nation-states with few virgin tracts of land to be claimed, it seems the task of defining territorial boundaries should be quite an easy one. However, the task becomes somewhat arduous when we try to approach it in terms of ethical perspectives that have religious sanctions. After all, if ethics is "the study of the right and the good, i.e., right conduct in the affairs of human life and the pursuit of the good life,"[1] then the question arises whether or not the current territorial boundaries that determine the position of the nation-states are all ethical. This chapter will attempt to define territorial boundaries and their ethical implications from Islamic points of view. Since the principal focus of the exposition in this chapter is on Islamic legal traditions, a brief introduction to the various schools of jurisprudence in Islam is imperative.

The two basic sources of Islamic thought and legal system are the divine revelation, the Qur'an, and the *sunna* (or the way of life) of the prophet Muhammad consisting of what he said, did, advised, and agreed to,[2] as documented by later generations in the *hadith* literature. From these two sources, jurists deduced rules and injunctions through various interpretive processes, including *qiyas* (analogical reasoning based on Qur'an and hadith), *ijtihad* (systematic original thinking),[3] *ijma'* (consensus among jurists), and *ra'y* (reasoning based on equity or public welfare).[4] The fruit of these early jurists' efforts was the emergence by the end of the ninth century of four schools of jurisprudence within the majority Sunni tradition, the Hanafi, Maliki, Shafi'i, and Hanbali.

Beyond the ninth century, no other school of law was able to gain a wide following within Sunni Islam. The Shi'i legal tradition evolved independently of developments in Sunni Islam, but this school— which itself was divided into several schools—always remained a distinctly minority tradition. We will, therefore, focus on Sunni thought in this chapter, although it should be mentioned that the differences between Sunni and Shi'i lawyers on most topics are not great.

Why the focus on law—and medieval law at that—in a chapter discussing Islamic ethical approaches to questions of boundaries? The reason is that the fruits of the early lawyers' labors, the body of Islamic law (*fiqh*), is synonymous in the view of many contemporary Muslims with *shari'a*, which represents the divine will revealed to the Prophet as guidance for all dimensions of human life. Thus, "Law in the Islamic sense is a set of value-oriented guidelines directed toward the divine purpose of Allah. Islamic law, therefore, is primarily normative rather than prescriptive and is designed for moral education as well as for legal enforcement."[5]

Of course, various reformist movements have arisen throughout Islamic history, and beginning in the nineteenth century, modernist intellectuals sought to separate fiqh from shari'a, and thus open the door to legal innovation based upon fresh readings of the ethical imperatives of the Qur'an and sunna. Yet, as the continuing controversies in Muslim states on the meaning and status of shari'a in public life demonstrate, fiqh still remains for many Muslims intrinsically related to the shari'a and thus provides a normative standard for what constitutes "genuine" Islam. We will examine these issues further as we proceed with our interpretation of Islamic perspectives on autonomy and territorial boundaries.

Defining Boundaries

The term *boundary* refers to any or all of the following: "border," "limit," "bound," "confine," "end," and "frontier." Territorial boundary, therefore, defines the limit of the area in which individuals, groups, or societies exercise rights and/or controls. The "boundary" demarcates one property from another and, thus, makes it possible for the owner or the renter (in some cases, manager or operator) to enjoy the fruits of the products and services, or the sanctity the boundary provides.

Human beings need order and structure to nurture fully all of their potentials. The search for order is the reason we enact laws, set boundaries, and seek religion. In the absence of territorial boundaries we would have chaos and injustice. The struggle for mere survival would take all of our energies and resources. It is difficult to imagine what the nature of human civilization would have been were there no order or structure in socioeconomic relations between various groups of people. The need for redemarcation of agricultural plots washed away by the frequent floods in the Nile delta apparently prompted the Egyptians, as early as 2000 B.C., to develop what came to be known later (at around 550 B.C.) as Pythagorean geometry.[6] From the records of history we find that not only economic growth but also cultural and intellectual development flourishes where there exists a healthy respect for law and order and where there is an atmosphere that is conducive to the pursuit of personal growth and fulfillment. The existence of territorial boundaries provides the security that is needed to promote economic and social progress by making it possible for individuals to reap the benefits of their personal efforts and initiatives.

Islam emphasizes the sanctity of personal property. Prophet Muhammad, in his farewell pilgrimage, declared to the gathering: "O men, your lives and your property shall be as inviolate as this holy day and holy month. Remember that you will indeed meet your Lord, and that He will indeed reckon your deeds."[7] At the same time, Islam reminds its adherents that with the right to own personal property comes the responsibility to see that this right is not misused. The Qur'an (17:26–27) implores all, "Squander not thy wealth in wantonness and extravagance. Lo! The squanderers were ever brothers of the devil, and the devil was ever an ingrate to the Lord."[8] The Qur'an further emphasizes that those who live around the property—the deserving kinsmen, the needy, the wayfarer, and the orphan—all have rights to be assisted by the property holder, since it is God who provides sustenance in abundance for whom He pleases, and He provides in a just manner (17:28–30).

Islam puts responsibility not only on individuals to utilize their resources prudently, but also on communities to assure that the needs of all are attended to in a balanced manner.[9] Communal property rights, as manifested by territorial boundaries, allow communities free choice as to the disposal of their property, but societies also bear responsibilities to the needy similar to those indicated by the above Qur'anic verses.

Ownership

Islam emphasizes individual initiative in property ownership and management, but with clear reminders, as found in numerous Qur'anic verses, that: "To God belongs all that is in the heavens and on earth" (2:284; see also 3:180, 4:126, 48:7, 53:25, 63:7).[10]

Human beings, as God's vicegerents on earth, are entitled to own and use God-given resources for their legitimate needs. The uniqueness and individuality of man is such that inequality in the accumulation of wealth and resources is inevitable.[11] "And it is He who hath made you His representatives on the Earth, and hath raised some of you above others by various grades, that He may test you by His gifts" (6:165). Whatever degree of wealth individuals possess, God reminds them: "And know you that your possessions and your progeny are but a trial; and that it is God with whom lies your highest reward" (8:28). Further, "And do not eat up your property among yourselves for vanities, nor use it as bait for the judges, with intent that you may eat up wrongfully and knowingly a little of [other] people's property" (2:188).

While encouraging Muslims to own and operate properties to meet their earthly needs, Islam urges them to share the fruits of their labor and wealth with the poor and the needy and for the common good.[12] Muslims who have *nisab* (income adequate for an acceptable standard of living) must pay the obligatory charitable levy, called *zakat*, to purify their wealth. They are also advised repeatedly to give to charities voluntarily.[13]

Ownership rights imply the presence of territorial boundaries. The question is, how does one acquire ownership of landed property?

At the outset of the Islamic state in Medina, Prophet Muhammad set the principles of property ownership and rights on the following basic principles: (1) All land belongs to God, and as such, all humans, as creatures of God, have a right to use it for their personal and societal benefit; (2) already occupied and tilled land belongs to its rightful owner, and the owner's rights to sell or transfer or give it in trust are to be recognized and protected by the state. Any fraudulent transaction or forced occupation is to be rendered null and void by the authority.[14]

As the Islamic state expanded over the following centuries beyond Medina to distant lands, the rules were expanded and sometimes adjusted, but with the same underlying principle of protecting property rights. According to the schools of Islamic jurisprudence, ownership can be achieved in a number of ways:[15]

On payment of land tax, kharaj, *to the* imam, *the Islamic state's ruler.* The laws of *kharaj* were formulated in response to the conquest of large amounts of territory by the early Muslim armies. At the time of the conquest, a payment of *kharaj* levy confirmed the right of the tiller to the land. The Islamic laws prevented the development of serfs by transforming land into a commodity and the payment of *kharaj* tax by the peasant cultivators as the proof of their land ownership. Although it originated as a tax on non-Muslim landholders, *kharaj* continued to be assessed even after the landholder converted to Islam or the property was sold to a Muslim. In addition, Muslims were assessed the *'ushr*, a levy of one-tenth the value of the produce on the land.

Through the allocation or assignment (iqtaʿ) *of wasteland* (mawat) *by the leader.*[16] Lands assigned in this way then become subject to the *kharaj* and/or *'ushr* levies. Uninhabited and unoccupied land is open to reclamation by any person. Whatever a person can till or build on, within certain reasonable limits, would be deemed as that person's property. Previously occupied but now abandoned (*'adi*) land can be taken or allotted to anyone who wants to resettle there. If resettled land is not used for three years or more by the present owner/occupier, it is deemed "abandoned" and can be reclaimed by another settler. When the state has granted land from its holdings (land that fell into the state coffers as a result of conquest or through bequests, etc.) on certain conditions or for a limited period, the ownership reverts back to the state, in case the conditions have not been met or at the expiration of the term.

On the other hand, the caliphs as well as local governors could permanently allocate public lands to those who desired to cultivate or settle on them. Once properly occupied or granted by the authority, the property would legally belong to the owner, and could not be reclaimed by the administration. Land designated for "public" use (such as a prairie, pond, or salt mine) could never become "personal" property, but must be preserved for unrestricted public use.

Through various types of gifts, such as (a) donation, (b) bequest, or (c) inheritance. Ownership of landed property can be transformed into a trust, or *waqf*, for charitable purposes.[17] All legal experts agree that the condition for such an endowment is that it be established in perpetuity, so long as the original intent or benefit of the endowment remains. For example, if a piece of land is dedicated to the construction of a mosque, it cannot be claimed as the property of the original owner or his/her heirs, or sold or transferred to other owners, so long as the mosque continues to function as a place of worship. The jurists are divided, however, on what happens to the *waqf* once the property falls into disuse. Some maintain that in this event it should revert to the original owner or his/her heirs. Others argue that the establishment of a *waqf* alienates the property rights of the original owner forever, and therefore unused endowments revert to the possession of the state. These rulings generally applied to both Muslims and non-Muslims.

Through various channels of exchange for a commodity, such as (a) sale or (b) preemption (shufʿa). Because of the sanctity of personal territorial boundaries guaranteed by Islam, there are some limitations on transfers of properties that have common borders and shareholders. The principle of *shufʿa*, or

preemption, needs to be addressed here briefly to demonstrate how the
sanctity of territorial boundaries puts some limit on the owner's right to
dispose of property as he or she pleases. Under the law of preemption it is
the right of a third party, the preemptor, to step in when a contract is made
between the seller of the property (a Muslim) and the purchaser (a Muslim
or a non-Muslim), and to claim the place of the buyer and take possession
of the property according to the terms and conditions of the sales contract.[18]
Since it is the Islamic laws of inheritance which tend to create fragmentation of landed property by requiring distribution of property among all
heirs, the laws of preemption tend to mitigate the situation by allowing the
joint owners (co-sharers) to claim property being sold to outsiders. The preemptory rights can be used to prevent inconveniences that an outsider
might cause to the co-sharer or to keep away a disagreeable neighbor.[19]

In the majority of the Sunni schools of law, the right of preemption can
be claimed by: (1) a co-owner, or a partner of the property sold; (2) "a
participator in the immunities and appendages of the property, such as the
right to water and roads or a common access";[20] (3) a neighbor or owner of
the adjoining property (confined to adjoining houses, gardens, and small
tracts of land, but not large landholdings). According to the Shafi'i school
and in Shi'i law, however, the preemptory right is limited to co-sharers
when their number is only two. "It does not recognize the right on the
ground of vicinage or on the ground of participation in appendages."[21] In
all schools the right of preemption exists only for immovable property such
as land, buildings, or trees.[22]

To summarize, ownership of landed property is confirmed by the
payment of tax (kharaj and/or 'ushr), which entitles the owner to
dispose of his/her property through various channels of transfer discussed above, including setting up of awqaf (plural of waqf). Ownership entails the creation of territorial boundaries that makes it possible to transform landed property into a commodity and subject it to
the various methods of exchange. The state in a Muslim country does
not own all the land; it only owns the land that does not belong to
anyone else. The state, however, may assert its rights to own and
control land and other natural resources deemed necessary for the
welfare and progress of the general public. Finally, it is important to
emphasize that under Islamic law, state property is not the property
of the imam. His personal property is distinct and must be acquired in
the same manner as that of any other person.

For more than a millennium, Muslim rulers in various parts of the
world essentially followed these basic principles, as evinced in the
elaborate revenue records they maintained. When the countries were
colonized during the eighteenth and nineteenth centuries, the colonial

authorities sometimes modified these laws according to European codes, but in general they allowed traditional Islamic patterns of land ownership to remain in place under new administration. Modern Muslim states by and large maintained this colonial legacy while in some cases attempting various redistribution schemes for the sake of economic development and social welfare.

Distribution

In an Islamic state, not all resources can be owned individually. The society collectively (i.e., states in modern times) is responsible for maintaining and managing environmental (natural) resources such as water, minerals, and forests for the collective good of all.[23] All members of the society who are living in peace in a Muslim state are entitled to the benefits to be derived from these natural resources. The state is responsible for ensuring the distribution of resources by developing infrastructure to promote economic activities. Creation and distribution of public goods are part of the obligatory duties of the state (*furud kifaya*). It is also incumbent upon the state to ensure adequate living spaces with defined boundaries for all of its citizens, irrespective of their diversity in faith and social characteristics. While the Muslims are prohibited from certain products and services (alcohol, pork, intoxicants, gambling, etc.), the non-Muslims may be permitted to use them under stipulated conditions. As the representative of the society, the state has the right and obligation to promote welfare for all.

Certain aspects of the Islamic penal code which appear overly harsh may in fact be understood only in the context of the full social welfare system that the religion enjoins. The Qur'an states on the subject of stealing, for example: "Now as for the man who steals and the woman who steals, cut off the hand of either of them in requital for what they have wrought, as a deterrent ordained by God" (5:38). Yet this punishment is grounded in "the fundamental principle of Islamic law that no duty (*taklif*) is ever imposed on man without his being granted a corresponding right (*haqq*); and the term 'duty' also comprises in this context, liability to punishment."[24] Thus, before anyone's hand can be cut off, the Islamic state must ensure that every citizen, Muslim as well as non-Muslim, has economic, social, and political protection and security. Thus, the nation's economic resources must be shared in such a way that everyone is able to meet his or her basic needs. If, after a basic minimum standard of living is met, someone steals to accumulate wealth, only then may the prescribed punishment even be considered, after due attention is given to mitigating circumstances. Thus, we see that the second caliph, 'Umar b. al-Khattab, waived the punishment during a period of famine.

From the opinions of jurists it is clear that "the cutting-off of a hand in punishment for theft is applicable only within the context of an already existing, fully functioning social security scheme, and in no other circumstances."[25] Establishment of a functional social security system for all citizens is an obligatory duty of the Islamic state. This can be done only when there is distributive justice in the state. Islam provides specific means for this in a number of ways. First, the role of the state in the creation and distribution of public goods has already been mentioned above. Second, the state is responsible for the collection of zakat from the Muslims who possess wealth above a standard minimum and for distribution of the proceeds to specific categories of people—the first two of which are the indigent and the needy—Muslims as well as non-Muslims. It is true that the various schools of Islamic fiqh interpret differently what exactly is to be collected and distributed by the state (e.g., how to differentiate between apparent and non-apparent wealth, *amwal zahira* and *amwal batina*). But there is no doubt that the Muslims must pay zakat on their wealth as part of the five pillars of Islam. The non-Muslims do not pay zakat because it is a religious duty for the Muslims only. Yet the indigent and the needy among them are entitled to share the benefits.

Ironically, many governments in Muslim states today, especially the oil-rich countries of the Middle East, do not make serious attempts to collect zakat because they either feel zakat proceeds are not needed to carry out some rudimentary charitable work for the benefit of the disadvantaged, or do not think it is worth the bother for them. It took a concerted effort over a number of years in the early 1980s to convince the Kingdom of Saudi Arabia not to burn the hundreds of thousands of cattle slaughtered during the annual pilgrimage (*hajj*), but to process them and distribute the meat among the poor outside Saudi Arabia. Similarly, such an oil-rich country could collect zakat from its citizens for distribution of proceeds to the poor Muslim countries if it had the desire to do so.[26] But Saudi officials have resisted acknowledging any international distributive justice claims on their vast oil wealth, preferring to operate within the framework of "foreign aid," rather than Islamic zakat. The Saudi state is one of the largest foreign aid donors in the world, as determined by percentage of GNP. Yet whether such aid serves the poorest and neediest Muslims is open to question, because under the foreign aid regime, most of the wealth goes into the hands of corrupt government officials in recipient states. The average wealthy citizen, motivated by a sense of pious obligation to the disadvantaged, is often more effective in promoting social welfare in poorer countries.

The Islamic system contains a number of other distributive measures aimed at maximizing the circulation of wealth. Apart from collecting zakat, the Muslim state is entitled to assess other types of taxes for social welfare purposes. Zakat is not strictly speaking a government "tax"—it is a religious levy to bring distributive justice only.[27] The Qur'an exhorts Muslims repeatedly to give as much as feasible in voluntary charities (*sadaqa*) above the zakat due in order to attain piety. Kind words or deeds to benefit others are also considered as charities. The goal is to make the life of the members of the society in general a fair and pleasant one, because in the absence of that, human beings cannot achieve spiritual well-being.

The state is also obligated to undertake other measures aimed at promoting distributive justice. Prevention of fraud and illegal transactions are major responsibilities of the state, since only in their absence can economic justice and fair play be realized. For this, medieval Islamic civilization introduced the institution of *hisba* and made it the responsibility of a government functionary, the *muhtasib*, to ensure ethical and spiritual conduct by the citizens. One of the muhtasib's most important duties was to prevent usurious transactions (*riba*) in the marketplace. Usury brings undue economic hardships to the poorest borrower, and justice requires its absence from the economic scene.

Finally, Islamic laws of inheritance—one of the most complicated aspects of the shari'a—have the purpose of widely disseminating wealth among the deceased's heirs. All heirs, male and female, have a stake in the inheritance according to formulae intended to meet the various needs and responsibilities of family members.

Diversity and Autonomy

Islam emphasizes the unity of human origin, as can be seen from the following Qur'anic verse: "O mankind! We created you from a single [pair] of a male and a female, and made you into nations and tribes, that you may know each other [not that you may despise each other]. Verily the most honored of you in the sight of God is he who is the most righteous of you. And God has full knowledge and is well acquainted with all things" (49:13).

Islam refers to *umma*, the Muslim community, in all deliberations about political entities. All Muslims, regardless of their place of origin or abode, language, and ethnicity, are part of the same umma. National boundaries, unlike personal territorial boundaries, are anathema to Islam. "Territorial nationalism, with its emphasis on what is called national characteristics,"[28] is of Christian-European origin and, as I discuss below, still enjoys only limited support among Muslim thinkers.

The maintenance of the unity of the umma has been a moral concern of Muslim thinkers throughout Islamic history, even after in reality the Islamic world fragmented into many separate political units. When Abu Bakr, the first caliph, declared war against rebel bedouin tribes in Arabia, the Muslim elites all sided with him so that the central authority of *khalifa* (caliph) could be enforced. The internal strife following the murder of the third caliph ʿUthman and the succession of ʿAli produced the most serious divisions within the early Islamic community. These conflicts brought the Umayyad dynasty to power, which then managed to maintain the unity and central authority of the Muslim state, keeping the umma together for another century.[29]

The perceived necessity to maintain the unity of the umma, as enjoined by the Qurʾan (see esp. 3:103–5), prompted the majority of Muslim jurists to support the office of the khalifa, despite the character and disposition of its incumbent, so long as he proclaimed in public loyalty and submission to the shariʿa. To classical political theorists like Abu Yusuf (d. 798), al-Baghdadi (d. 1037), al-Mawardi (d. 1058), and Abu Yaʿla (d. 1065), the communal unity of the umma could only be possible under political and legal unity. In order to preserve this unity, they were willing to compromise with the political realities of their time, which often included giving allegiance to less than ideal rulers.[30] Nevertheless, many of the jurists played the role of the loyal opposition to corrupt caliphs.

The Abbasid revolt against the Umayyads in the middle of the eighth century ushered in a new period of increasing political fragmentation of the Islamic empire. The jurists were forced to reconcile the power struggle between the center and the breakaway areas on the periphery of the Islamic empire with the ideal of the unified caliphate. Grudgingly, some approved "the existence of more than one legitimate independent political unit and authority. Some jurists approved of this when the units were far apart geographically and thus difficult to run under a single administration. The jurists no longer paid much attention to the question of the office of the khalifah when it could no longer be preserved."[31]

The tension between the political authority to govern and the legal authority to legislate that evolved from the dynastic periods of Islam (from the Umayyad period onward) continued throughout the medieval period. Further development of the shariʿa was seriously limited when Abbasid jurists curtailed legal innovation in order to prevent political meddling from the rulers. As a result, the shari'a became less and less relevant to Muslim practice, especially in administrative or constitutional matters. Medieval works dating back to the eleventh century were still read as representative of the Islamic ideal even though Muslim realities had long since diverged from it. Al-Mawardi's theory of the state, for example, dominated Islamic political thinking for centuries, up to the time of the gradual encroachment of Western colonial powers in Muslim lands during the eighteenth and nineteenth centuries.

It fell upon Jamal al-Din al-Afghani (d. 1897) to issue clarion calls to all Muslims to wake up and face the dangers of Western expansionism. He urged Muslims to go back to the study of science and reasoning and adapt medieval Islamic concepts to meet the needs of modern times. His call for the political unification of the Muslim world, known as pan-Islamism, revived the concept of one umma. While he understood the importance of constitutional governments as the bulwark against Western power and intrigues and, hence, the necessary growth of national states, he abhorred nationalism that was narrowly based on race, language, or culture, and consequently, transformed into secular states. While he realized that modern political developments would lead to nation-states, he wanted to keep the door open for the eventual and progressive unity of the Muslim umma. His ideas were mirrored in the works of other contemporary Muslim intellectuals, such as Sayyid Ahmad Khan of India (d. 1898) and Muhammad 'Abduh of Egypt (d. 1905). The political thought of these modernists still reverberates throughout the Muslim world. Support for purely secular national states among Muslim thinkers is wanting. They are still reeling from the secularization of Turkey by Mustafa Kemal Ataturk.[32]

As in previous centuries, some contemporary Muslim scholars have attempted to reconcile Islamic ideals with prevailing political realities. The modern Muslim states can still pursue the concept of one umma, these intellectuals suggest, by following the basic precepts of the shari'a to enforce equal treatment of their subjects—Muslims as well as non-Muslims—and through treaties and agreements (in modern times, diplomatic relations) with other nation-states, following the footsteps of the Prophet and the covenant that the second caliph, 'Umar b. al-Khattab, enacted with non-Muslims after the conquest of Egypt.[33] James Piscatori suggests that "over time authoritative Muslim writers have come to elaborate a new 'consensus of speech' (imja' al-qawl), which argues that the territorial state is a natural and even worthy institution."[34] With the diffusion of the nation-state model throughout the world during the twentieth century, the function of the state is now to enforce and promote the "reformatory program which Islam has given for the betterment of mankind."[35]

From its very origins, the Islamic worldview acknowledged and embraced the existence of non-Muslim communities, some living within *dar al-Islam* (the area in which Islamic sovereignty prevailed and where the shari'a was enforced), others outside of it. The classical Islamic theory provided recognition for the autonomy of non-Muslims living within dar al-Islam. The non-Muslims were "protected minorities," as were the Jews under the so-called Constitution of Medina contracted by the Prophet shortly after his arrival in the town. Similarly, Christians and other Jewish tribes living in the Arabian peninsula were recognized as autonomous communities during the lifetime of Prophet Muhammad. These "protected minorities" were collectively called *ahl al-dhimma* (people receiving protection), and an individual living in such a community was known as a *dhimmi*. Protected minorities under the Ottoman Turks were known as *millet*.[36] Millet or *milla* (the original word in Arabic) may be defined as a religious society, and Islamic society, or *dar al-Islam*, is composed of not only the Muslims, but also Christian, Jewish, Magian (Zoroastrian), Sabaean, Buddhist, and even Hindu religious communities, because all of them identify themselves by their religious affiliations. Isma'il al-Faruqi writes, "Islamic jurisprudence equally recognizes those people who opt for non-religious identification provided they have a legacy of laws (even if secular) by which they wish to order their lives. The only group which may be barred from membership is that whose law is anti-peace. . . . Islamic jurisprudence thus enables one to affirm today that any group claiming itself to be a *millah* on whatever grounds is entitled to membership."[37]

The Arab tradition (dating back to the pre-Islamic period) of a strong tribe protecting a weaker tribe in return for certain consideration seems to underlie the concept of ahl al-dhimma. W. Montgomery Watt asserts that Islamic states on the whole had an excellent record of tolerance and treatment of non-Muslim minorities.[38] The dhimmis, in return for taxes and tributes agreed to by treaties, were accorded protection from external enemies, and the same protection internally as was guaranteed to the Muslims.

The most significant special tax imposed upon dhimmis, according to the shari'a, was the *jizya*, or poll tax. The payment of jizya guaranteed non-Muslims protection by the Islamic state without having to give their lives defending the state against its enemies. If the state proved unable to defend the non-Muslims, the jizya was returned. If the non-Muslims chose to fight alongside the Muslims against a common enemy, the jizya was not collected. Likewise, in modern times, when Muslims and non-Muslims coexist peacefully within a Muslim state, there is no reason why non-Muslims could not opt to join hands with the Muslims in defense of the country and in maintaining internal law and order. The rationale for levying jizya would therefore no longer exist.

According to the classical theory, protected minorities enjoyed a large sphere of autonomy in their own affairs, with the Muslim rulers serving as arbiters when disputes needed to be settled between various parties. The religious head of each minority community was responsible for collecting tributes and taxes, and for administering law courts dealing with its religious matters. While the status of "protected minority" originated during the Prophet's lifetime as a way of dealing with the "people of the book" (*ahl al-kitab*, principally Jews and Christians), it was eventually extended to people of other religions, including Hinduism. Of course, the preceding discussion does not mean that intolerance towards dhimmis was unknown in Islamic history. But most of the cases of widespread intolerance and discrimination can be ascribed to political weakness or strife within the Islamic state, when Muslims and non-Muslims suffered for their lives and property.

To summarize the main points of the Islamic view toward communal autonomy: Ethnicity, culture, language, and even religion do not provide grounds for the division of living space between communities under Islam. Once a non-Muslim community accepts the sovereignty of the Islamic state and becomes *ahl al-dhimma*, it acquires defined rights and duties vis-à-vis the state, the Muslims, and other non-Muslims living within dar al-Islam. While some Muslim cities have contained "quarters" for one religious community or another, this pattern of urban settlement was largely a voluntary development rather than a policy of segregation by the state. By and large, Muslims and non-Muslims have mixed freely in the public spaces of Muslim cities.

The Islamic state cannot regulate the moral practices of non-Muslims until they conflict with those of the Muslims. Unless the non-Muslims themselves choose to practice their different lifestyle away from the personal living spaces of the Muslims, or their moral practices are a threat to the way of life and beliefs of the Muslims, the state has no right to herd them together within any designated territorial boundaries.

The classical Islamic approach to questions of diversity and political autonomy beyond dar al-Islam must be studied with reference to the Islamic theory of international relations, known as *siyar*. This

worldview was the product of persistent persecution of Muslims, first
by the Meccan idolators, principally by the rich tribe of Quraysh and
its allies; then by the frequent betrayals of non-Muslim tribes of Medina; followed in the final years of the Prophet's life by conflict with
the Byzantine empire to the north. The unceasing hostility towards
the Muslims by their non-Muslim neighbors forced the early Muslims
to struggle for survival and, thus, war and fighting became an integral part of the relationships with non-Muslims. As a by-product of
the struggle, Muslim jurists took excessive recourse of the concept of
naskh (abrogation) in formulating their views on external relations
with non-Muslim enemies, and ignored some of the very basic Qur'-
anic verses dealing with persuasion (*husna*), patience (*sabr*), tolerance
(*la ikrah*), and the right to self-determination (*lasta 'alayhim bi-mus-
aytir*), in favor of an aggressive conception of *jihad*.[39]

Since fiqh is the interpretation of the Qur'an and sunna, there has
not been unanimity of opinion among the various schools of thought
on all issues, especially regarding siyar and jihad. *Siyar* describes the
rules of conduct for Muslims in dealing with the unbelievers of
enemy territory or those with whom they have established treaties of
nonaggression. The Qur'anic verses and the Prophetic traditions on
jihad address how Muslims should respond to the hostilities of the
enemies of Islam. The principles of siyar follow from them.

The conditions for and conduct of jihad are issues that have historically created controversy among Muslim jurists. Islamic legal precedents that were set during the time of the Prophet and his immediate
successors, the first four "rightly guided" caliphs (*al-khulafa' al-
rashidun*), served the Muslim community well until the advent of the
Umayyad dynasty in A.D. 661. The people of the newly conquered
territories could not shed entirely their pre-Islamic customs and culture and acted, in some cases, contrary to the standards set forth by
the jurists and the government.[40] For all practical purposes, from the
rise of the Umayyads through the rest of the dynasties of Muslim
history, fiqh more often than not ceased to represent actual policies or
regulations of the Muslim state. Fiqh essentially has been nothing
more than legal opinions of various scholars of divergent schools of
jurisprudence, and they differ on the nature of jihad and the conduct
of international relations generally.

A few additional related concepts need to be defined here before
we investigate the principles of jihad and siyar. Beyond the frontiers
of dar al-Islam, medieval jurists conceived the existence of other territories or realms, including *dar al-harb* (world of war, i.e., non-Muslim
territory hostile to Muslims);[41] *dar al-aman* (non-Muslim territory
which is at peace with Muslims);[42] and *dar al-'ahd*, otherwise referred

to as *dar al-sulh*[43] (non-Muslim territory which pledges through treaty to acknowledge Muslim sovereignty, but maintains local autonomy by paying some land taxes in lieu of jizya, or poll tax).

The *harbis*, or inhabitants of dar al-harb, are enemies of Islam and, as such, have no right to enter into Muslim territories without express permission. However, a harbi who receives a guarantee of safe passage (*aman*) from even the poorest and the weakest Muslim is secure from harm for at least one year. At the expiry of that date, the harbi is bound to depart—unless, of course, he or she converts to Islam and becomes a part of the Muslim *umma* (community or society). The inhabitants of dar al-aman, the *musta'mins*, are treated according to the conditions of treaty between them and the Muslim state. The musta'mins are governed by their own laws, are exempt from taxes, and enjoy other privileges.[44]

Historically, the question of whether or not the Islamic state (dar al-Islam) is obligated to wage jihad against dar al-harb raised contradictory opinions from the various Sunni schools of jurisprudence. Abu Hanifa (d. 767), the founder of the Hanafi school, and Sufyan al-Thawri (d. 778) state that fighting against non-Muslims is not obligatory unless they themselves initiate it, in which case it becomes obligatory on Muslims to fight back.[45] Al-Sarakhsi (d. 1097), a Hanafi jurist, on the other hand, asserts that the commands for fighting the nonbelievers were revealed in the Qur'an by stages. At the final stage it was made mandatory to subdue the Arab polytheists, as well as other non-Muslims, and previous verses permitting peaceful coexistence were abrogated. Al-Shafi'i is of a similar opinion.[46]

The jurists are also divided on the issue of whether or not a harbi who is granted aman (safe conduct or protection) to enter dar al-Islam but who commits a crime while in Islamic territory is subject to Islamic legal punishment; Abu Hanifa asserts that such harbis are not subject to Muslim legal punishments, al-Shafi'i says that they are. Similarly, contradictory views are expressed on whether or not a Muslim who kills a non-Muslim subject is liable to be executed or required to pay the blood money to the victim's family. Juristic opinions also vary on who may be legitimately fought and killed during jihad, and on the treatment of enemy populations after their defeat.[47] In fact, if all the legal opinions of Muslim jurists are compared, it would not be surprising to find many contradictory assertions. To quote Abu Sulayman, a contemporary scholar of Islamic approaches to international relations: "The parts of *fiqh* manuals dealing with the question of international relations—the chapters on *al-jihad* and related matters such as *al-jizyah* and *al-siyar*—actually deal with matters that are highly political and can hardly be looked upon as simply enforcements or the carrying out of opinions of the ʿulama [religious scholars], who had become more and more removed from the center of power and decision making."[48]

The early Muslim political thinkers, whether Abu Yusuf, deriving his political theories based on the practices of the Abbasid caliphs, or al-Mawardi, basing his on those of the Buwayhids and Abbasids,[49] paid more attention to the political realities of their times than to the fiqh of their respective schools of thought.[50] Some modern writers like Majid Khadduri have selectively chosen to emphasize one school of thought (Shafiʿi) while ignoring others. In his *Islamic Law of Nations*, Khadduri asserts that jihad is made incumbent by God upon all Muslims to slay all polytheists wherever they are found, and that the "law of Islam" allows granting a treaty with the harbis for no more than ten years.[51] Khadduri presents the extreme views of al-Shafiʿi and ignores the equally authoritative views of Abu Hanifa, who asserts that peace treaties, initially contracted for ten years, can be renewed as any other contract, as long as it serves the interest of the Muslims. Ibn Rushd (d. 1198) is of the opinion that not only Abu Hanifa, but also Malik ibn Anas (d. 795) and Ibn Hanbal (d. 855), the founders of the Maliki and Hanbali schools of fiqh, supported the notion of an indefinite peace treaty as long as it served the interest of the Muslim state.[52] Undoubtedly, as these jurists realized, everyone's interest is served in peace rather than war. Thus, we see that the majority of the founders of the Sunni schools of jurisprudence did not agree with the idea that jihad against dar al-harb was necessary or inevitable.

As regards Khadduri's point about polytheists, jurists like Abu Hanifa and Malik believe that the injunctions in the Qurʾan and sunna referred only to the Arab polytheists such as Quraysh, who worshiped idols without believing in a supreme deity. Many of the jurists argue that the jizya could be collected from all polytheists except the Arab pagans, especially the Quraysh, who had repeatedly incited war against the Muslims in the lifetime of the Prophet.

It appears that the injunction about jihad against idolaters is not an obligation unless they initiate fighting, and only then does it become the duty of the Muslims to fight back in fulfillment of God's decree. Let us examine the Qurʾanic verses that explain the position of Islam with respect to jihad:

And so when the sacred months are over, slay those who ascribe divinity to any being but God [i.e., slay the pagans] wherever you may find them, and seize them, beleaguer them, and lie in wait for them in every conceivable place. But if they repent, and take to prayers, and render the purifying dues, let them go their way: for behold, God is much-forgiving, a dispenser of grace. (9:5)

This verse is sometimes referred to as the "verse of the sword" by those who want to project Islam as a belligerent religion. They add another Qur'anic verse to strengthen their position: "O you who believe! Fight those of the disbelievers who are near to you, and let them find harshness in you" (9:123). But these verses are only two among scores that deal with the subject of Muslim treatment of non-Muslims. They must be read in conjunction with such other Qur'anic verses as the following: "Let there be no coercion in matters of faith" (2:256); and "Fight in God's cause against those who wage war against you; but do not commit aggression, for verily God does not love aggressors" (2:190).

Taken in its entirety, the Qur'an makes clear that war (jihad) is permissible only in self-defense: "If they do not let you be, and do not offer you peace, and do not stay their hands, seize them and slay them whenever you come upon them. It is against these that We have clearly empowered you [to make war]" (4:91). But, "If they desist— behold God is much-forgiving, a dispenser of grace; and if they desist, all hostility shall cease" (2:192–93).

Verses must be read in context; that is, the time and circumstances for the revelation of various Qur'anic verses have to be considered before any given verse can be generalized as the "Islamic" view. Verses like 2:190 and 2:256 are general ethical injunctions, applicable to all times, whereas verses 9:5 and 9:123 specifically refer to the Quraysh and other pagan Arab tribes who were bent upon destroying Islam and the Muslims at the time of the Prophet.[53]

With reference to dar al-ʿahd, a non-Muslim territory may acknowledge by treaty or other agreement (ʿahd) the sovereignty of the Islamic state, thereby maintaining its local autonomy. The ʿahd defines the rights and obligations of both parties. There have been disagreements among the jurists whether or not the Islamic state may renounce such treaties if conditions are in their favor. Since the ʿahd can be a major diplomatic tool to regulate foreign affairs, such as peace agreements with non-Muslim states, it is an important issue in modern times, where nation-states establish diplomatic relations and live, more or less, in peace with each other. The Shafiʿi school invalidates any treaty with a duration of more than ten years, while the other Sunni schools place no such restrictions. Most jurists, except those of the Hanafi school, assert that the Islamic state cannot break any lawful treaty unless it is broken first by dar al-ʿahd.

It should be noted here that while political issues related to truce agreements with non-Muslim states are determined by political authorities, with or without reference to legal opinions of Muslim jurists, personal contacts between Muslims and non-Muslims living inside and outside dar al-Islam for trade or other reasons are left to individuals to decide via aman. According to all the legal schools, any Muslim man or woman could extend the rights and privileges of aman to any non-Muslim who requested it, allowing that person to reside and travel unimpeded in Muslim lands.[54]

Mobility

With the rise of an international system based on sovereign nation-states, Muslims have been forced to adapt Islamic principles to modern conditions. Dar al-Islam is today largely a cultural-religious construct, an ideal of the spiritual, if not political, unity of Muslims around the world. The political reality is of the existence of some fifty-six independent Muslim states which frequently find themselves bitterly divided and sometimes at war with each other.

Still, significant moral issues arise in any attempt to reconcile a world of sovereign territorial states with the Islamic ideals of a universal commonwealth including diverse races, religions, and linguistic groups. We have already seen one important concern in our preceding discussion, that of international distributive justice claims. Another issue, and one related to distributive justice, is that of mobility of peoples.

In the early centuries of Islam, Muslim communities traveled easily from one geographical boundary to another in search of their livelihood. Political frontiers meant little in their search for food and water. Individual Muslims also traveled easily and widely, sometimes holding positions in governments of various states without the complications of immigration and naturalization laws and regulations. Even non-Muslims were allowed to travel freely within and between the Muslim states. The Muslim centers of learning in Cordova, Granada, Fez, Salerno, Cairo, Baghdad, Damascus, and Bukhara were frequented by scholars and students of various religious persuasions from all over the world.[55] It was not uncommon for a noted religious personality or jurist to wander easily from one center to another, an itinerant scholar whose passport was his scholastic reputation. Two of the best-known figures from Islamic history are Ibn Khaldun, the historian and jurist who taught and held government posts in Tunis, Fez, Granada, and Cairo, and Ibn Batuta, whose name is synonymous in the Muslim world with the irrepressible traveler. Ibn Batuta's travelogues of his visits to one Muslim land after another are packed with information on the people, flora and fauna, and natural and manufactured products, and are written with a flair that still makes them among the best works in this genre.[56]

Up to the period of the three great modern Muslim empires, the Ottoman, Safavid, and Mughal, Muslim states placed little restriction on the movement of their peoples within and outside their territorial boundaries. Even though Islamic laws permitted Muslims to impose restrictions on the movements of harbis without aman, in practice these laws were not strictly enforced after Islam became the dominant power in the eighth century.

Ironically, though, in modern times some of the Muslim countries even treat Muslims from outside their political boundaries as if they are harbis. Some Middle Eastern states not only have imposed severe restrictions on the entry and domestic travel of Muslims from other countries within their territories, but also prevent them from owning landed property, and determine when they may leave their host countries through the issuance of exit visas. From the Qur'anic teachings and from the life and practices of the Prophet and the early Muslim rulers, we find this behavior, at best, contrary to Islamic values and deplorable. As long as the nonresidents do not engage in activities that are harmful and repugnant to the residents, there is no moral or religious reason to impose restrictions on them. Unfortunately, modern nation-states that justify their existence on the basis of national characteristics (race, ethnicity, language, religion, etc.) do impose upon nonresidents, and in some cases on their own citizens, limits on movements, ownership of property, and encroach upon their personal space. The ideals of the religion and the practices of Muslim governments are often in conflict in the real world.

Conclusion

Boundaries are essential for the growth and fulfillment of an individual's pursuit of life, liberty, and happiness. Islam encourages Muslims to acquire wealth, while bidding them to be mindful of the needs of others. It sanctifies ownership of landed property (and, hence, territorial boundary), yet places the responsibility of utilization and development of natural and environmental resources on the society (i.e., on the state) for the common good.

Islamic teachings make it clear that differences in ethnicity, culture, language, religion, and moral practices cannot be the basis of allocation (or assignment) of specific living spaces for specific communities. The minorities living in peace within the boundary of an Islamic state are entitled to receive protection of life and property and are to be treated humanely.

Muslims are part of the Islamic *umma*, no matter what their origin or nationality. Ideally, there should be no restrictions on the movements of nonresident Muslims from one country to another. People of other faiths, when they are not at war with the Muslims, cannot be considered as *harbis* and, as such, there should be no restriction on their movements either. Unfortunately, because of the rise of nation-states, but more so because of the rise of corrupt governments and/or ruling classes or families, the realities are just the opposite of the ideals.

Notes

1. William S. Sahakian and Mabel L. Sahakian, *Realms of Philosophy* (Cambridge, Mass.: Schenkman, 1965), 75.

2. See Taha Jabir al-ʿAlwani, *Usul Al-Fiqh Al-Islami: Source Methodology in Islamic Jurisprudence* (Herndon, Va.: International Institute of Islamic Thought, 1990).

3. See Fazlur Rahman, *Islam*, 2nd ed. (Chicago: University of Chicago Press, 1979), chap. 4.

4. See also al-ʿAlwani, *Usul al-Fiqh al-Islami*; N. J. Coulson, *A History of Islamic Law* (Edinburgh: Edinburgh University Press, 1964); and Majid Fakhry, *A History of Islamic Philosophy*, 2nd ed. (New York: Columbia University Press, 1983), intro.

5. For further detail, see Abdulhamid A. Abu Sulayman, *The Islamic Theory of International Relations: New Directions for Islamic Methodology and Thought* (Herndon, Va.: International Institute of Islamic Thought, 1987), 5.

6. The Pythagorean theorem of geometry was apparently known by the Egyptians as early as 2000 B.C., even though the record of its clear-cut deductive proof dates back only to the time of Pythagoras, around 550 B.C. See James R. Newman, ed., *The Harper Encyclopedia of Science*, rev. ed. (New York: Harper & Row, 1967).

7. Muhammad H. Haykal, *The Life of Muhammad*, 8th ed., trans. Ismaʿil R. al-Faruqi (Indianapolis: North American Trust Publications, 1976), 486–87.

8. Abu al-Aʿla Mawdudi, *Islamic Law and Constitution*, 3rd ed. (Lahore: Islamic Publications, 1967), 202.

9. Syed Nawab Haider Naqvi, *Ethics and Economics: An Islamic Synthesis* (Leicester, U.K.: The Islamic Foundation, 1981), chap. 2.

10. I have used the translation and commentary of Muhammad Asad, *The Message of the Qurʾan* (Gibraltar: Dar al-Andalus, 1993).

11. It is the uniqueness and individuality of each person that makes it impossible for one to bear the burden of another and, as such, the idea of redemption is rejected by Islam. See Muhammad Iqbal, *The Reconstruction of Religious Thought in Islam* (Lahore: Sh. Muhammad Ashraf, 1968), chap. 4.

12. Qurʾanic references on this subject are 1:78, 2:2–7, 7:1–3, 20:6, and 32:9.

13. See Qurʾan 2:43, 83, 110, 177, 277; 4:77, 162; 5:13, 58; 7:156; 9:11, 18, 60, 71; 19:55; 22:78; and 30:39.

14. See Imam Abu ʿUbayd al-Qasim ibn Sallam, *Kitab al-amwal* (Beirut: Dar

al-Hadathah, 1988). Originally published in the eighth century, this book remains a fundamental reference for ownership rights in Islamic law.

15. Baber Johansen, *The Islamic Law on Land Tax and Rent* (London: Croom Helm, 1988), 11–12.

16. For the Qur'anic injunctions with respect to the distribution of conquered land and war booty, see 8:41, 67–69. See also M.A.Z. Nawawi, *Minhaj et Talibin: A Manual of Muhammadan Law According to the School of Shafii*, trans. E. C. Howard (London: W. Thacker, 1914), bk. 31.

17. Though waqf is a kind of charitable trust, there are material differences between the two. Nasir (1986) points out eight characteristics that differentiate the two. See Jamal J. Nasir, *The Islamic Law of Personal Status* (London: Graham & Trotman, 1986), 252.

18. See B. Ahmed and A. D. Mahajan, *Questions and Answers on Mohammadan Law (Including Leading Cases)*, 14th ed. (Allahabad, India: Allahabad Law Agency, 1974).

19. Ibid., 91–92.

20. Ibid., 93.

21. Ibid. See also Charles Hamilton, *The Hedaya: A Commentary on the Mussulman Laws* (Delhi: Islamic Book Trust, 1982), 547–65 for details on laws of preemption.

22. See Nawawi, *Minhaj et Talibin*, bk. 18.

23. See Hasan Askari, *Society and State in Islam: An Introduction* (New Delhi: Islam and the Modern Age Society, 1978). See also M. Raquibuz Zaman, "Economic Justice in Islam, Ideals and Reality: The Case of Malaysia, Pakistan, and Saudi Arabia," in *Islamic Identity and the Struggle for Justice*, ed. N. H. Barazangi, M. R. Zaman, and O. Afzal (Gainesville: University Press of Florida, 1996), chap. 4.

24. See the commentary on this Qur'anic verse by Asad, *Message of the Qur'an*, 149.

25. Ibid., 150.

26. A proposal for collection of *zakat* and distribution of some of the proceeds to poor countries like Bangladesh was prepared by this author in 1981–82 while he was on sabbatical leave to teach at the King Abdulaziz University in Jeddah, Saudi Arabia. See M. Raquibuz Zaman, *Some Administrative Aspects of the Collection and Distribution of Zakat and the Distributive Effects of the Introduction of Zakat in Modern Economies* (Jeddah, Saudi Arabia: Scientific Publishing Center, King Abdulaziz University, 1987).

27. For a detailed exposition of the subject, see M. Raquibuz Zaman, ed., *Some Aspects of the Economics of Zakah* (Indianapolis: American Trust Publications, 1981).

28. See Iqbal, *Reconstruction of Religious Thought in Islam*, 141.

29. See Abu Sulayman, *Islamic Theory of International Relations*, 29.

30. See Manzooruddin Ahmed, *Islamic Political System in the Modern Age: Theory and Practice* (Karachi: Saad Publications, 1983), 73.

31. Abu Sulayman quotes the discourse of Imam al-Haramayn (d. 1085) on this subject. See Abu Sulayman, *Islamic Theory of International Relations*, 30, and 53, n. 44.

32. For an eloquent discussion of the modern political thinking in Islam,

see Rahman, *Islam*, 226–31. See also W. Montgomery Watt, *Islamic Political Thought* (Edinburgh: Edinburgh University Press, 1968).

33. See Ann K. S. Lambton, *State and Government in Medieval Islam* (New York: Oxford University Press, 1981), 203.

34. See James Piscatori, *Islam in a World of Nation-States* (Cambridge: Cambridge University Press, 1986), 45.

35. See Mawdudi, *Islamic Law and Constitution*, 248.

36. See W. Montgomery Watt, *The Majesty That Was Islam* (London: Sidgwick and Jackson, 1974), 46–49.

37. See Isma'il R. al-Faruqi, in his intro. to Abu Sulayman, *Islamic Theory of International Relations*, xxv–xxvi.

38. See Watt, *Majesty That Was Islam*, 47–48.

39. See Abu Sulayman, *Islamic Theory of International Relations*, 30–35.

40. Ibid., 7.

41. Treatment of non-Muslims in a Muslim society has been a subject of interest to Muslims as well as non-Muslims. Among the non-Muslim writers who are critical of Islamic laws, one may consult Bat Ye'or, *The Decline of Eastern Christianity under Islam: From Jihad to Dhimmitude: Seventh–Twentieth Century*, trans. M. Kochan and D. Littman (Madison, N.J.: Fairleigh Dickinson University Press, 1996); and Bat Ye'or, *The Dhimmi: Jews and Christians under Islam*, trans. D. Maisel and P. Fenton (Rutherford, N.J.: Fairleigh Dickinson University Press, 1985). For a Muslim point of view, see Syed Amir Ali, *The Spirit of Islam* (Karachi: Pakistan Publishing House, 1976). For other viewpoints, see Nicolas P. Aghnides, *Mohammedan Theories of Finance* (Lahore: Premier Book House, n.d.); and Gustave E. von Grunebaum, *Classical Islam: A History—600–1258*, trans. K. Watson (New York: Barnes & Noble, 1970).

42. See Ali, *Spirit of Islam*, 212–16, for details on dar al-aman.

43. This category is coined by Shafi'i. See Abu Sulayman, *Islamic Theory of International Relations*, 17.

44. Ali, *Spirit of Islam*, 215.

45. Abu Sulayman, *Islamic Theory of International Relations*, 8.

46. Ibid.

47. Ibid., 10.

48. Ibid., 11.

49. The Buwayhid sultans controlled Iraq and Persia between 932 and 1062. The Abbasids succeeded the Umayyads in 749 and ruled the Muslim empire until 1258, when the Mongols overran Baghdad.

50. See Qamaruddin Khan, *Al-Mawardi's Theory of the State* (Delhi: Idarah-i Adabiyat-i Delhi, 1979).

51. See Majid Khadduri, *The Islamic Law of Nations*, trans. from Arabic of Muhammad al-Shaybani's *al-Siyar al-kabir* (Baltimore: Johns Hopkins University Press, 1966), 16–17.

52. See Abu Sulayman, *Islamic Theory of International Relations*, 18.

53. For a detailed explanation, see the commentaries by Asad, *Message of the Qur'an*, on the Qur'anic verses cited. He has cited *hadiths* as well as earlier commentators on the subject.

54. See Majid Khadduri, *War and Peace in the Law of Islam* (Baltimore: Johns Hopkins University Press, 1952), 162–69.

55. See Ali, *Spirit of Islam*, 397.

56. On the life of Ibn Khaldun, see Franz Rosenthal, *The Muqaddimah: An Introduction to History*, 2nd ed. (Princeton: Princeton University Press, 1967), vol. 1, xxix–lxvii. For an account of the journeys of Ibn Batuta, see Ross E. Dunn, *The Adventures of Ibn Batuta: A Muslim Traveler of the 14th Century* (Berkeley: University of California Press, 1989).

5

Religion and the Maintenance of Boundaries

AN ISLAMIC VIEW

SULAYMAN NYANG

RELIGION is one of the oldest sources of boundaries among human beings. It remains one of the most important means of demarcating and maintaining boundaries in our time. The necessity of taking account of religious values is particularly acute for men and women living in states and societies where notions of boundaries—geographical and metaphysical—are related to notions of divine will, expressed through revelation of a sacred law, as is the case in Islam. M. Raquibuz Zaman's review of the Islamic tradition in the preceding chapter highlights this way of thinking, for he cites several Qur'anic verses and Prophetic statements to justify the right of ownership and the sanctity of private property. This treatment is certainly warranted, for the *shari'a* prescriptions for ordering human relations remain perhaps the first and most essential consideration that most Muslims employ. I want to approach the topic in a slightly different manner, however, focusing on both the metaphysical and physical aspects of boundary formation and maintenance from an Islamic point of view.

Religion as a Source of Boundaries

Religions claim transcendence beyond time and place. But the historical fact is that in most human societies religions arose from and responded to the conditions of specific human groups. These ethnic or geographic origins of religious beliefs have been well documented by anthropologists, historians, and social scientists.[1] Boundary lines in the early human communities were erected and maintained through some ritualistic expression of shared faith. Since one human being cannot read the mind of another, the only way to determine belief is by some explicit profession and affirmation of membership in a belief system.

Some religious systems have erected elaborate means of admission to their community. Others make fewer demands on those who would enter their fold. Nevertheless, all religious systems create boundaries between their believers and outsiders by requiring some overt demonstration of conviction. In Islam, the means of crossing the boundary from non-Islam to Islam is relatively straightforward: through the *shahada* or the profession of faith that "There is no god but God, and Muhammad is the messenger of God." This first pillar of the Islamic faith is the moral equivalent of a public declaration delimiting the borders of one's mind. A non-Muslim who decides voluntarily to embrace Islam is making both a mental and a social/physical decision. By declaring his faith as a Muslim, he is telling members of his immediate family and the rest of society that the mental borders defining his family and the culture with which he identifies have been redrawn in accordance with the teachings of his newly adopted faith.

This geography of the mind has a number of social consequences. The new believer must now be trusted by all members of his new religion. His faithfulness to Islam cannot be challenged within the community because no other believer can directly probe his mind and know absolutely whether he is a true believer or not. From the point of view of external verification of his faith, the only means by which the border guard of the faith can attest to his fidelity and sincerity is through his compliance with the rituals of the new faith. This is why rituals are crucial for the maintenance of boundaries and in the perpetuation of social solidarity among the members of a particular religion. We will return to the role of ritual in maintaining boundaries shortly.

Religions not only establish boundaries between believers and unbelievers, they also frequently create or legitimate boundaries among believers. I am referring now not to spiritual boundaries, which shared conviction is supposed to tear down, but to physical boundaries such as the rights of property ownership. As Zaman's elaboration of the Islamic laws on property demonstrates, Islam has been closely aligned through the centuries with private property. Under the shari'a, property may be acquired in three ways: by *iktisab* (earning), *wiratha* (inheritance), and *hiba* (gift). Maulana Muhammad 'Ali, a leading Indo-Pakistani intellectual of the twentieth century, describes the right of an individual to acquire property as "one of the basic laws regulating human society."[2] The Qur'an makes clear that this right is enjoyed by both men and women: "Men shall have the benefit of what they earn and women shall have the benefit of what they earn" (4:32). Both sexes also have a right to inherit property: "Men shall have a portion of what the parents and the near relatives leave and women shall have a portion of what the parents and the near relatives leave" (4:7). While no formal legal limitations are placed upon the property or wealth that an individual may acquire or dispose of, moral injunctions certainly circumscribe the behavior of the faithful in this area.

The Qur'an warns Muslims not to seek wealth through immoral means, such as through deceit (e.g., 4:29), bribery (2:188), usury (2:275–76), and the misappropriation of wealth held in trust (4:58)—for example, the property of orphans (4:6). Moreover, a number of other proscriptions in Islam may be seen as related to honest dealing in property acquisition. For example, the strong condemnation of gambling is coupled with a rebuke against consumption of alcoholic beverages in Q. 2:219. The connection between gambling and obtaining or losing property is obvious, but the connection with intoxicants is perhaps not so straightforward. Certainly, consumption of alcohol may be condemned for other reasons as well. In Q. 4:43 Muslims are told not to approach their daily prayers in a state of intoxication. But finally when the Qur'an proscribes intoxicants altogether in a later revelation (5:90), alcohol is once again linked with gambling because "they excite enmity and hatred among you." Producing, selling, and imbibing liquor and other forms of intoxicants are all condemned, like gambling, because they promote, among other things, fraudulent and harmful exchanges of wealth, potentially threatening the stability of society.

The Qur'an gives full rights of disposal of property to its legitimate owners, whether male or female, but at the same time it requires that the owners be most careful in spending the resulting wealth.[3] There are many injunctions of a general nature to this effect. Thus, the Qur'an describes the righteous servants of Allah ('ibad al-Rahman) as "they who, when they spend, are neither extravagant, nor parsimonious, and keep between these the just mean" (25:67). And elsewhere: "And do not make your hand to be shackled to your neck [in miserliness], nor stretch it forth to the utmost limit of its stretching forth, lest you should [afterwards] become blameworthy and destitute" (17:29). These restrictions on the exercise of rights of property by individual owners is described as hajr in a number of hadiths from the prophet Muhammad. One widely cited report from Imam Bukhari's collection of hadith reads as follows: "There is no charity unless a man has sufficient to give, and whoever spends in charity and he is himself in want or his family is in want or he has a debt to pay, it is more in the fitness of things that the debt should be paid than that he should spend in charity or free a slave or make a gift, and such a gift or charity shall be annulled, for he has no right to waste the wealth of the people (amwal al-nas)."[4] The reference to the "wealth of the people" in this hadith is a clear example of the Islamic view that though an individual owns property, that ownership *in the moral sense* is not exclusive to him or her. Spending one's wealth in even the worthiest of causes, as in charity, may be objectionable if the prior claims of one's dependents are not met.

In short, we can conclude that the owner of movable or immovable property, whether male or female, has the right to sell, barter, or bequeath it in any fashion deemed moral in light of Islamic teachings. Overarching all such transactions is the fundamental Qur'anic injunction: "Woe to the defrauders, who, when they take the measure from men, take it fully; but when they measure out to others or weigh out for them, they are deficient" (83:1–3).

The preceding discussion of private property rights is fundamental to our discussion of territorial boundaries, not only because individual owners are the building blocks of any national economy, but because the legal rulings and the general moral precepts we have outlined above apply equally to the state in its own business transactions. What is permitted the individual is permitted the state; what is prohibited the individual is prohibited the state. On the basis of the Qur'anic statements discussed above, general agreement has existed among Muslim scholars that in light of Islam's protection of individual property rights, governments have no right to deprive citizens of such ownership. This is not to say, of course, that the moral purview of the state is not broader than that of the individual. Whereas the individual is responsible to family and perhaps immediate neighbors, the state must take account of the welfare of all those residing within its jurisdiction. This obligation was historically fulfilled through the collection and distribution of the alms tax (*zakat*), which has already been discussed in the previous chapter. During the past two centuries, under the influence of socialist ideologies from Europe, a few Muslim intellectuals have sought to portray the Qur'anic vision of mutual obligations in society as a form of proto-socialism, while rejecting some of the more extreme aspects of Marxism. As Maulana Muhammad 'Ali argues: "Islam is thus opposed to Bolshevism, which recognizes no individual rights of property; but it is at the same time socialistic in its tendencies, inasmuch as it tries to bring about a more or less equal distribution of wealth."[5] The question is, how far does Islamic ethics permit the state to move down the path of distributive justice?

The debate among Muslims on this issue is rich and ranges along the spectrum from total rejection to acceptance of various degrees of state intervention. Much of the controversy centers around the right of modern nation-states to nationalize private property in the name of social welfare and economic development. All modern Muslim states have to various degrees pursued such policies, and, in the face of religious opposition, have mobilized religious supporters to provide Islamic sanction for their policies. Thus, when Nasser undertook his Arab socialist schemes in Egypt, Mahmud Shaltut, the shaykh of al-Azhar, the leading religious functionary of the state, produced a treatise arguing that Islam and Arab socialism were compatible. Other, "independent" Muslim intellectuals, such as Mustafa Siba'i, a leader of the Syrian Muslim Brotherhood, and the Indo-Pakistani scholar Khalifa 'Abd al-Hakim, have also promoted the idea of "Islamic socialism." In their view, the goal of state intervention should be to alleviate poverty and class differences, not eradicate them as the Communists wanted to do, because such goals are contrary to the natural order described in the Qur'an.[6]

Such arguments have been strongly challenged by other Muslim thinkers, and in some cases of state intervention, the 'ulama, the guardians of the religious law, have led a conservative backlash. Particularly susceptible to challenge from the 'ulama have been land reforms, which represent an obviously dramatic claim on the part of the state to reinterpret shari'a laws for the sake of the national good. When the shah of Iran undertook land reforms as part of his White Revolution in the mid-1960s, the Iranian 'ulama, including Ayatollah Khomeini, were almost unanimous in their opposition to the redistribution of private property.[7] Such reactions have been evident in other major instances of land reform, including in Pakistan and Egypt. In the case of Iran, the 'ulama's mobilization against the shah during the White Revolution (which incidentally did little to improve the condition of the nation's peasant farmers) proved a harbinger of the revolution that came fifteen years later.

Religion as a Maintainer of Boundaries

Linking religion to private property, as most Muslims have done over the centuries, produces significant social and political consequences. The right to enjoy private property is meaningless without the existence of law and order. Hence, Islamic political thought has historically emphasized the need for law and order, leading even some of the greatest Muslim thinkers to accept tyrannical or, in modern parlance, authoritarian rule. "For," as al-Ghazali (d. 1111) famously put it, "if we were to decide that all wilayat [political authority] are now null and void, all institutions of public welfare would also be absolutely null and void. How should the capital be dissipated in straining after the profit?"[8] The "capital" al-Ghazali refers to here is the shari'a, which establishes and regulates all institutions of public welfare.[9] These institutions allow men and women in society, both individually and collectively, to carry out the primary purpose of life, the worship of the Most High God. But they also promote social peace and harmony through the regulation of human institutions, including the right to own and dispose of one's property. Surely, the preservation of such physical boundaries would be among the chief "profits" al-Ghazali had in mind.

All religions, no matter how universalistic their claims, are in the final analysis boundary maintainers, not just in the physical domain as discussed with regard to property, but also in the metaphysical realm.[10] This is largely because of their doctrine and their definition of reality. In the particular case of Islam, though Muslims claim that all human beings are the creatures of Allah and descendants of Adam and Eve, they strongly emphasize the line demarcating believers from unbelievers. Hence the juristic terms discussed by Zaman, *dar al-Islam* and *dar al-harb*. The first realm is that which harbors the men and women who embrace the belief in one God (*tawhid*), and the other is inhabited by the unbelievers (*kafirun*). Dar al-Islam and dar al-harb are as much metaphysical as physical constructs. We see clearly in these concepts how boundary lines are drawn not on geographical or biological differences, but on matters of faith. These concepts require us to distinguish between mental and physical boundaries among humans.[11]

Mental boundaries are those boundaries that are visible only to the perceiving agent. One can never know with certainty who else shares one's mental boundaries. This raises some acute problems for ideologically based human groupings whose physical and metaphysical integrity rests on trusting others who claim to hold the same convictions.

Hypocrisy and dissimulation have been the two most formidable threats to the integrity and security of social formations in human history. All religions as social groups have historically tried to maintain and protect their boundaries from penetration and infiltration. We know, for example, that the ancient Israelites were very much aware of the dangers posed by infiltration. According to linguists familiar with the Israelites' language, the Hebrew word *shibboleth* was used to distinguish aggressors and hypocrites from the devout; although the word simply meant "stream," its special use, as a test of pronunciation, gave it a special function (as can be seen in its English meaning). The very creation of a word like this reveals the strategic and social consciousness of the Israelites that the preservation of their community required both physical and mental tests.

In the case of Islam, inner acceptance of the faith has entailed the public performance of various ritual obligations, such as the pilgrimage, alms-giving, fasting, and most conspicuously, prayer. Yet from its very origins as a social phenomenon, Islam has grappled with the problems of false expressions of faith. The Qur'an repeatedly warns the faithful to beware the deceptions of hypocrites, who may give physical indications of their sincerity, but have not fully crossed the mental boundary separating believers and unbelievers: "Woe to the worshippers, those who are neglectful of their prayers, those who [want but] to be seen [as Muslims], but refuse [even] the small kindnesses" (107:4–7).

In more extreme cases, that of the renegade apostate (*murtadd*) who renounces his religion, the penalty adduced by most medieval jurists was execution. The legal rationale for this penalty was that his apostasy signified that he was either a hypocrite or an unbeliever disguised as a believer. In either event, he was a spy who posed a danger to the physical integrity of the Muslim community rather than to its spiritual integrity. This danger was considerable in the early days of Islam—from which the punishment is derived—because the community was constantly threatened by enemies from within and without.[12]

Cases like this one illustrate how the ethical questions are virtually indistinguishable from the legal and political ones. Since membership in an ethnic, national, or religious community confers social, political, and psychological protection and benefits upon those who are eligible and certified, it becomes problematic if someone who was at one time deemed worthy of privileges turns out to be an outsider posing as an insider. This is why words become an important means by which Muslims hold one another accountable for their deeds in this life. Historically, under Muslim rule, those who converted to the faith by declaring the shahada immediately became eligible for all the rights and prerogatives of the community, including ownership of land, just as those who were born Muslim. Conversely, those who recanted became subject to sanctions.

The problem of dealing with hypocrites and renegades was not confined to legal disputations. The early history of Islam witnessed philosophical and theological controversies among Muslim intellectuals trying to demarcate the mental boundaries, especially as these boundaries influenced the social and physical realms of human belief and action.[13] The question was: What actions signify an absence of faith? How can the community discern the true believer from the hypocrite? The intellectual contests between the Mu'tazilites and other schools of thought during the ninth and tenth centuries is perhaps the best-known case of such philosophical wrangling. The Mu-'tazilites believed that human beings are responsible for their actions within the human realm, producing a view of human agency and hence responsibility that is not contingent on external factors. The Ashʿarites took the view that a combination of human will and divine sanction underlie all human activity, that no result in the physical or metaphysical universe is the product simply of human intent. This view leads logically to a predeterministic view of one's own place in the universe. The Murjiʾites sought to chart a middle course on the question of human agency. Their leaders preferred to defer judgment to the end of time, when the Truth will be known only through divine revelation. This metaphysical "fence-sitting"—eventually adopted as a sort of compromise position among Muslim theologians—could well be construed as a sanction for the politics of indifference. Such a theological attitude of course yields a variety of outcomes. On the one hand, it promotes an ethic of toleration by removing judgment on matters of faith from human hands. But on the other hand, this position can easily become the basis for the acceptance of the status quo and the unenthusiastic conformity with changes brought about by revolutionary means. It may yield as fatalistic a view of human life as some of the predestinarian principles of the Ashʿarites, making the maintenance of mental and physical boundaries not a human activity, but a divine will.

Regardless of how one feels about the different strategies developed by religious communities to maintain their boundaries, the fact remains that social and political order can only become a reality when men and women live in peace. This is where Islam provided the ancient world with a new paradigm of social definition and identification. Using what we might term "Adamic" and "Abrahamic" criteria to determine who belongs where and why, Islam holds all human beings to be essentially the same because they are all the children of Adam. This universal category confers upon all human beings the attributes of a creature deemed as God's representative on earth through genetic links to Adam and Eve.

However, a being devoid of faith in the Creator is considered *kafir*, a word which conveys both the sense of lack of belief and lack of gratitude. For this and other related reasons, he or she is excluded from the Abrahamic commonwealth. This commonwealth consists of the Islamic *umma* and those members of the human race who are called *ahl al-kitab* (peoples of the book)—a category including Jews and Christians, who also began with the Abrahamic ethic, but in one crucial way or another departed from it in the course of their evolution. As Zaman points out in the preceding chapter, the category was extended to include Zoroastrians, Hindus, and Buddhists when Islam expanded east of the Arabian peninsula. In describing the Islamic view of boundaries, therefore, we can argue that Muslims at the height of their power—when they might have succumbed to the temptations of exclusivism—recognized the utility and reality of both mental and physical boundaries, and they tried to defend and protect the rights of members of the various groups under their rule by formulating a public policy which allowed mental space to determine physical space. This is to say that the Muslims in their quest for a just order among human beings saw the relationship between the geography of religion and the theology of space.

The Islamic geography of religion made it impossible for the Islamic conquerors of the Middle East to uproot and relocate the vanquished as other conquerors had done in the ages before them. It also enabled them to articulate a policy of accommodation which respects the property rights of the defeated through the assessment of a special kind of tax (*kharaj*). The theology of space, it must be emphasized, allowed the Muslims to recognize and protect the rights of all property owners, Muslim and non-Muslim.[14]

Two points made by Zaman bear repeating in our discussion of the Muslim approach to property rights. The first issue relates to the belief that the universe is a created *entity*, with humans as temporary custodians of this world. Unlike many Western exponents of the principle that a piece of land belongs to the person who mixes his labor with it, the Islamic view categorically states that private ownership is justifiable, but it is and must be seen always as holding property in trust. In his exposition, Zaman has shed ample light on the different schools of jurisprudence and their rulings on ownership.

What needs to be emphasized here is the second point, that the ethics of ownership in this case is so religiously bound that the believer's acts can be read ethically and legally simultaneously. In other words, ownership cannot in itself be the goal of a righteous individual; it is always merely a means to the pursuit of higher goals, and Islam always enjoins the promotion of family and communal well-being as among the highest. The Qur'an and the hadith literature identified with the prophet Muhammad convey to Muslims that this life is temporary and human beings should not be too fixated upon it. However, Islam does not teach its followers that this life is an illusion, as some creeds maintain. Rather, it teaches that compared to the next life (*al-akhira*), this life is insignificant. This is why Muslims pray for success in this life and success in the next life.

No strand of Muslim thought has grappled so deeply with the moral importance of physical and mental boundaries as has that of the Sufis, who came to the understanding that ownership is socially acceptable but mentally unnecessary. To most Sufi masters the idea of owning a thing is acceptable, but one must not forget that ownership brings only temporary utility. Investing too much emotional and psychic energy in such items of passing value can be spiritually counterproductive. In the logic of the Sufi master, material things, which are seen by many human beings as extensions of their egos, erect unwarranted boundaries among people. To the Sufi master, the only boundary worth preserving is that which separates the believer from the unbeliever. Though unbelievers share with believers common ancestry from Adam and Eve, their lack of faith in the Creator disqualifies them as reliable associates in this world. Again we return to the ingratitude implied in the term *kafir*: The unbeliever does not give credit to the very one who gives his life and ultimately takes his life in death. By being an unbeliever the neighbor who shares physical space with the Muslim in a human society is a traveling partner on the highway of life, but one fated sooner or later to part ways with the believer. The Muslim's destination is heavenward, whereas that of her unbelieving neighbor is earthbound.

Notes

1. For a discussion of the variety of human religious thought and the impact of ethno-cultural history on human societies, see Ninian Smart, *Worldviews: Crosscultural Explorations of Human Beliefs* (New York: Charles Scribner's Sons, 1983).

2. Maulana Muhammad ʿAli, *The Religion of Islam* (Columbus, Ohio: Ahmadiyya Anjuman Ishaʿat Islam, 1990), 509.

3. Ibid., 510.

4. *Sahih al-Bukhari*, bk. 24 (*kitab al-zakat*), chap. 17, cited ibid., 511.

5. Ibid., 509.

6. For a convenient anthology of Muslim arguments on socialism, see John J. Donohue and John L. Esposito, *Islam in Transition: Muslim Perspectives* (New York: Oxford University Press, 1982), 98–139.

7. See Ervand Abrahamian, *Khomeinism: Essays on the Islamic Republic* (Berkeley: University of California Press, 1993), 10, 55.

8. Quoted in H.A.R. Gibb, "Constitutional Organization," in *Law in the Middle East*, ed. Majid Khadduri and Herbert Liebesny (Washington, D.C.: Middle East Institute, 1955), 19.

9. Ibid., 20.

10. Almost all students of religion will agree that, though the world religions claim to be universal, their distinctiveness demarcates them from others making similar claims. For some recent discussions on this phenomenon and

the challenge of pluralism, see Harold Coward, *Pluralism: Challenge to World Religions* (Maryknoll, N.Y.: Orbis Books, 1985).

11. For a discussion by modern Muslims of the relevance of these terms, see Hasan Moinuddin, *Charter of the Islamic Conference* (New York: Oxford University Press, 1987), 42–53; and Mohammad Talaat al-Ghunaimi, *The Muslim Conception of International Law and the Western Approach* (The Hague: Martinus Nijhoff, 1968), 184.

12. Al-Mawardi summarizes some of the opinions regarding the treatment of renegades who departed from the Islamic fold but later recanted. Abu al-Hasan al-Mawardi, *al-Ahkam al-Sultaniyya: The Laws of Islamic Governance*, trans. Asadullah Yate (London: Ta-Ha Publishers, 1996), chap. 5.

13. For details on these medieval theological disputes, see Fazlur Rahman, *Islam* (Chicago: University of Chicago Press, 1979), chap. 5.

14. For a balanced discussion on the treatment of religious minorities by both Muslims and Christians in the medieval period, see Mark R. Cohen, *Under Crescent and Cross: The Jews in the Middle Ages* (Princeton: Princeton University Press, 1994).

Part III

PLURALISM AND INTERNATIONAL SOCIETY

6

Islam and Ethical Pluralism

DALE F. EICKELMAN

THE QUR'AN offers a distinctly modern perspective on the role of Islam as a force for tolerance and mutual recognition in a multiethnic, multicommunity world: "To each among you, We have ordained a law and assigned a path. Had God pleased, He could have made you one nation, but His will is to test you by what He has given you; so compete in goodness" (5:48).[1] Other verses reinforce the concepts and practices of tolerating religious difference: "Had your Lord willed, He would have made mankind one nation: but they will not cease differing" (11:118). Another reads: "O mankind! We created you from a male and a female and made you into nations and tribes, that you may know one another" (49:13).

The contextual interpretations of these verses are multiple, but in contemporary Muslim discussion and debate, the point of departure is increasingly the Qur'an itself and not the many layers of scholarly interpretation that have accumulated over the centuries. It would be incorrect to say that there is a single, dominant view among Muslims concerning religious and ethical pluralism. As Khalid Masud argues in the next chapter, modern Muslims proclaim with pride that there is no "church" in Islam, no prevalent "official" or "authoritative" view. He writes that there have always been several moral traditions in Islam, some of which—as in other religious traditions—are more tolerant and open to alternative ethical positions.[2] As part of this use of reason, however, many Muslim voices call for a return to understanding the Qur'an and Prophetic tradition in their historical context. For example, Sohail Hashmi argues that Muslims must "disentangle Islamic ethics from medieval Islamic law" and treat the Qur'an as "a complete ethical system" in order to elaborate new principles for Muslim participation in international society.[3]

Had this chapter been completed entirely prior to the events of September 11, 2001, its main theme would have been that increasing levels of education, greater ease of travel, and the rise of new communications media are rapidly developing a public sphere in Muslim-majority societies in which large numbers of people—and not just an

educated, political, and economic elite—want a say in religion, governance, and public issues. The consequent fragmentation of religious
and political authority challenges authoritarianism. This can lead to
more open societies, just as globalization has been accompanied by
such developments as Vatican II and secular transnational human-
rights movements. These movements show the positive side of globalization, in which small but determined transnational groups work
toward goals seen to improve the human condition. The leaders of
such movements, including religious interpreters, sometimes lack
theological and philosophical sophistication. They can, however, mo-
tivate a minority and persuade a wider public of the justice of their
cause, changing implicit, practical understandings of ethical issues in
the process.

There is, however, a darker side to globalization, the fragmentation
of authority, and the growing ability of large numbers of people to
participate in wider spheres of religious and political debates and
practical action. This darker side is epitomized by Osama bin Laden
and the al-Qaʿida terrorist movement. The movement is not noted for
its theoretical sophistication. In quality of thought, Bin Laden and his
associates, such as the Egyptian physician Ayman al-Zawahiri, are no
match for Thomas Hobbes or Martin Heidegger. They have, however,
demonstrated a public relations genius that, combined with massive
and dramatic terrorist acts, have caught the world by surprise.

As James Piscatori argues, the Bin Laden/al-Qaʿida view of world
politics is powerfully timeless—appealing to unity and faith regardless of a balance of power against them, attributing the evils of this
world to Christians and Jews, and to "Muslims" who associate with
them and thus pervert the goals of the *umma*, the worldwide community of true believers. Does not the Qurʾan say that polytheists should
be fought until they cease to exist (Q. 9:5) and that those who do not
rule by God's law are unbelievers and, by implication, should be resisted (Q. 5:44)?[4]

These interpretations of scripture are highly contestable. Only a
tiny but lethal minority has been inspired to action by such interpretations. As Piscatori explains, the "theology" of this group is basically an update of that of the Egyptian Islamic Jihad group, best
known for its assassination of Anwar al-Sadat. Some elements of its
message, including that of injustices perpetrated against the worldwide Islamic community—in Palestine, Chechnya, Kashmir, and elsewhere—capture the imagination of wider numbers of people, although
their accord with some elements of the al-Qaʿida view of world politics
and repression by state authorities does not get translated into action.

This chapter highlights the circumstances and potential of voices and practices in the Muslim world that contribute to more open societies and religious interpretations. We must accept that there will always be ideas available to justify intolerance and violence, and there will also always be ways for terrorists to manipulate open societies for their own nefarious ends. Countering radical ideologies and theologies of violence is not easy. Yet the proliferation of voices arguing in open debate about the role of Islam in the modern world and in contemporary society contributes significantly to defusing terrorist appeals. Because the advocates of ethical pluralism are less well known outside of the Muslim world than, for instance, the views of Solidarity activists in Poland or the advocates of liberation theology, this chapter is focused on them. Even if challenged by much less tolerant views from what is sometimes called the "street," the courage of those who advocate toleration, or who practice it without articulating their views in public, merits more attention than it has received to date.

Islam's "Remarkably Modern" Origins

Writing in the 1960s, sociologist Robert Bellah argued that Islam in its seventh-century origins was for its time and place "remarkably modern . . . in the high degree of commitment, involvement, and participation expected from the rank-and-file members of the community."[5] Its leadership positions were open, and divine revelation emphasized equality among believers. Bellah argues that the restraints that kept the early Muslim community from "wholly exemplifying" these principles of modernity underscore the modernity of the basic message of Qur'anic Islam, exhorting its initial audience in seventh-century Arabia to break through the "stagnant localisms" of tribe and kinship.[6] Indeed, Bellah argues that "the effort of modern Muslims to depict the early community as the very type of equalitarian participant nationalism is by no means entirely an unhistorical ideological fabrication."[7]

Of course, these "stagnant localisms" offered powerful resistance to the Qur'anic vision of community in the seventh century. Another often-cited Qur'anic verse emphasizes that there is "no compulsion in religion. Whoever . . . believes in God has grasped a firm handhold of the truth that will never break" (2:256). Other verses nonetheless appear to justify coercion and severe punishment for apostates, renegades, and unbelievers who break their agreement with the prophet Muhammad (for example, 4:89, 9:1–16).

Some commentators conclude that such coercion is specific to the context of the early Islamic community and grounded in "emergency conditions." In this view, coercion was needed to emphasize such "basic moral requirements" as keeping promises and treaties, and protecting a community's "basic welfare and security against aggression."[8] The overall emphasis is on voluntary consent to the will of God "which is prompted by the universal guidance that is engraved upon the human heart." The Qur²an advises even the prophet Muhammad to show tolerance toward his opponents: "If it had been your Lord's will, they would all have believed, all who are on earth. Would you [O Muhammad] then compel mankind against their will to believe?" (10:99).[9]

More specifically, as Fazlur Rahman argues, the prophet Muhammad "recognized without a moment of hesitation that Abraham, Moses, Jesus, and other Old and New Testament religious personalities had been genuine prophets like himself." Their different messages, coming to different peoples and nations at different times, were "universal and identical."[10] Indeed, Muhammad is made to say in the Qur²an, "I believe in whatever book God may have revealed" (42:15), because "God's guidance is universal and not restricted to any nation or nations."[11] The idea of "book" (*kitab*), as Rahman points out, is a generic term in the Qur²an, "denoting the totality of divine revelations."[12]

What Happened in History

The modern era has accelerated the intensity and pace of interaction among believers in different religious traditions. However, as the above Qur²anic verses indicate, intense awareness of and interaction with other faiths have been present in the Islamic tradition from its inception and are not characteristics unique to the modern era. For much of Islamic history, Muslim societies have been remarkably open to the outside world, incorporating through bricolage many preexisting and coexisting elements. Indeed, the vast expanse of the Muslim world inevitably meant that it came to encompass a variety of civilizational and cultural forms. By the tenth and eleventh centuries, the Muslim-majority world showed a remarkable variety of institutional forms from North Africa to South Asia, up to and including the hinterland of the Chinese empire, and soon thereafter emerged as a dominant force in Southeast Asia.[13] Likewise, the Mediterranean, far from being a barrier between civilizations in the early modern era, facilitated sharpened awareness of differences and similarities among both Muslim and non-Muslim "others." As Masud points out, the Islamic tradition incorporated many pre-Islamic tribal values. The "literary moral tradition" called *adab*, to which he refers derives its ethical values from multiple sources, both Muslim and non-Muslim. The same is the case for philosophy and the Sufi moral tradition. Even legal ethics (*fiqh*), incorrectly (in Masud's view) excoriated by some Islamic modernists as rigid and fixed, developed out of multiple customary legal traditions. Even before the advent of the modern state, Muslim jurists resisted the efforts of political rulers to reduce this pluralism, regarding it as an attack on their freedom to interpret. Moreover, most jurists were acutely aware that local customary laws continued to prevail in rural and tribal areas, even non-Muslim laws in the case of Mughal India and parts of the Ottoman empire.

Pluralism was also encouraged by the fact that the boundaries of the Muslim world were not sharply delineated. It was not only the boundaries between the Mediterranean Muslim world that were fluid and indistinct but also those of other areas of the Muslim world. In India, the great Mughal ruler Akbar (1542–1605) ruled over Muslims, Hindus, Jains, Sikhs, Parsees, Christians, Jews, and others. It was only by the end of the sixteenth century that the intellectual and material conditions for a symbolic duality between the West and the Muslim "Orient" began to take hold. It reached full form by the seventeenth and eighteenth centuries, when it conveyed the idea that the Muslim world was "distinct" from Europe and the West. Even after this period, however, an awareness of the "other" continued to be available to the elites and many ordinary people of the Muslim-majority world, from Indonesia to the Maghrib.[14]

Contrary to the tolerance and awareness of other religions set forth in the Qur'an, the record of Muslim attitudes in history toward other religions and different interpretations of Islam is as uneven as that of the followers of other religious traditions. A nadir of intolerance within the Muslim community was the inquisition (*mihna*) of 833–848. In its fifteen years, four successive caliphs supported the views of some jurists that the Qur'an was created, in spite of intensely held popular support for the traditionalist view that the Qur'an had always existed. This authoritarian imposition of doctrine through state violence and torture met fierce resistance, and the effort was abandoned after 848. A lasting result of this episode, however, was that later caliphs and other temporal rulers intervened only with caution in religious disputes.

Muslim awareness of the other was not always neutral and tolerant, but neither was it unremittingly hostile. Indeed, when the Christian rulers of the Iberian peninsula broke the treaties they earlier signed allowing freedom of worship, expelling the Jews from Spain in 1492, and in Portugal ordering their forced conversion to Christianity in 1497, the majority took refuge in Morocco and the other North

African principalities.[15] Likewise, Morocco's Muhammad V protected
Jews of Moroccan nationality during World War II from the threat of
deportation by the Vichy French. Jews with French nationality had no
such protection.[16]

The basis for openness to different religious interpretations within
the Muslim tradition and for other religious traditions antedates European modernity. In Andalusia, for example, the jurist Abu Ishaq al-
Shatibi (d. 1388) advocated the centrality of human reason for interpreting Islamic law and applying it to specific social, economic, and
political contexts.[17] Such a formulation recognized the possibility of
multiple and coexisting interpretations. In India, Akbar the Great developed Islamic institutions, but also advocated the "cult of reason"
(rah-i 'aql), insisting on open dialogue and free choice among religions.[18] At one point he even sponsored a universalistic cult called
"Divine Religion" (Din-i Ilahi), with himself as master of a religious
order synthesizing Islam and Hinduism.[19] Indian villagers often fused
Hindu and Muslim religious practices, but Akbar used reason to represent himself as a ruler whose government and values transcended
specific religious traditions. He deliberately set about creating an empire in which the followers of various religions could coexist. Akbar
argued that "morality can be guided by critical reason" and that "we
must not make reasoning subordinate to religious command."[20]

The historical antecedents for tolerance and the use of reason to
achieve it facilitate understanding Islam in history and how Muslims
interpret, accommodate, and explain differences in religious belief
and practice. The historical experience of al-Shatibi in jurisprudence
and Akbar the Great in governance also indicate that the multiple
paths to "modernity" do not necessarily depend on replicating or em-
ulating the European historical experience. The modernization theories of the mid-twentieth century assumed that "the cultural program
of modernity as it developed in modern Europe and the basic institutional constellations that emerged there would ultimately take over
in all modernizing and modern societies."[21] A concomitant of this
assumption was that religion had no place in the "modern" public
sphere. In the words of philosopher Richard Rorty, outside of circles
of believers, it usually functions as a "conversation stopper."[22]

Rorty's observation reminds us that any discussion of religion and
tolerance involves three dimensions: tolerance within the various currents of a religious tradition, tolerance among religions, and the tolerance of religion itself.[23] As Masud notes, sectarian violence in Pakistan, and religious and ethnic violence in Indonesia, Kosovo, Bosnia,
northern Nigeria, southern Sudan, and Northern Ireland are only
some of the more obvious indications that religiously based intol-

erance persists. The so-called headscarf dispute in France in 1989, mirroring the unease of the Turkish republic with religion in the public sphere, suggests intolerance for the public expression of some religious identities.[24] Indeed, the intolerance of some of Turkey's secular elite for any form of public religious expression serves as a reminder that elements of the secular tradition can be highly intolerant.

There are significant antecedents for religious tolerance and for the use of reason to interpret religious traditions in the premodern era, and in the next chapter Masud persuasively sets out the evidence, sometimes ignored by Islamic modernists themselves, that supports this view. However, the trend over the past two centuries has been for a heightened awareness of religious difference. It is seen both in how intellectuals talk about religious belief and practice and in the ordinary, taken-for-granted language by which we perceive the world. It was only in the early nineteenth century that the notion of "religions" to reflect different religious systems came into common use in English, with a parallel development taking place in other languages, including Arabic. The naming of specific "religions"—such as Hinduism, Buddhism, and Taoism—came into common currency only by the 1840s.[25] This was also when the idea of "religion" as separate from other aspects of life—in other words a de facto secularization—became general.

Contemporary Understandings

In the Muslim world, as elsewhere, the spread of printing in vernacular Muslim languages in the nineteenth century accelerated the process of large numbers of people thinking of their religion as one set apart from other traditions in doctrine and practice.[26] Since the mid-nineteenth century, the dramatic rise in mass higher education, the greater ease and rapidity of travel, and the proliferation of means of communication enabled large numbers of people to raise questions such as "What is my religion?" "Why is it important to my life?" and "How do my beliefs guide my conduct?" This interest in such basic, abstract questions of doctrine and faith by large numbers of people, as opposed to a small elite, is new. The result, at least for the Muslim world, has not been a homogenization of faith, but rather an intensified, multipolar struggle over people's imaginations—over the symbols and principles of "Islam." Many different voices assert that they speak for "Islam," and not all these voices offer a vision of tolerance and mutual understanding, either among Muslims themselves or between Islam and other religious traditions.

Some contemporary Muslim intellectuals argue that Islam offers a timeless precedent of "peace, harmony, hope, justice, and tolerance, not only for the Muslims but also for the whole of mankind," and that tolerance is a problem only for "those who belong to other than the Islamic faith."[27] Others, such as Masud, shift between sociologically and historically aware perspectives of the social and political contexts in which ethical ideas are shaped, reformulated, and practiced. As he writes in chapter 7, "pluralism derives its legitimacy and acceptance by justifying universal values in local contexts. Ethical pluralism [in Islam] is thus a concept that is constantly negotiated between universal and local ethical values." Or, as an Arabian peninsula intellectual argues, the notion of *shura* (consultation), the Qur'anic equivalent to democracy, expands and develops over time and remains incomplete. He makes an explicit analogy with the American democratic experience—an analogy certainly not part of the standard analogies of an earlier era. The essentials of the American democratic experience, he argues, were expressed at the founding of the republic, but the principles of equality and of voting rights were elaborated and expanded over time and continue to develop to this day.[28]

Similarly, Islamic concepts of conduct are subject to elaboration and expansion over time. As Robert Wuthnow argues, all religious traditions have a "problem of articulation."[29] If their ideas and practices do not articulate closely enough to their social settings, "they are likely to be regarded by their potential audiences of which these settings are composed as irrelevant, unrealistic, artificial, and overly abstract." But if they "articulate too closely with the specific social environment in which they are produced, they are likely to be thought of as esoteric, parochial, time bound, and fail to attract a wider and more lasting audience."[30]

Any system of ethics acquires legitimacy as supposedly "timeless" moral presuppositions interact with, and are interpreted by, specific moral experience. Charles Taylor refers to the background understandings of person, authority, and responsibility on the basis of which explicit systems of beliefs and practices are formulated as the "social imaginary."[31] In ideology, Islamic law (the *shari'a*—a concept much wider than legislated jurisprudence) is eternal and enduring. In practice, however, it is the Muslim world's equivalent of the social imaginary. Even judges in contemporary Saudi Arabia practice a de facto, if not a de jure, form of case law, even as they deny that they do so.[32] Likewise, most Muslims assume that their accepted local practices are part of the shari'a.

Even when Islamic thinkers advocate a separation of Islamic thought and practice from other traditions, including European colonialism and economic domination, they encourage the elaboration of habits of thought and practice that facilitate introducing new elements and practices. Thus activist thinkers such as Sayyid Qutb (1906–1966) wrote of Islam as a "system" or "program" (*minhaj*), an open, manifest, and clear system of thought and practice that could be distinguished from other systems of belief, including nonreligious ones. For Qutb, as for other activists, it is not sufficient simply to "be" Muslim and to follow Muslim practices. One must reflect upon Islam and articulate it. When activists declare that they are engaged in the "Islamization" of their society, the sense of thinking of religious beliefs as an objective system becomes explicit. Such thinking is increasingly reflected at the popular level by the proliferation of catechism-like "new" Islamic books, the printed sermons and audio cassettes of popular preachers, and books "proving" the compatibility of modern science and medicine with the Qur³an.[33]

A Religious Movement in Turkey

Turkey is an especially pivotal Muslim-majority country because it is where debates about secularism and modernity, and Islam and the West, have become most public and spirited. A salient indication of the ways in which the pervasive trend toward the systematization of belief and practice and the advocacy of conscious reflection on faith can be used to pave the way to a greater openness toward other religious traditions is Turkey's Nurculuk movement. It began in Turkey in the early twentieth century and today has followers in Germany, California, Central Asia, and elsewhere. The teachings of its founder, Bediüzzaman Said Nursi (1873–1960)—originally written and passed on by hand because of government hostility in republican Turkey— have been collected in pamphlets with titles such as *The Miracles of Muhammad*, *Belief in Man*, and *Resurrection in the Hereafter*.[34] These pamphlets have "the function of explaining, in accordance with the understanding of the age, the truths of the Qur³an."[35] Nursi insisted that books, not people, "have waged a battle against unbelief."[36]

Nursi stressed the importance of direct contact with texts and encouraged his followers to adopt his own approach, which emphasized exploring multiple combinations of knowledge, including those outside the Islamic tradition. In 1910 a policeman in Tiflis, asking Nursi about his plans for building a religious school, said that it was hopeless to envision a unity of the "broken up and fragmented" Muslim world. Nursi replied: "They have gone to study. It is like this: India is an able son of Islam; it is studying in the high school of the British. Egypt is a clever son of Islam; it is taking lessons in the British school for civil servants. Caucasia and Turkestan are two valiant sons of Islam; they are training in the Russian war academy. And so on."[37] In 1911, a half century before the Second Vatican Council urged Christians and Muslims to resolve their differences and move beyond the conflicts of the past, Nursi advocated such a dialogue, and his successors have taken significant steps to engage in interfaith discussions.[38]

Another element in Nursi's writing sets him apart from earlier religious intellectuals such as Muhammad ʿAbduh (1849–1905) and Jamal al-Din al-Afghani (1838/9–1897). As much as these two predecessors appealed to the learned classes throughout the Muslim world and sought to popularize their message, their primary audience remained the educated, urban cadres. They, like other religious modernists, distanced themselves from popular belief and rhetorical styles. Nursi, in contrast, never lost his rural roots and often employed the metaphors and imagery of Turkey's rural population.

Although familiar with the structure and content of modern scientific knowledge, Nursi recognized the value of fable and metaphor in shaping his message. His use of them facilitated understandings of his message in different social and historical contexts. Thus in the early part of Nursi's career, his writings and messages were listened to by audiences as they were read aloud, either directly by him to his disciples or by "persons who had already acquired religious prestige." Moreover, in spite of the "official terror and persecution" carried out against those caught reading and teaching books in the old (Arabic) script in the 1920s and 1930s, the practices continued.[39] The *Risale-i Nur*, the collection of Nursi's principal writings, was first disseminated by "thousands" of women and men, young and old, who made copies by hand, and by 1946 or 1947 through the use of duplicating machines.[40] After 1956, when Nursi's books were taken off the banned list and published in modern Turkish, his audience broadened to include those whose primary engagement with the *Risale-i Nur* was through reading it, and not necessarily the face-to-face or hand-to-hand contact of an earlier era.[41]

The *Risale-i Nur* is modern in the sense that its texts encourage reflection on ideas of society and nation. In countries other than Turkey, religious intellectuals also spoke of constitutionalism, justice, and the relation of Islamic belief to modern science, morality, public responsibilities, and the application of faith to public life and spiritual development. Moreover, after 1923 Nursi made a distinctive contribution to the sense of public space. The Syrian translator of Nursi's writings, Said Ramadan al-Buti, remarks on the disjunction in Nursi's career between his early political activism and his post-1923 writings and activities. After 1923, Nursi encouraged reasoned reflection and action based on core ethical and religious values without prescribing particular, context-specific political action.[42] Nursi's message, more than that of many of his contemporaries, was accessible not only to religiously oriented educated cadres but also to the less educated, who saw in his message a means of integrating faith with modernity, nationalism, and social revitalization.

The other defining feature of his message, especially in the earlier part of this century, was its success in speaking to the conditions of Turkish society, especially rural Turkish society, when the hold of local leaders was rapidly giving way to an increasingly effective state apparatus, improved communications, and centralization. His message was sufficiently adaptable in structure and content, however, so that it subsequently spoke to the Turkey of later eras and, increasingly, to an international audience. Produced at first in manuscript form and faithfully copied by disciples despite long-standing official prohibitions, Nursi's work is now communicated in multiple languages and publications and through a multilingual website (*www.nesil.com.tr*).

Nursi's style is readily accessible to these multiple audiences, and women are taking an increasingly active role in promoting the message. For some readers, the specifics of Turkish historical development help explain the nuances of certain passages and the context for which they were originally intended. For others, however, the rich metaphors and imagery offer a point of departure for religious understanding that requires only minimal familiarity with the specifics of the times and places in Turkey where the various elements of the *Risale-i Nur* first came into existence.

In the current era, the Nurculuk movement has succeeded in attracting significant followers from all social classes in Turkey. Especially as articulated by one of Nursi's leading contemporary disciples, Fethullah Gülen (b. 1938), Nursi's interpretation of Islamic values offers a union between religion and science, and tradition and modernity, stressing the compatibility of Islamic ideas and practices with Turkish nationalism, education, and the market economy.[43] His followers control a complex web of businesses and significant broadcast and print media in Turkey and in Central Asia. The movement has over three hundred schools in Turkey and the countries of the Commonwealth of Independent States, especially in Central Asia. Within Turkey, the only religious classes are those prescribed by the Turkish national curriculum. The schools do not explicitly promote a particular interpretation of Islam, but rather instill a morality and sense of discipline intended to pervade personal conduct and public life. This teaching advocates a public role for women in society. As Gülen has stated, to the consternation both of conservative Muslims and Turkey's secular elite, the wearing of the headscarf by women is a matter of personal choice. It is not prescribed by faith.

The businessmen, teachers, journalists, students, and others to whom his message appeals stress the combination of knowledge and discipline to empower Muslims and, at least within Turkey, the Turkish state. Less a centralized network than loosely affiliated clusters of organizations, those inspired by Gülen's ideas stress discipline and dialogue.[44] The disciplined use of reason and acquisition of knowledge are stressed within Turkey itself, and are combined with highly publicized and sustained dialogues with Christian and Jewish religious leaders, which stress tolerance, electoral politics, moderation, and participation in a market economy.

In spite of efforts of some elements of Turkey's militantly secularist elite to consider all those who advocate a public role for religious expression as antidemocratic "fundamentalists," most Turks consider Islam an integral part of their social identity. Indeed, the "background" understandings of Islam appear to be on the side of Gülen and others who see Islam as a religion of dialogue, tolerance, and reason. In this respect, rising educational levels, strengthened ties between Turks living in Turkey and in Europe, and the proliferation of media and the means of communication not necessarily mediated by state elites favor these more open interpretations. For example, in 1992, 1993, and 1994, a sample of rural and urban Turks (N = 1,363) was asked whether Turkey was "Muslim," "European," or "both"; roughly the same number, 20–21 percent each year, said "European." The number who said that Turkey was primarily Muslim, however, declined from 37 percent in 1992 to 25 percent in 1994, while the number who answered "both" increased from 25 percent to 36 percent.[45] More recently, in a survey conducted by TESEV, a Turkish think tank,

> 97% of those questioned identified themselves as Muslim, 92% said they fasted during the holy month of Ramadan, and 46% claimed to pray five times a day. But 91% also said different religious beliefs should be respected, and clear majorities thought it did not matter if Muslims consumed alcohol, failed to fast or pray or, if they were women, went outside without covering their heads. Only 21% called for an Islamic state, and once the implications were pointed out to them, some were not so sure.[46]

The Turkish experience does not represent the entire Muslim world, but it serves as a reminder of the diversity of the Muslim experience, both among intellectual formulations of Islamic thought and among the practical, implicitly shared understandings of large numbers of people.

Tolerance Today

Many Muslim thinkers interpret the Islamic tradition as enjoining a continuous dialogue over meaning, one that explicitly enjoins tolerance among Muslims and among Muslim and other religious traditions. For example, Morocco's Said Binsaid, speaking out against the intolerance of some Muslim fundamentalists in the early 1990s, wrote that religious radicals, by coercing their opponents into silence, seek to "worship God in ignorance." He argues that a proper understanding of the principles of Islam enjoins dialogue, a willingness to understand the opinions of others, and a disposition toward good relations (*husna*) with them. This dialogue entails adaptation and the continual renewal of religious understandings within a framework of civility.[47] Said Binsaid in Morocco, Syria's Muhammad Shahrur, Turkey's Fethullah Gülen, Iran's Muhammad Khatami, and Indonesia's Nurcholish Madjid are but a few prominent Muslim thinkers who advocate this ongoing "internal" dialogue of reason among Muslims, often paralleled by discussions with both secularists and the followers of other religious faiths.

In a similar vein, Syria's Muhammad Shahrur, whose *The Book and the Qur'an: A Contemporary Interpretation* became a best seller throughout the Arab world since its publication in 1990, argues for the use of reason in interpreting Islamic doctrine. He advocates religious tolerance both from Qur'anic precedent and "in its spirit."[48] On inheritance laws, for example, which some scholars argue are fixed for all times, Shahrur suggests that the various Qura'nic verses have been interpreted in such a way as to give women lesser shares in most instances. Shahrur argues that jurists in earlier eras reached wrong conclusions based on the limitations of the human knowledge of their time. Using the more sophisticated understandings of mathematics available in the current era, for instance, he argues for new interpretations of Islamic law concerning inheritance.

Such arguments will not win Shahrur friends among most jurists, but legal scholars such as Wael Hallaq state that of all contemporary reformers, Shahrur is the most persuasive.[49] Shahrur also argues that the *hadd* punishments, which include penalties such as stoning and the amputations of limbs for certain offenses, are not prescriptive but rather serve as the "outer limits" permitted by divine law, and invite modification as societies mature. Indeed, Shahrur's thinking is imbued with the idea of the evolution of human societies. He argues that implicit in Qur'anic thought is the idea that humankind is now beyond prophecy and revelation, and is now prepared to "go it alone" in the spirit of divine precept. Shahrur's solution for the multiplicity of religions is that we are all Muslims—Muslim-Christians, Muslim-Jews, and "believing Muslims" (al-muslimun al-mu'minun, those who accept the prophecy of Muhammad), and that all must be treated equally, even atheists and apostates. It is God's responsibility alone to judge human conduct.[50]

Shahrur shares a common feature with many other contemporary Islamic thinkers. Scholars trained in the Islamic religious sciences remain important, but authoritative religious interpretations, once the monopoly of religious scholars who had mastered recognized religious texts, is now replaced by direct and broader access to the printed word. More and more Muslims take it upon themselves to interpret the textual sources—classical or modern—of Islam. Hasan al-Turabi (b. 1930), the Sorbonne-educated leader of the Muslim Brothers in the Sudan and a former attorney general, forcefully makes this point: "Because all knowledge is divine and religious, a chemist, an engineer, an economist, or a jurist are all 'ulama."[51] Turabi implicitly builds on an Islamic tradition that affirms the authority of those who possess religious knowledge ('ilm) over the faithful. He expands the idea of valued knowledge, however, to include any scientific endeavor.

The approach to authoritative knowledge articulated by Turabi captures the public imagination throughout the Muslim world. Indeed, the more unfettered broadcast media, such as Qatar's al-Jazeera satellite TV, which has a wide audience throughout the Arab world, finds that its discussion programs dealing with religious issues are highly popular.[52] Such arguments proceed not from traditional jurisprudence, the form used by most madrasa-trained clerics, but by expounding directly from the actual Qur'anic text, linking it to contemporary issues and approaches and drawing on many other sources.

Thus powerful arguments can be elaborated from the Qur'an to show how its divine message forms the basis for a complex moral language that encompasses all mankind, not just Muslims. In Shahrur's words, Islam (islam, or submission to God) is a covenant "between God and the whole of humanity," and the specifically Islamic faith (iman) "is a covenant between God and the believers who specifically follow Muhammad's prophecy."[53] Thus, for Shahrur and others, religious and ethical pluralism is divinely approved.

Some Iranians now write of a "post-Islamic" Iran. Iranian anthropologist Fariba Adelkhah, for example, writes that a "religious public sphere" (espace public confessionel) has emerged in Iran in which politics and religion are subtly intertwined, and not always in ways anticipated by Iran's established religious leaders. In this post-Islamic society, vigorous and increasingly public debates center on such issues as the role of religious leaders in politics, women in public spaces, and other vital issues influencing daily life.[54]

Qur'anic interpretation and the Islamic tradition can be used to elaborate a notion of civil society and a public sphere in which Islam can play a role, alongside other religious and secular perspectives, free from coercion and guaranteeing individual dignity and personal liberty. The idea of citizenship as a bundle of rights and obligations to the state is firmly incorporated into the social imaginary, even in regions where authoritarianism prevails. Counting Muslims in India (about 200 million, nearly double the number of Muslims in the Arab Middle East) and Indonesia (the most populous Muslim-majority country), many Muslims live under democratic rule. Masud points to a prominent twentieth-century Muslim intellectual, Muhammad Iqbal, who even defined Islam as a civil society. Many Muslims may live under authoritarian rule, but this is not due to any inherent link between Islam and authoritarianism.

The Islamic Republic of Iran, in which elections are assuming increasing significance, suggests the contours of the ongoing dialogue concerning religion and democracy. The substantive clauses of the Iranian constitution display the coexistence of two contrasting notions of sovereignty. Principles 2 and 56 affirm the conventional concept of the absolute sovereignty of Allah, but elsewhere the constitution accommodates the very different idea of popular sovereignty in acknowledging the people's right to determine their own "destiny" (Principle 3:8), and allowing for occasional referenda (Principle 59) and a popularly elected assembly (Principle 62).[55] The constitution of Pakistan shows a similar dual sovereignty, and in many countries, the status of the shari'a versus legislated law remains unresolved.

Islam as a moral tradition, as Masud argues, favors ethical pluralism both because it appeals to human reason and because the value of pluralism is widely accepted. The opportunity and scope to apply reason to solving ongoing practical problems, such as human sexuality, decisions over life and death, organ transplants, gender relations, and international relations is uneven. This unevenness is itself an indication of pluralism. Throughout the Muslim-majority world, there is a patchwork of incremental practical decisions that affect issues of tolerance both within and among religious traditions. In Indonesia, for example, legal decisionmaking related to issues of family law and other issues of civil society are no longer confined exclusively to religious jurists.[56] Likewise, there is an overall trend, although not without resistance, for women to play increasingly public roles in society.

Attitudes toward homosexuality and same-sex unions indicate the challenges facing greater openness toward individual choice and responsibility in personal issues. At one level, homosexuality meets with profound religious disapproval, as is also the case in the orthodox Jewish tradition and among many Christians. At another level, however, as Masud points out, there is a long history of de facto tolerance for homosexuality. Only contemporary Turkey has a public tolerance for homosexuality, and hosts an openly gay website. In Europe, however, debates among Muslims over the legitimacy of homosexual lifestyles have become increasingly common. In Spring 2001 a highly publicized homophobic statement by the Moroccan *imam* of a mosque in Rotterdam, in response to the Dutch legalization of same-sex unions (voted for by all three Muslim members of parliament), set off a national debate over the role of Muslims in Dutch society. It also, however, led to the creation of a support group for gay Muslim youth. States in the Middle East, such as Egypt, are wary of any societies or organizations not under state supervision.

From the perspective of some states, homosexual and women's rights organizations are as much of a threat as human rights groups and nongovernmental organizations that advocate the monitoring of elections.[57] The overall trend toward the fragmentation of religious and political authority favors greater openness and toleration in all spheres of social action. In sexual politics as in other forms of expression, however, the road ahead is uneven and rocky. Some will argue that such practices should not be condoned, but leave judgment to God, not human justice. In some U.S. jurisdictions, laws against sodomy were only removed from statutes in recent years, and only two states allow same-sex unions.

The fact that decisions and debates on issues of personal status are made on a country-by-country basis indicates the absence of a pan-Islamic or doctrinal consensus. Local cultural practices often allow for a spectrum of de facto autonomy on decisions that affect private life, including the expression of sexual orientation.[58] The prevalent practical approach in many societies is "Don't ask, don't tell," but in some respects the lack of open debate on all issues of personal choice can pragmatically allow for a greater liberty by denying extreme conservatives the opportunity to silence minority voices.

The prevailing secularist bias of many theories of society has alternatively marginalized and demonized religious forces and religious intellectuals. The Muslim world has been characterized as especially resistant to "modernity" and intolerant of other religious traditions.

Yet the Muslim-majority world is as open as that of any other civilizational domain. We live in a world in which an Islamic leader such as Fethullah Gülen meets popes and patriarchs, advocating diversity and tolerance in the public sphere more than many of those who are secular. Far from compromising the public sphere, religious movements and religious intellectuals in the Muslim majority world can advocate compromise and a mutual agreement to persuade by words rather than by force. Religious intellectuals may claim strong links with the past, but their practice in the present conveys significantly different and more open ideas of person, authority, and responsibility.

Notes

1. Quotations from the Qur'an are based on Ezzidin al-Hayek, *Approximate Translation of the Meaning of the Qur'an* (Damascus: Dar al-Fikr, 1996).

2. All references to Khalid Masud in this chapter, unless otherwise noted, are to his essay "The Scope of Pluralism in Islamic Moral Traditions," chap. 7 below.

3. Sohail H. Hashmi, "Islamic Ethics in International Society," chap. 8 below.

4. I am grateful to James Piscatori for generously sharing with me an unpublished paper-in-progress concerning the Bin Laden/al-Qa'ida view of world politics.

5. Robert N. Bellah, *Beyond Belief: Essays on Religion in a Post-Traditional World* (New York: Harper & Row, 1970), 150–51.

6. Ibid., 160.

7. Ibid., 151.

8. David Little, "The Development in the West of the Right to Freedom of Religion and Conscience: A Basis for Comparison with Islam," in *Human Rights and the Conflict of Cultures: Western and Islamic Perspectives on Religious Liberty*, ed. David Little, John Kelsay, and Abdulaziz A. Sachedina (Columbia: University of South Carolina Press, 1988), 30.

9. This is the argument of Abdulaziz A. Sachedina, "Freedom of Conscience and Religion in the Qur'an," in Little, Kelsay, and Sachedina, *Human Rights*, 68, 74.

10. Fazlur Rahman, *Major Themes of the Qur'an* (Minneapolis: Bibliotheca Islamica, 1980), 163.

11. Ibid., 164.

12. Ibid.

13. Paul Wheatley, *The Places Where Men Pray Together: Cities in Islamic Lands, 7th–10th Centuries* (Chicago: University of Chicago Press, 2000).

14. See Dale F. Eickelman and James Piscatori, "Social Theory in the Study of Muslim Societies," in *Muslim Travellers: Pilgrimage, Migration, and the Religious Imagination*, ed. Dale F. Eickelman and James Piscatori (Berkeley and Los Angeles: University of California Press, 1990), 3–25.

15. Mikhaêl Elbaz, "La diáspora Sefardí a través del Meriterráneo y el Maghreb tras la expulsión de España en 1492," in *Atlas de la inmigración magrebí en España*, ed. Bernabé López García (Madrid: Ediciones Universidad Autónoma de Madrid, 1996), 18.

16. Robert Assaraf, *Mohammed V et les Juifs du Maroc à l'époque de Vichy* (Paris: Plon, 1997).

17. See Muhammad Khalid Masud, *Shatibi's Philosophy of Islamic Law* (Islamabad: Islamic Research Institute, 1995).

18. Iqtidar Ali Khan, "Akbar's Personality Traits and World Outlook—A Critical Appraisal," in *Akbar and His India*, ed. Irfan Habib (Delhi: Oxford University Press, 1997), 95.

19. Ira M. Lapidus, *A History of Islamic Societies* (Cambridge: Cambridge University Press, 1988), 456.

20. Amartya Sen, "East and West: The Reach of Reason," *New York Review of Books*, July 20, 2000: 33.

21. S. N. Eisenstadt, "Multiple Modernities," *Daedalus* 129:1 (Winter 2000): 1.

22. Cited in John Keane, "The Limits of Secularism," *Times Literary Supplement*, January 9, 1998: 12–13.

23. This distinction is noted by Muhammad Khalid Masud, "Religions and Tolerance: Islam," paper presented at a symposium on "Religions and Tolerance," May 8–10, 2000, Potsdam and Berlin, Germany, 2 (cited here with permission).

24. Ibid., 1–2. See also Dale F. Eickelman and James Piscatori, *Muslim Politics* (Princeton: Princeton University Press, 1996), 3–4.

25. See Wilfred Cantwell Smith, *The Meaning and End of Religion: A New Approach to the Religious Traditions of Mankind* (New York: Macmillan, 1963), 48–50, 60–62.

26. Francis Robinson, "Technology and Religious Change: Islam and the Impact of Print," *Modern Asian Studies* 27:1(January 1993): 229–51.

27. Syed Othman Alhabshi and Nik Mustapha Nik Hasan, introduction to *Islam and Tolerance*, ed. Syed Othman Alhabshi and Nik Mustapha Nik Hasan (Kuala Lumpur: Institute of Islamic Understanding Malaysia, 1994), 1–2.

28. Sadek J. Sulaiman, "Democracy and *Shura*," in *Liberal Islam: A Sourcebook*, ed. Charles Kurzman (New York: Oxford University Press, 1998), 96–98.

29. Robert Wuthnow, *Communities of Discourse: Ideology and Social Structure in the Reformation, the Enlightenment, and European Socialism* (Cambridge: Harvard University Press, 1989), 3.

30. Ibid.

31. Charles Taylor, "Modernity and the Rise of the Public Sphere," in *The Tanner Lectures on Human Values*, vol. 14 (Salt Lake City: University of Utah Press, 1993), 213.

32. Frank Vogel, *Islamic Law and Legal System: Studies of Saudi Arabia* (Leiden: E. J. Brill, 2000).

33. See Yves Gonzalez-Quijano, *Les gens du livre: Édition et champ intellectuel dans l'Égypte républicaine* (Paris: CNRS Éditions, 1998), 171–98.

34. Bediüzzaman Said Nursi, *The Miracles of Muhammad*, trans. from Turk-

ish by Ümit Şimşek (Istanbul: Yeni Asya Yanıları, 1985); Nursi, *Belief and Man*, trans. from Turkish by Ümit Şimşek (Istanbul: Yeni Asya Yanıları, 1985); and Nursi, *Resurrection and the Hereafter*, trans. from Turkish by Ümit Şimşek (Istanbul: Yeni Asya Yanıları, 1985).

35. Bediüzzaman Said Nursi, *Nature: Cause or Effect?* trans. from Turkish by Ümit Şimşek (Istanbul: Yeni Asya Yanıları, 1985).

36. Cited in Şerif Mardin, *Religion and Social Change in Modern Turkey: The Case of Bediüzzaman Said Nursi* (Albany: State University of New York Press, 1989), 4.

37. Sükran Vahide, *Bediüzzaman Said Nursi: The Author of the* Risale-i Nur (Istanbul: Sözler Publications, 1992), 89–90. For a further discussion of the structure of Nursi's ideas and their appeal to different audiences, see Dale F. Eickelman, "Qur'anic Commentary, Public Space, and Religious Intellectuals in the Writings of Said Nursi," *Muslim World* 89:3–4 (July–October 1999): 260–69, from which part of this section is adapted.

38. Thomas Michel, "Muslim-Christian Dialogue and Cooperation in the Thought of Bediüzzaman Said Nursi," *Muslim World* 89:3–4 (July–October 1999): 325.

39. Vahide, *Bediüzzaman Said Nursi*, 217.

40. Ibid., 219.

41. Mardin, *Religion and Social Change in Modern Turkey*, 6.

42. Muhammad Said Ramadan al-Buti, "Bediüzzaman Said Nursi's Experience of Serving Islam by Means of Politics," in *The Reconstruction of Islamic Thought in the Twentieth Century and Bediüzzaman Said Nursi: Third International Symposium on Bediüzzaman Said Nursi, 24th–26th September 1995, Istanbul*, vol. 1, trans. from Turkish by Şükran Vahide (Istanbul: Sözler Publications, 1997), 111–21. Al-Buti is a prominent Syrian religious scholar who broadcasts a popular weekly television program in Damascus.

43. For an excellent overview of the significance of the movement, see M. Hakan Yavuz, "Towards an Islamic Liberalism? The Nurcu Movement and Fethullah Gülen," *Middle East Journal* 53:4 (Fall 1999): 584–605. See also Bülent Aras, "Turkish Islam's Moderate Face," *Middle East Quarterly* 5:3 (September 1998): 23–29.

44. Yavuz, "Towards an Islamic Liberalism?" 600.

45. Sources: PIAR Gallup, polls conducted November 1992, November 1993; DAP/Yankelvitch poll, Turkey, August–September 1994. I wish to thank the United States Information Service, Washington, D.C., for providing me with these polls in February 1996.

46. Cited in "Fundamental Separation," in special supplement: "Ataturk's Long Shadow: A Survey of Turkey," *Economist*, June 10, 2000: 11.

47. Said Bensaid, "Al-Hiwar wa'l-fahm la al-qat'iyya wa'l-jahl" (Dialogue and understanding, not alienation and ignorance), *Al-Sharq al-awsat* (London), July 7, 1993: 10.

48. Muhammad Shahrur, *Al-Kitab wa'l-Qur'an: Qira'a mu'asira* (The Book and the Qur'an: A Contemporary Interpretation) (Damascus: Dar al-Ahali, 1990).

49. Wael B. Hallaq, *A History of Islamic Legal Theories* (Cambridge: Cambridge University Press, 1997), 253.

50. See Muhammad Shahrur, *Proposal for an Islamic Covenant*, trans. from Arabic by Dale F. Eickelman and Ismail S. Abu Shehadeh (Damascus: Dar al-Ahali, 2000). This book is also available online at *www.isim.nl/isim/publications/ other/shahrur*. For an introduction to Shahrur's thinking, see Dale F. Eickelman, "Islamic Liberalism Strikes Back," *Middle East Studies Association Bulletin* 27:2 (December 1993): 163–68.

51. Hasan al-Turabi, "The Islamic State," in *Voices of Resurgent Islam*, ed. John L. Esposito (New York: Oxford University Press, 1983), 245.

52. See John F. Burns, "Arab TV Gets a New Slant: Newscasts without Censorship," *New York Times*, July 4, 1999: A1, A6.

53. Shahrur, *Islamic Covenant*.

54. Fariba Adelkhah, *Being Modern in Iran* (New York: Columbia University Press, 2000), 105–38.

55. Islamic Republic of Iran, "Constitution of the Islamic Republic of Iran" (ratified December 2–3, 1979), *Middle East Journal* 34:2 (Spring 1980): 181–204.

56. John R. Bowen, "Legal Reasoning and Public Discourse in Indonesian Islam," in *New Media in the Muslim World: The Emerging Public Sphere*, ed. Dale F. Eickelman and Jon W. Anderson (Bloomington: Indiana University Press, 1999), 80–105.

57. For an argument on personal liberty linking gay rights to the right of female students to wear headscarves, see Bahar Öcal Düzgören, "Neyim Ki, Kimim Ki Ben?" *Sözleşme*, July 9, 1998: 47–49. For ethnic Turkish homosexual organizations in the Netherlands ("Strange Fruit"), Moroccans ("Ipoth"), and Arabs in general ("Yusuf"), see Oussama Cherreibi, "Imams d'Amsterdam: À travers l'example des imams de la diaspora marocaine," Ph.D. dissertation, University of Amsterdam, 2000, 164–67.

58. See Stephen O. Murray and Will Roscoe, eds., *Islamic Homosexualities: Culture, Homosexuality, and Literature* (New York: New York University Press, 1997).

7

The Scope of Pluralism
in Islamic Moral Traditions

MUHAMMAD KHALID MASUD

DALE EICKELMAN argues in the previous chapter that the Qur'an offers a modern perspective of a multiethnic and multicommunity world. Despite the fact that over time localisms have resisted the full realization of this Qur'anic perspective, Muslim societies have nevertheless continuously demonstrated their belief in this principle, as illustrated by the thought of the jurist Abu Ishaq al-Shatibi in fourteenth-century Spain, the Mughal ruler Akbar in sixteenth-century India, and the Nurculuk movement in twentieth-century Turkey. Eickelman has very significantly noted that on various Islamic issues, the point of departure in contemporary debates is the Qur'an itself, not the interpretations of the ʿulama in the past or present.

I should begin my comments saying that I fully support Eickelman's thesis, especially the point that modern Muslims do not support the concept of an "official" or "authoritative" view. They often proclaim with some sense of pride that there is no church in Islam. Inevitably, this claim implies accommodating pluralism. In my remarks, I would like to present an overview of the several moral traditions in Islam. I would also like to comment with specific reference to the issues of social regulation, citizenship, life-and-death decisions, and human sexuality that Muslim ethical positions may differ with others, and these differences should be regarded as part of ethical pluralism on the global level.

Modern Muslim writings on pluralism are clearly apprehensive of the possible anarchy and schism to which it may lead, threatening the unity of the Muslim *umma*.[1] They particularly stress that pluralism in Islam is conceived within a framework of unity. This apprehension reflects the distinct attitude of these Muslim thinkers toward prioritizing society over the individual.

In my view, pluralism is a part of the project of modernity that favors the freedom of the individual. Pluralism does not stress multiplicity per se as much as it is concerned with questioning the traditional monopoly of certain persons, groups, or institutions on pre-

scribing ethical values authoritatively. In this sense, pluralism is not
against the idea of unity and universalism on the basis of rationalism
and humanism. It aims also at the growth of these values on the
transnational and global level. This does not, however, mean that pluralism should ignore local or religious values. In fact, pluralism derives its legitimacy and acceptance by justifying universal values in
local contexts. Ethical pluralism is thus a concept that is constantly
negotiated between universal and local ethical values.

Ethical Traditions in Islam

Islam as a moral tradition has never been monolithic.[2] Quite early in
its history, it developed several approaches to moral issues. These approaches vary in their sources of authority, methods of interpretations, and emphasis. They sometimes oppose one another but often
continue to function side by side, even complementing each other. It
is therefore appropriate to review, even if briefly, these various moral
traditions in Islam.

The *hadith* literature reflects a very significant moral tradition. It
offers the prophet Muhammad and his companions as models for
moral behavior. This tradition developed a very comprehensive ethical system of the *sunna* (norms) of the prophet Muhammad. The tradition frequently refers to the pre-Islamic tribal sunna, even if it is
only to elaborate its assimilation or rejection into the Prophetic sunna.
The definition of the sunna not only included the sayings and the
practice of the Prophet, but also the practices to which the Prophet
did not raise any objection.

The outstanding aspect of this ethical tradition is that it is essentially oriented to issues of religion and authenticity. The fact that this
tradition produced dozens of compendia, however, each of them accepted as authoritative, stresses the principle of ethical pluralism
within the tradition itself.

Pre-Islamic tribal values such as manliness, honor, forbearance, and
tolerance were part of the Arab sunna that operated at the level of
custom and usage in the literary moral tradition called *adab*. The adab
tradition represents a humanist moral approach to morality. Most
probably, writings in this tradition were initiated by Ibn Muqaffaʿ (d.
756), and carried on by several other well-known writers like Ibn
Qutayba (d. 889), al-Mawardi (d. 1058), and al-Qalqashandi (d. 1418).
The tradition expresses itself in the literary genre that comprises
guidebooks for rulers or civil servants, laying down principles of
model behavior for them. This tradition is more open than hadith, as

it derives its ethical values from various sources: pre-Islamic Arabic as well as Persian literature, the Qur'an, Islamic history, ancient Persian history, and Greek and Indian literature. Ibn Muqaffa‛ translated into Arabic *Kalila wa Dimna*, a book of moral stories that originated in India. The adab tradition continues in arts and literature, but also as etiquette literature that provides a code of ethics for various professions, such as musicians.[3]

The philosophical tradition in Islam dealt with ethical issues on a more abstract level than the adab tradition. One of the essential questions with which this tradition was engaged was that of ethical obligation and its origins. The issue was whether it was only religion that defined rights and obligations, or whether human reason on its own could also differentiate between ethically good and bad. The Muslim philosophers explored the nature of prophethood, revelation, the role of reason, and other such themes. From Ibn Sina (d. 1037) to Ibn Rushd (d. 1198), the Muslim philosophers generally argued that there was no conflict between reason and revelation. The most interesting examples of the discussion of this problem are the treatises entitled *Hayy bin Yaqzan* (The Living, Son of Awake) by Ibn Sina and Ibn Tufayl (d. 1185).[4] Ibn Tufayl's story presents Hayy as a human child growing up on an island among animals without any contact with humans. By instinct and experience, he develops a moral code for himself. Later, he finds out that his moral values are no different from the religious values in the neighboring island inhabited by humans. Jurist-philosophers such as Shatibi[5] and Shah Waliullah (d. 1762)[6] also hold that human reason reaches similar conclusions during the absence of revelation.

The philosophical tradition developed a system of practical or applied ethics that came to be known as *akhlaq*. It received its recognition as a system of Islamic ethics proper as early as the eleventh century. It is a synthesis of pre-Islamic Arab moral values and Qur'anic teachings, and has Persian, Indian, and Greek elements. Miskawayh's (d. 1030) *Tahdhib al-akhlaq* offers a comprehensive and systematic treatment of ethical values in this tradition. It is obviously influenced by Greek ethical literature. Miskawayh explains that Greek ethics is more in accord with Islamic teachings than is pre-Islamic Arab morality. Jalal al-Din al-Dawwani (d. 1501) and Nasir al-Din al-Tusi (d. 1274) followed Miskawayh in their writings on ethics. Their books, popularly known as *Akhlaq Jalali* and *Akhlaq Nasiri*, respectively, were used as textbooks in the religious institutions.

The Sufi moral tradition is more popular than the other Islamic moral traditions. The Sufis were critical of the literal and exoteric approach to obligations by the jurists and theologians. Al-Harith al-Muhasibi (d. 857) wrote *Kitab al-ri'aya li huquq Allah* (The Book of Observance of the Rights of God). He treats ethical obligations as surrender to the will of God and speaks of moral values such as *taqwa* (fear of God), *tawba* (return to God), *mahabba* (love), and others. Muhasibi stresses the need to abide by the laws of prescription and prohibition in the Qur'an and sunna, but he also stresses a more conscious effort to control the self from its propensity toward evil. Al-Ghazali (d. 1111) also followed Miskawayh in his ethical writings. His books on ethics, namely *Ihya 'ulum al-din* and *Kimiya-yi sa'adat*, have been more popular than his other works.

The Sufis became more and more critical of the legal and theological approaches to obligations in later local traditions. The folk literature stresses the inner and humanist meanings of obligations, and emphasizes tolerance, love, and sincerity.

Kalam (theology) is another tradition that dealt extensively with moral questions. Looking at the theological debates in the second and third centuries of Islam, one cannot fail to notice the diversity of the opinions even on such questions as the nature of divine attributes and the scope of human reason. It took up very early the question of whether the ethical values of good and bad were known only by revelation and religion, or whether human reason can also discover them. The Mu'tazilite school maintained that ethical values are rational and that revelation never contradicts them. The Mu'tazilites developed an entire system of theology and jurisprudence on this basis. They believed in the principle of justice to the extent that they argued that it was an obligation even for God. Revelation, specifically the Qur'an, was not sempiternal because it conformed to the findings of human reason.

The theologians were also divided on the nature of divine attributes. On the question of divine knowledge, for example: Does it exist eternally with God, is it in the essence of God, or is it independent of His essence? Anthropomorphists had an easy solution: humans can understand God only in human terms. The divine attributes are like human attributes. The Mu'tazilites, as strict monotheists, rejected the anthropomorphist view. They also rejected the position of those theologians who held that the divine attributes had an eternal and independent existence apart from God. Such an idea, in their view, could not be reconciled with the idea of God's unity (*tawhid*). They explained the problem in linguistic terms: The attributes were like adjectives. They only denoted a quality that is part of the entity. God's knowledge is part of his essence. When we say God is all-knowing, we are only saying that knowledge is a quality of His essence.

The Mu'tazilites came into conflict with other Muslims, especially those championing hadith, such as Ibn Qutayba, who accused them of denying divine attributes.[7] The Ash'arites, another group of theologians, broke away from the Mu'tazilites, denouncing their theology of human reason. The Mu'tazilites eventually lost the caliphal support they had initially enjoyed, and other groups gained strength. Although a consensus developed within Sunni Islam, the kalam tradition was never monolithic; it continued to develop multiple voices. It was not pluralist in the strict sense, however, as each group claimed authenticity only for itself.

Finally, we come to the tradition of *fiqh* (legal ethics). Although it is the closest Islamic equivalent to Western positive law, fiqh is generally regarded as a tradition that created moral obligations more than legal rights. Snouck Hurgronje even defined Islamic law as a doctrine of ethics and duties.[8]

Regardless of whether it is law in the strict sense or merely a moral tradition, what is significant is that the fiqh tradition also evinces diverse origins and interpretations. In fact, fiqh developed initially as multiple local customary legal traditions. The plurality of views in the fiqh traditions is proverbial. The hadith tradition questioned the authenticity of fiqh traditions and described them as mere opinions (*ra'y*) as opposed to the hadith, which was based on scientific knowledge (*'ilm*). The fiqh traditions produced more than nineteen schools, all of them recognizing one another's validity. The multiplicity of views continues within the schools and is regarded as a blessing. The principle of legal reasoning (*ijtihad*) encourages differences of opinion, because the struggle of the jurist to derive the right ruling is considered religiously commendable even though he may arrive at an erroneous conclusion. Adherence to these different schools of law is reflected in the diverse personal laws in Muslim societies.

It is significant that the caliphs in early Islamic history were apprehensive about the conflicting views of the Muslim jurists that produced diverse court judgments. Several Abbasid caliphs, and later other Muslim rulers, tried to unify laws. Resistance to such attempts often came from the Muslim jurists themselves. They feared that such attempts would mean state interference in this tradition, and they wanted to preserve their freedom. They considered their rulings enforceable by the state, but they never agreed to codify them as state laws. As a result, Muslim societies continuously practiced legal pluralism before the advent of the modern state.

The rural and tribal areas continued their local customary laws, sometimes even non-Muslim laws (as, for example, in Mughal and Ottoman villages). In cities, as well, there were different types of courts. The courts of complaints (*mazalim*) differed from ordinary courts even in their procedural laws. Different state institutions like the police also had their own legal system and procedures. The *hisba* (public censor) courts had jurisdiction over business ethics in the market as well as over offenses against public morals.

Fiqh soon came to stand for *shari'a* (divine law) and defined moral as well as legal obligations. This position of fiqh came about mostly through the function of jurists as *muftis*. A mufti, even today, may be asked about any matter under the sun, and he is supposed to explain God's law on the points in question. Consequently, fiqh assumed a dominant position in Islamic ethical discourse. A mufti's response, called a *fatwa*, offers a social construction of shari'a, as most often it refers to a concrete social question. It evaluates a practice with reference to an ideal. Most often, we find muftis also adjusting ideals to practice in view of the prevailing social conditions. These practices are frequently assimilated into the tradition in such a way that they are sometimes hard to distinguish. In the following pages, we shall refer to some fatwas to illustrate this point.

To conclude this section, we may say that Muslim societies have in practice accommodated ethical pluralism. Modern scholarship, however, generally considers this phenomenon of pluralism a deviation from the ideal. The conservative 'ulama, while recognizing the validity of the different schools of Islamic law, nevertheless insist on *taqlid*, or adherence to one of them. They regard the ijtihad which produced these various schools of interpretation as an instrument of a bygone "golden age," but reject its exercise today because it would lead to anarchy and conflicting opinions. Even many of the reformist 'ulama criticize the plurality of customs and social practices as innovations (*bid'a*), which are contrary to the Qur'an and sunna.

Many Western scholars, among them Reuben Levy, Georges-Henri Bousquet, and Joseph Schacht, have also treated the pluralism in Muslim societies in terms of theory and practice. The theory or ideal is defined, for them, by the Qur'an, sunna, and fiqh. Muslim practices or customs (*adat*, *'urf*) that led to pluralism are defined as deviations. It is noteworthy that these Western scholars were studying this pluralism at times when colonialism or the centralizing nation-state stressed the unification of legal and ethical standards, and upheld it as the ideal. Similarly, Muslim societies also became more conscious of the plurality of societal practices during the reformist phases when unity of the umma was upheld as the ideal, and the ideal was defined in terms of unity of ethical standards.

In fact, I would argue, this "dichotomy" between theory and practice is more imagined than real because both are continuously readjusted in light of each other. The general or universal principles, which may determine the extent to which ethical pluralism is acceptable, are constantly redefined with reference to their local objectification.

Social Regulation

Muslim moral traditions evolved independently of state support. Each tradition expected the state to enforce the laws to ensure social regulations, but would never allow the state to arbitrate ethical differences. As we have mentioned above, the Mu'tazilites invoked the power of the state to regulate ethical differences. They failed. Such attempts on the part of the state were always resisted by society. Ibn Muqaffa' in Baghdad and some Indian 'ulama in Akbar's court tried to win for the ruler the right to arbitrate in case of differences among scholars. The majority of scholars disagreed and did not allow the ruler even the right to choose one among their different views. To them, the basis of authority was *ijma'*, or consensus of legal experts. This concept of consensus required the gradual acceptance of an idea by the whole community. This type of consensus was called *ijma' sukuti* (silent approval) in contrast to *ijma' qawli* (verbal approval), which rarely occurred.

Invocation of the state's power in these matters is more frequent today than previously in Muslim societies. This is perhaps because the concept of the state has changed. The modern concept of the state is that of a nation-state, which implies identity and unity of the polity. The state today frequently brings with it a reform agenda. It is also more encompassing in its function and operation.

Citizenship

Islamic moral traditions obviously support the idea of civil society. Muhammad Iqbal, a twentieth-century Muslim thinker, even defines Islam as a civil society.[9] Based upon this idea, Iqbal declared the necessity of a separate state for Muslims in the Indian subcontinent. In his view, the role of the state should be to provide facilities to promote an ethically based sense of rights and duties.

Modern political systems have introduced several new practices that did not exist in the past, and consequently some dissenting positions on these matters have emerged. One of the controversial issues is the civil status of women. It is significant to note that there is, for instance, no difference of opinion among most Muslim thinkers today on the education of women or their participation in elections. The 'ulama who oppose women's participation in these activities do so for other reasons. The following example will illustrate the point.

In response to a long query by the government of Afghanistan about the civil status of women, the Indian mufti Kifayatullah explained in 1924 that there should be no objection to the education of women, as it is one of the essential Islamic obligations for both men and women.[10] The requirements of modern times make education of women imperative. Muslim societies are losing advantages and opportunities due to their lack of education. The point of controversy lies in the modes of education, which might disregard Islamic requirements of veiling and prohibition of the free mixing of the sexes.

In answer to various other questions about the status of women by several other inquirers, the mufti explained on other occasions that a Muslim woman could go outside the home to cast ballots in elections, provided she observed the veiling requirement.[11] He was, however, reluctant to allow women to contest elections because it would not be possible for them to observe all religious requirements. He did not explain what these requirements were. Apparently, he meant mixed gatherings, but in another fatwa, he allowed a Muslim woman to address a gathering of men if she observed the veil.[12]

We can see that as far as the civil rights of women are concerned, the areas of dissent do not lie in the rights themselves but in some cultural considerations, which these scholars regard as religious requirements. The particular ethical values of veiling and the separation of sexes are explained in view of the corruption of society in modern times. The time of the Prophet, the ideal time, was not corrupt and hence women frequented mosques and participated in social and religious events.

Life-and-Death Decisions

I will discuss issues related to bioethics with reference to a recent study by Vardit Rispler-Chaim.[13] According to Tristram Engelhardt Jr., bioethics is an element of a secular culture and a product of the Enlightenment. In this sense, it forms a venture in secular ethics. Rispler-Chaim disagrees with this conclusion and argues that solutions to problems of life and death must be provided locally and independently in each society and religious community.[14] She explains that there can be no one ethical code for these decisions. Even within particular religious traditions, including Islam, there exist several trends.

According to Rispler-Chaim, the modern Western code of medical ethics is informed by an emphasis on the rights of the individual. It is closely associated with the study of human rights, privacy, personal dignity, and individual freedom of choice in life and death. Islamic ethics, on the other hand, evaluates individual rights in relation to those of society. Not that Islamic ethics ignores human rights; it places more emphasis on society.

With regard to euthanasia, she finds a consensus emerging among Muslim scholars that the mercy killing of a terminally sick patient is forbidden in Islamic law.[15] Their justification is based not on a clear text but on analogy with suicide. They argue that a human being does not own a body, and therefore a person has no right to put it to death.

They also argue that killing oneself to escape suffering, even extreme pain, constitutes suicide. It is a sin because God alone causes death. It also defies the belief in God's ability to perform miracles and interferes with God's exclusive control over life and death.[16]

There is no clear prohibition of suicide in the Qur'an, especially in cases of extreme suffering. Qur'anic references to killing oneself do not always refer to suicide (e.g., 2:54 and 4:66). The jurists often explain the verse "Do not kill yourself" (6:29) as prohibition against mutual fighting among Muslims. The hadith literature, on the other hand, provides clear prohibitions of suicide, and regards it sinful to the extent that funeral prayers are not to be offered for such a person. Suicide is generally a rare occurrence in the history of Muslim societies.[17]

In his discussion of the nature of obligation, Shatibi goes into a detailed analysis of the concept of suffering. Distinguishing between suffering or hardship that is part of obligation and that which is not, he argues that hunger, thirst, sickness, bodily harm, and the like are not part of the concept of obligation. It is therefore obligatory to remove or prevent these types of hardships. He observes, however, that suffering caused by incurable illness is not included in this category. Its removal or elimination is not an obligation. It must be endured as the will of God.[18]

The recent controversy over the legitimacy of suicide attacks by Palestinians as a military tactic against the Israelis has added a new dimension to ethical perspectives on suffering. If Muslims find themselves in the position of extreme suffering and have lost hope of any solution, can they decide to commit suicide in a way that results in the death of other innocent persons? The shaykh of al-Azhar, Muhammad Sayyid al-Tantawi, has declared that suicide attacks against the Israelis are not a legitimate tactic or form of *jihad*. They are simply suicide. Islam does not allow killing civilians in this or any other direct way, in any city or country, even in Israel. Another prominent scholar, Yusuf Qaradawi, disagrees with the shaykh and considers such attacks against the Israelis as justified because all Israelis are involved in the occupation of Palestinian land and in the oppression of ordinary Palestinians.[19]

Human Sexuality

Several studies on sexuality in Islam have recently appeared.[20] Among the issues relating to this topic, homosexuality (*liwat*) attracts the most attention. In view of the Muslim jurists' position on this issue, it is difficult to say if they would ever allow same-sex unions as a form of marriage. Nevertheless, homosexuality has undoubtedly existed in Muslim societies. There is, however, a distinction between sexual relations and simple cohabitation, as well as between this practice as a perversion and debauchery and as an incurable habit.

The Qur'an refers repeatedly to the people of Lot and their practice of sodomy, leaving little doubt that they suffered divine punishment for this pervasive practice (e.g., 11:77–83). There are, however, fleeting references to *ghilman* (52:24) and *wildan* (56:17, 76:19), the "youth" in paradise, but these are not in an explicitly sexual context.

Sexual relations between members of the same sex are harshly condemned in the hadith. The opinions of the jurists, based on the practice of the Prophet's companions, are divided on the exact punishment for sexual offences, and depend largely on the circumstances surrounding such relations. First, most jurists distinguish liwat (same-sex relations) from *zina* (fornication, adultery, or rape). Second, they also distinguish between a married and an unmarried person. Ibn Hazm (d. 1064) recommended lesser punishment for an unmarried person. Ibn Abdun recommended expulsion from the town instead of corporal punishment.[21]

The generally harsh view toward homosexuality is probably due to the fact that the practice appeared, in the minds of many early scholars, to be a corruption of Muslim society in the wake of prosperity during the Abbasid period. Al-Jahiz (d. 868) cites a poem glorifying homosexuality as a sign of sophisticated civilization; normal sex was a practice of the primitive.[22] It is significant to note that in the past Christians attacked Muslim culture particularly for the frequency of homosexual relations.[23] One should not, however, take such descriptions of Muslim culture literally. It is possible that the authors in fact wanted to condemn the Christian monks who took a lenient view toward this practice. It is also possible that the authors of these stories attributed this practice to Muslims in order to stress that it was un-Christian, and that the Christians should not indulge in it.[24]

If one believes the popular literature, the practice also existed among Muslim religious brotherhoods and educational institutions. These stories probably reflect the fact that because of the separation of sexes—stressed so much by Muslim ethical traditions—intimate same-sex relationships inevitably evolved. Such relationships may not necessarily have been sexual. Frequent references in poetry to what may be construed as platonic love show the general acceptance of this form of intimacy.

Conclusion

Islam as a moral tradition favors pluralism on two grounds; first, because it appeals to human reason. The Qur'an attaches pivotal significance to individual rational choice and responsibility. To be a Muslim is a matter of rational choice and an admission of responsibility. "There is no coercion in religion. The truth stands out clear from error" (2:256). "By the soul, and the order given it, He has inspired it to its wrong and to its good" (91:7–8). "To each is a goal to which He turns it. Then strive for what is good" (2:178). "Say, 'The truth is from your Lord,' then believe who wills and deny who wills" (18:29). The emphasis here is not so much that ethical values are rational and scientific but that they are reasonable and understandable by all humans. Because the level of understanding may differ from person to person and from community to community, a multiplicity of views is inevitable.

The second basis for pluralism is social acceptance of Islamic values as understood by different persons and different communities. This basis also regulates the permissible scope of dissent from what are widely accepted social norms. For the Qur'an calls the "good" *ma'ruf* (that which is well known) and "evil" *munkar* (that which is rejected). Social dialectics develop and enforce the acceptable definition of ethical values.

Notes

1. For instance, see Muhammad Ammara, *Al-Ta'addudiyya: Al-Ru'ya al-Islamiyya wa'l-tahaddiyyat al-gharbiyya* (Cairo: Dar Nahdat Misr li'l-Taba'a wa'l-Nashr, 1997), introduction; Zaki al-Milad, *Al-Fikr al-Islami: Qira'at wa muraja'at, al-ta'addudiyya* . . . (Beirut: Mu'assasat al-Intishar al-'Arabi, 1999).

2. See R. Walzer, "Akhlak," in *Encyclopaedia of Islam*, new ed. (Leiden: E. J. Brill, 1986), 1: 325–29.

3. Barbara D. Metcalf, ed., *Moral Conduct and Authority: The Place of* Adab *in*

146

MASUD

South Asian Islam (Berkeley and Los Angeles: University of California Press, 1984), especially Brian Silver, "The *Adab* of Musicians," 315–29.

4. See A.-M. Goichon, "Hayy b. Yakzan," in *Encyclopaedia of Islam*, new ed. (Leiden: E. J. Brill, 1986), 3: 330–34.

5. Muhammad Khalid Masud, *Shatibi's Philosophy of Islamic Law* (Islamabad: Islamic Research Institute, 1995), 157 ff.

6. Shah Waliullah, *Hujjatullah al-baligha* (Lahore: Maktaba Salafiyya, n.d.).

7. Ibn Qutayba, *Al-Ikhtilaf fi'l lafz wa al-radd 'ala al-Jahmiyya wa'l-mushabbiha* (Cairo: Matba'a al-Sa'ada, 1930), 23. Ibn Qutayba argues, "There are others who examined the issue in depth. They presumed that by rejecting anthropomorphism (*tashbih*) of the Creator they were correcting the belief in His unity (*tawhid*). However, they denied the attributes like *hilm, qudra, jalal* and *'afw,* and so on. They said, 'We believe that He is *halim;* we do not believe in His *hilm.* We believe that He is all-knowing; we do not believe in His knowledge.' " See also Gérard Lecomte, *Ibn Qutayba (mort en 276/889); l'homme, son oeuvre, ses idées* (Damas, 1965), 220. For a detailed discussion of the problem, see Richard MacDonough Frank, *Beings and Their Attributes: The Teaching of the Basrian School of the Mu'tazila in the Classical Period* (Albany: State University of New York Press, 1978).

8. See for instance, Snouck Hurgronje, *Selected Works of C. Snouck Hurgronje,* ed. G.-H. Bousqet and Joseph Schacht (Leiden: E. J. Brill, 1957), 256. He says, "le droit musulman qu'on ferait mieux de désigner par le terme de déontologie (ou: doctrines des devoirs de l'homme)."

9. Muhammad Iqbal, *The Reconstruction of Religious Thought in Islam* (Lahore: Institute of Islamic Culture, 1986), 123.

10. Mufti Kifayatullah, *Kifayat al-mufti* (Multan: Imdadiyya, n.d.), 2: 25–40.

11. Ibid., 9: 371, 380.

12. Ibid., 2: 41.

13. Vardit Rispler-Chaim, *Islamic Medical Ethics in the Twentieth Century* (Leiden: E. J. Brill, 1993).

14. Ibid., 142.

15. Jalaluddin Umri, "Suicide or Termination of Life," trans. S.A.H. Rizvi , *Islamic and Comparative Law Quarterly* 7 (1987): 136–44; and Muhammad Rajab al-Bayumi, "Qatl al-marid al-mayus 'anhu," *Majallat al-Azhar,* January–February 1986: 674–78.

16. Rispler-Chaim, *Islamic Medical Ethics,* 95–97.

17. F. Rosenthal, "Intihar," in *Encyclopaedia of Islam*, new ed. (Leiden: E. J. Brill, 1986), 3: 1,246–48.

18. Masud, *Shatibi's Philosophy of Islamic Law,* 193–94.

19. See "Dr. Qaradawi criticizes the shaykh al-Azhar's fatwa forbidding suicide attacks in Palestine," December 5, 2001, at *www.qaradawi.net,* under "Fatawa wa Ahkam."

20. See for instance, G.-H. Bousquet, *La morale de l'Islam et son éthique sexuelle* (Paris: A. Maisonneuve, 1953); Salah al-Din al-Munajjid, *Al-Hayat al-jinsiyya 'inda al 'Arab* (Beirut: Dar al-Kutub, 1958); M. Abd al-Wahid, *Al-Islam wa mushkilat al-jinsiyya* (Cairo: 'Isa al-Babi, 1961); A. Bouhdiba, *La sexualité en*

Islam (Paris: Presses Universitaires de France, 1975); Basim Musallam, *Sex and Society in Islam* (Cambridge: Cambridge University Press, 1983).

21. For references, see "Liwat," in *Encylopaedia of Islam*, new ed. (Leiden: E. J. Brill, 1986), 5: 777.

22. Al-Jahiz, *Mufakharat al-jawari wa'l-ghilman*, cited in ibid.

23. Norman Daniel, *Islam and the West* (Edinburgh: Edinburgh University Press, 1960), 141–45.

24. For a detailed analysis of this aspect, see Rebecca Joubin, "Islam and Arabs through the Eyes of the *Encyclopédie*: The "Other" as a Case of French Cultural Self-Criticism," *International Journal of Middle East Studies* 32:2 (May 2000): 197–217.

8

Islamic Ethics in International Society

SOHAIL H. HASHMI

> [Mahomet] prit de la morale du Christianisme
> et du Judaisme, ce qui lui sembla le plus
> convenable aux peuples des climats chauds.
> —M. *Savary*, Le Coran, *1783*

FOR THE past fourteen centuries, Westerners have not known quite what to think of Islam. Western and Islamic civilizations are inextricably linked in origins, histories, and even, to a large degree, ethical values, and yet the encounter has been far from easy. Medieval Europeans considered Islam, as Albert Hourani has observed, "with a mixture of fear, bewilderment and uneasy recognition of a kind of spiritual kinship."[1] Modern Europeans puzzled over the place of Islam in their emerging "international society." Today, Islam still remains a source of confusion and concern for many in the West. At the end of the twentieth century, many scholars of international politics are returning to an emphasis on civilizations—not individuals or states—as the most significant unit of analysis for studying international relations. Often they conclude that international society will, for the foreseeable future, consist of civilizations that clash rather than cooperate.[2] Islamic civilization emerges in this literature as the most potent remaining threat to building a liberal international order.

My purpose in this chapter is not to enter this debate, at least not directly. Rather, I intend to present, first, the range of ideas that characterize both historical and contemporary Islamic thought on the character and structure of international society, and, second, my own suggestions for a normative Islamic framework for the evolution of international society. My suggestions assume the need for Muslims to disentangle Islamic ethics from medieval Islamic law (*shari'a*); to understand the Qur'an and the traditions (*sunna*) of the Prophet in their historical context; and to elaborate new principles of shari'a on issues relating to international society by treating the Qur'an as a complete ethical system.

Two points should be emphasized at the outset of any discussion of

Islam in contemporary international politics. First, it is important to appreciate the unity as well as diversity in Islamic ethical and political thought. The unity emerges from a consensus among virtually all Muslim communities on the authenticity of the Qur'anic text as it exists today. Moreover, there is general agreement among all four Sunni schools of jurisprudence as well as the dominant Shi'ite school on the authenticity of the Prophetic sayings and actions (*hadith*) as found in authoritative medieval collections. Although the interpretation of specific traditions has generated controversy among Muslim scholars since the earliest period, their disputes do not challenge the general and consistent moral framework that emerges from the corpus of the hadith literature.

The existence of a consensus among Muslims regarding the authenticity of the "canonical" sources for an Islamic ethical framework does not, however, lessen the significance of the diversity in medieval and modern moral reasoning. As critics of the "clash of civilizations" thesis have pointed out, the greatest danger of such an emphasis on civilizations is to make them into holistic, nonporous units. There is nothing, of course, more porous than the boundaries of civilizations. Islamic civilization is no exception. Indeed, Islamic civilization has historically evinced a strong syncretistic inclination, adapting easily to specific cultural conditions as the Islamic faith spread through Africa, Asia, and Europe. It is utterly meaningless today to speak of an Islamic "tradition" or "civilization" as a monolithic force operating in international politics.

This brings us to the second point: Islamic thought today is in a state of flux. This situation is particularly acute in Islamic political thought, for Muslims have yet to formulate a coherent response to European political ideas that began to spread in Muslim countries in the nineteenth century. Western thought has provoked opinions about the constitution of a legitimate Islamic political order across a wide ideological spectrum. The current "Islamic revival," manifested in diverse forms in virtually all Muslim societies, is part of a two-century-old Muslim response to a world order shaped and ruled by the West. Since no "authoritative" body exists to interpret and codify the "orthodox" Islamic position, this response is likely to be the source of controversy and conflict well into the next century.

Islamic Ethics: Universalistic or Particularistic?

The Qur'an is the source of Islamic ethics, yet it is not a book on Islamic ethics. Human beings have been left to discern God's purpose for His creation from within the 6,236 verses revealed in Arabic to the prophet Muhammad over the course of twenty-three years. Throughout this period, the Qurʾan addresses itself to *all* human beings (39:41); its ethical framework is presented as one of universal applicability, "a message to all the worlds" (81:27). For the Prophet's community, and for all successive Muslim communities, the Qurʾan was accepted as a matter of faith to be the basis of Islamic ethics and law, God's final revelation to man.

And yet what of those human beings who choose not to accept the Qurʾan as God's revelation or faith in God as the basis of any ethical system? How can a system of religious ethics, though claiming universal relevance, transcend the particularism of faith?

The Qurʾan is aware of this concern and implicitly addresses it in a single enigmatic verse:

> When your Lord drew forth from the Children of Adam, from their loins, their descendants, and made them testify concerning themselves [saying] "Am I not your Lord?" they said, "Yes, we do testify" [this], lest you should say on the Day of Judgment: "Of this we were unaware." (7:172)

Despite the human proclivity to stray from God's commandments or to deny them altogether, each human soul is party to a primeval covenant, a covenant linking it with all other created things who acknowledge their Lord. The covenant establishes the reality of a human conscience, an ingrained awareness within each human being not only of the existence of God, but also of God's laws, so that when divine justice is ultimately dispensed, no soul can plead innocence through ignorance.

How do human beings discern God's laws? For medieval Muslim scholars, the answer was self-evident: through God's final revelation, the Qurʾan, as interpreted and enforced by the traditions of the Prophet. But what if the Qurʾan and the sunna are silent or ambiguous on a specific issue? The legal controversy that inevitably arose on this point in turn fueled a broader theological controversy on the question: What makes God's laws "good" or "right"? Although the debate was conducted by a range of writers over two centuries, it centered on the ethical objectivism favored by the Muʿtazilites and the ethical voluntarism argued by the Ashʿarites.

The earliest schools of Islamic jurisprudence were established by men advocating *ijtihad al-raʾy* (legal judgment based on reason). The advocates of *raʾy* found support in the ethical objectivism of the Muʿtazilites. Revelation could be supplemented by reason, the Muʿtazilites argued, because truth and falsehood, right and wrong, are objective categories independent of God's will. Revelation supplements reason in confirming the value of certain actions, particularly those involving man's obligations toward God, such as prayer, fasting, etc. Nevertheless, reason unaided by revelation is adequate in confirming the specific dictates of revelation. Although the Qur'an presents alms-giving as good action by virtue of divine command, for example, reason also demonstrates the value of charity in fostering individual virtue and promoting social welfare.

The early juristic preference for ra'y was steadily challenged by later schools who espoused *ijtihad al-qiyas* (legal interpretation based on analogy). Instead of being guided by the public welfare and principles of equity, the jurist was to deduce law through strict analogy with cases in the Qur'an and sunna. This shift away from an emphasis on reason in legal interpretation was mirrored by the rise of the Ash-'arite school, which fiercely denounced the ethical objectivism of the Mu'tazilites. The Ash'arites held that God's power could not be subject to any objective ethical values; rather, ethical value was derived entirely from God's command. Man discovers right action through God's grace to His creation, through the scriptures, and through the actions of divinely inspired prophets. These sources of divine law are the only arbiters of the moral content of specific actions. "He who does not validly know the law," Abu al-Qasim al-Ansari (d. 1118) wrote, "does not validly know that a bad action is bad."[3]

By the twelfth century, in part for political reasons that had nothing to do with the intellectual merits of either position, the Ash'arite view had emerged as the orthodoxy in Sunni intellectual circles. The triumph of the Ash'arites had profound consequences for the evolution of Islamic conceptions of ethics, philosophy, and law in general, especially with regard to questions concerning international society. The emphasis on revelation placed those most familiar with revelation, the *'ulama*, in a privileged position, while increasing political instability coupled with pressures from various Abbasid rulers forced the 'ulama toward greater conservatism in their legal interpretation.[4] In the tenth and eleventh centuries, further development of the law was seriously curtailed with the "closing of the gates of ijtihad." While this event was more mythical than real—for legal interpretation continued—the ethos that gripped Islamic scholarship was deeply resistant to critical inquiry and change. The consequences for Islamic political thought were particularly dire. The fact that the work of an eighth-century jurist, al-Shaybani (d. 804), remains today an essential source on international relations typifies the stagnation of Islamic political thought.

Another consequence of the Ash'arites' victory was emphasis on the particularistic over the universalistic aspects of the Qur'anic reve-

lation. Human beings could gain true knowledge of right and wrong
only by strict adherence to God's revealed will, as codified in the
shari'a. This emphasis on the law, as George Hourani has observed,
"must have undermined the confidence of ordinary Muslims in their
ability to make sound ethical judgments."[5] Moreover, it could only
have heightened perceptions of the exclusiveness of the Muslim community: if even the ordinary Muslim could not be confident of ethical
behavior without strict conformity to shari'a, then how much more
astray must the non-Muslim be?

Although the Mu'tazilites ceased to exist as a distinct theological
school by the thirteenth century, their arguments continued to figure
in later theological disputes. Their emphasis upon reason as a source
of knowledge of God's will decisively influenced, in particular, the
development of Shi'ite theology and law. In Sunni Islam, echoes of
the Mu'tazilite-Ash'arite controversy may be heard in the discourse of
the Islamic revival beginning in the mid-nineteenth century. For modernists like Sayyid Ahmad Khan (d. 1898), Muhammad 'Abduh (d.
1905), and Muhammad Iqbal (d. 1938), the rejuvenation of Islamic
culture could occur only through a reexamination of the shari'a in
light of modern conditions. This reexamination required the dis-
avowal of two cherished principles of Islamic orthodoxy: the literal
interpretation of the Qur'an and predeterminism. In reopening the
Qur'an to interpretation, the modernists resorted to the instrument of
the earliest Muslim jurists, ijtihad al-ra'y, human reason guided by
principles of equity and public interest. In opposing predeterminism,
they found scriptural support in the Qur'anic verse: "Truly God does
not change the state of a people until they change their own state"
(13:12). Muslim history went horribly astray, the modernists argued,
when Muslims abjured a central principle of Islamic ethics: man's
moral responsibility for his own fate.

Among contemporary intellectuals, Fazlur Rahman (d. 1988) has
made particularly important contributions in applying a rationalist,
modernist approach to Islamic reform. In several essays on Islamic
ethics, Rahman argues that the Qur'anic message should be seen not
as a series of legal pronouncements, but essentially as a moral code
upon which a legal system can be constructed. The "right" legal principles, Rahman suggests, are those that foster the just and equitable
social order that the Qur'an consistently promotes, when it is considered as a complete and consistent ethical system. He is, in effect, rejecting Ash'arite voluntarism when he writes: "This is where the Muslim
legal tradition, which essentially regarded the Qur'an as a lawbook and
not *the religious source* of the law, went so palpably wrong."[6]

Of course, opening the Qur'an to reinterpretation will not lead all

Muslims to the same conclusions. Thus it was inevitable that the Islamic revival would be characterized by two competing visions, the second—for lack of a better word—being the fundamentalist. Fundamentalist thinkers such as Sayyid Qutb (d. 1966) and Abu al-Aʻla Mawdudi (d. 1979) share the modernists' concern with the malaise afflicting Islamic civilization. They also share the modernists' conviction in ijtihad as a necessary instrument for rethinking Islam. They diverge fundamentally from the modernists, however, on the substantive conclusions to which their ijtihad leads. Their reinterpretation of the Qurʾan ends not with a general moral code or an ethical framework; it ends with the confirmation of divine law, albeit a law more in keeping with the "authentic" message of the Qurʾan. The duty of the Muslim community (and ideally the Islamic state) is to apply this law, for "the basis of the Islamic message is that one should accept the shariʻa without any question and reject all other laws. . . . This is Islam. There is no other meaning of Islam."[7]

Both the modernist and the fundamentalist positions are based upon the claim of Qurʾanic authenticity. Both can be derived from the Qurʾan. How then are we to resolve the issue of the universality or particularity of Qurʾanic ethics? Are Muslims fated to remain forever mired in theological disputes on this point? Perhaps. But before we leave altogether confused the topic of Islamic ethics, we should turn to the Qurʾan itself.

A superficial reading of the Qurʾan readily indicates why Ashʻarite voluntarism and even more literalist schools emerged as the orthodoxy in medieval theology.[8] First, the Qurʾan clearly rejects human subjectivism as the basis of ethical value. The "good" or "right" are not simply what human beings believe them to be. The human intellect is incapable of *always* discerning truth from error. The Qurʾan frequently links right knowledge (*ʻilm*) with faith (*iman*) and contrasts it with following human desires and passions (*hawa*) (see in particular 35:8; 45:18, 23). Clearly the Qurʾanic message is that an individual or communal life not based on faith and submission to God's laws (*islam*) is one fraught with actual or potential moral turpitude.

But does the Qurʾan foreclose the possibility of *any* independent right moral judgment by human beings? Can there never be a righteous unbeliever in the Islamic view? The Qurʾan never directly addresses this issue, focusing instead on its central message: the virtues of faith over disbelief. As Hourani observes, "From its unquestioning simplicity, much of its religious force is derived."[9] Read straightforwardly, the Qurʾan again seems to preclude the possibility of righteousness without faith, consistently linking the two in the formulaic phrase: "Those who believe and do good deeds."

At the same time, the Qur'an accepts the fact that there will always be unbelievers. They are also part of God's unknown plan for humanity. Is the Muslims' relationship to them to be determined simply on the basis of their faith or lack thereof, or upon their actual behavior determined by their own moral understanding? I will explore some of the answers that Muslims have historically given to these questions in more detail below when considering the issues of human rights and international diversity. Here suffice it to say that I agree with the argument developed by George Hourani and implicitly embraced by the modernists. The Qur'anic text stresses the perils of a moral system based entirely on natural reason, but nowhere does it preclude the exercise of reason in the search for moral truths. Indeed, several verses suggest that reason is a correlate to revelation. God's presence and the truth of His laws are presented as accessible through human contemplation of nature and nature's laws. Several verses on this theme are prefaced by: "What will make clear to you (that is, your reason) . . . ?" and again "Have you not considered . . . ?" The rejecter of faith (*kafir*) commits a double act of rebellion, one against revelation, the other against his own reason.

Since the Qur'an leaves open the possibility of right moral judgment based upon reason, it must at the same time leave open the possibility that human beings are capable of moral action without faith. The objection that lack of faith will *sometimes* lead to wrong moral judgments and hence wrong actions can easily be dismissed. For not even faith can assure *absolute* knowledge of the truth or even more freedom from wrong actions. Whether good deeds alone are sufficient to earn God's grace in the afterlife is a question the Qur'an never addresses. But surely the Qur'an does envision, *in this life*, the possibility of an international society consisting of good believers and unbelievers as well as bad believers and unbelievers, each to be "brought back to God." "Then shall every soul be paid what it earned, and none shall be dealt with unjustly" (2:281).

Constitution and Legitimate Authority

Medieval Islamic thought on international relations was built on the premise that the Muslims form a distinct and separate community. This belief was derived from unambiguous Qur'anic verses and the practice of the Prophet. It led to the elaboration by medieval jurists of an international law (*siyar*) whose foundation was the bifurcation of the world into two spheres: *dar al-Islam* (the abode of Islam) and *dar al-harb* (the abode of war). Contemporary Islamic thought on international relations, I will argue, has moved away from this medieval bifurcation. Yet contemporary Muslim theorists—modernists as well as fundamentalists—agree that the Muslims are and should form a distinct multinational society within international society. I will begin, therefore, by considering the constitution of the Muslim community and then move on to Muslim views on the constitution of international society generally.

The Muslim Community

Shortly after his arrival in Medina in 622 c.e., the Prophet concluded a series of agreements that historians have preserved collectively as the "Constitution of Medina." These documents comprised, in essence, a "social contract," freely entered by all parties, that outlined the mutual rights and obligations of members of the Muslim community, the role of the Prophet, and the Muslims' relationship with non-Muslim residents of Medina. They established the framework for the first Islamic state and its dealings with outsiders. They also diminished tribalism as the basis for Muslim identity and society and replaced it with the community of the faithful, the Muslim *umma*. From that day, the belief that all Muslims everywhere form a single community has agitated Muslim theorists and activists, with far-reaching political implications.

The Qur'an endows the word *umma* (or its plural, *umam*) with a variety of meanings. The common element that emerges from its use with regard to human beings is that of moral community. Thus, mankind in its primordial state is described as having being "one umma" (2:213). It has since lost this unity, having splintered into a multiplicity of communities professing or denying faith in God. The disputes that divide human beings, the Qur'an suggests, arise from human folly, since God Himself is consistent in revealing His true nature to man through a series of prophets, each of them *muslim* (2:132, 128; 21:92). There is no objective basis for ethical diversity, only willful human distortion.

The Muslim umma, by accepting the truth of the Qur'an as revealed to Muhammad, is heir to the primeval contract that God made with all human souls on the day they witnessed, "Truly you are our Lord." All human beings are therefore potentially members of the Muslim umma. And now that the umma has been realized, it is the Muslims' duty, the Qur'an admonishes, to remain a cohesive community witnessing God's truth: "And hold fast, all together, by the rope which God [stretches out for you] and be not divided among yourselves" (3:103). The Qur'anic injunctions are augmented by several Prophetic traditions, including the famous "Farewell Sermon": "Every Muslim is the brother of every Muslim and the Muslims constitute one brotherhood."[10]

Historically, of course, this ethical injunction went unfulfilled almost immediately after the death of the prophet Muhammad in 632 C.E. The Muslim community was rent by disputes stemming from both politics and dogma, the most serious and enduring of these being the Sunni-Shi'ite split on the issue of legitimate authority. For the Sunni majority, the Muslim umma was viewed as constituting not just a moral or social community, but a body politic as well. Legitimate authority was invested in the single *imam*, who, as the *khalifat rasul Allah* (successor to the Messenger of God), was theoretically the man considered by the community to mirror most closely the qualities of the Prophet. But with the murder of the fourth caliph, 'Ali ibn Abi Talib, in 661 C.E., political power passed to a series of traditional dynasties.

Although historical realities diverged almost at once from the ideals of the united umma and the just imam, Sunni theory was slow to assimilate such changes. Al-Mawardi (d. 1058), the author of one of the most important Sunni treatises on political theory, still explicitly denies the possibility of two imams simultaneously existing, thus foreclosing the possibility of legitimate political divisions in the umma.[11] This theory is taken to an extreme by Ibn Jama'a (d. 1333), who suggests that anyone able to install himself in power, even though he is otherwise not qualified, is the rightful imam and Muslims are bound to obey him. The reason given for obedience to the usurper is, remarkably, so that the unity, and presumably the stability, of the Muslim community would not be disturbed.[12] The one check left upon the imam was the shari'a, whose integrity was to be guarded by the 'ulama. Any ruler who systematically violates or repudiates the shari'a ceases to be imam and it is incumbent upon the Muslim community to find another.

The theory problematically assumes that a usurper is not necessarily a tyrant. Better to tolerate the corruption of one law, that pertaining to legitimate authority, than to risk the overthrow of the law altogether. Though other theorists did not formulate the issue in such stark terms, the practical impact of Sunni theory was to establish an autocracy with little recourse available to the ordinary Muslim except an "appeal to heaven." That Sunni theorists would accept it reflects the extreme political instability that characterized the central Islamic lands throughout the medieval period.

An attempt to merge the ideals of caliphal authority with the realities of kingly power was made by Ibn Khaldun (d. 1406) in the *Muqaddima*. Royal power is subsumed under the authority of the caliph, because his duty is to establish an order that promotes the Muslims' well-being in this world as well as in the next. Ibn Khaldun notes differences of opinion concerning the possibility of more than one imam, but concludes that the welfare of the Muslims may require the presence of many imams ruling distinct and far-removed territories. This view, he acknowledges, is disputed among scholars.[13]

Six hundred years later, disputes over the constitution of the Muslim world and legitimate authority within it continue. Such disputes have, if anything, become even more vigorous in the twentieth century, as Muslims face the challenge of defining Islamic political life in a world shaped by others, and particularly according to the Western idea of territorial nationalism.

The ongoing discourse on the connections between nationalism, the territorial state, and Islam is exceedingly complex. We may, however, divide Muslim political thought into three categories. The first may be called the "statist" because it fully embraces the legitimacy of the territorial state. Its proponents tend to be secularists, and may be further divided into two groups. One strand of "Islamically sensitive" secularists attempts to appropriate, coopt, or coexist with Islam in mutually supportive but separate spheres. Islam is regarded as a key source of national identity but otherwise devoid of practical political significance. Another strand sees organized Islam as a threat to national integration or modernization and therefore attempts to eliminate Islam from public life. The secularists have yet to disentangle convincingly the link between religion and politics in Islam. Not surprisingly, they remain peripheral to Islamic political discourse.

The second category is that of the "Islamic internationalists." Its advocates are mostly modernists whose aim is to reconcile Islamic ethical ideals with prevailing realities. Their argument favors accepting separate Muslim states as the best way of meeting the needs of the different Muslim peoples. Yet they are quick to assert that their vision of nationalism does not eliminate the existence of international obligations that transcend the interests of individual states. Several modernist thinkers, including Muhammad Iqbal, ʿAbd al-Razzaq al-Sanhuri (d. 1971), and Mohammad Talaat al-Ghunaimi, have suggested that the concept of the umma requires at least some degree of transnational cooperation—a "Muslim League of Nations," to borrow Iqbal's characterization.[14] The existence of the Organization of the Islamic Conference (OIC) and a host of other multilateral Islamic institutions is testimony to the influence of these internationalist ideals.

The third category comprises those who may be called the "Islamic cosmopolitans," and who are often drawn from the ranks of fundamentalist thinkers. The latter argue that the division of Muslims into sovereign, territorially delimited states has no legitimacy in Islam because it violates the Qurʾan's ethics of Islamic universality and Muslim solidarity, and because it is a vestige of European imperialism intended to maintain the weakness of the Muslim community. Abu al-A'la Mawdudi, the founder of the most important Islamic party in South Asia, actively campaigned on these grounds against the creation of Pakistan during the 1940s. He was supported in this by a broad spectrum of religious opinion in India. Likewise, Ayatollah Khomeini described the territorial state system as the "product of the deficient human mind."[15] Iran was to be the center for the propagation of the universal Islamic revolution that would sweep away "unIslamic" regimes everywhere. Mawdudi and Khomeini eventually reconciled themselves to existing realities: Mawdudi settled in Pakistan and played a significant role in that country's politics for nearly three decades. Khomeini's later speeches extol the unique virtues of the Iranian nation. But even though Mawdudi and Khomeini proved willing to accommodate to political conditions, it would be incorrect to assume that they fundamentally altered their conceptions of Islamic political order, or that they ended their lives as Pakistani or Iranian nationalists.

The details of an Islamic international system and the legitimate means to bring it about remain only vaguely defined in the works of both modernists and fundamentalists. There is broad consensus on one point, however: judged according to Islamic ideals, the current state of Islamic international politics is woefully defective. The history of the Organization of the Islamic Conference illustrates the general discontent. In 1969, twenty-four Muslim states voted to establish an international organization to further mutual cooperation on the basis of the "immortal teachings of Islam." Ever since its founding, the OIC has been repeatedly assailed, particularly by the fundamentalists, for failing to act as an instrument of the collective Muslim community, rather than the assortment of fifty-six states who are today its real constituents. As the first truly universal Muslim organization, the OIC has come to be viewed by many as a "proto-caliphate," the potential embodiment of a distinct Islamic subsystem within the international system. Despite the vociferous attacks upon it in recent years for its dismal performance in the Gulf War and in the conflict in Bosnia, many Muslim activists continue to hope that the OIC may yet evolve into a political manifestation of the united Muslim umma, as the Islamic revolution triumphs in other Muslim states.

Islam in the International Arena

In the Constitution of Medina, Jewish tribes living in the town are declared to be an umma alongside the Muslim umma. Their religious autonomy is specifically guaranteed and they are brought within a "collective security" framework for the defense of Medina. Since the Jews entered the pact as a free and equal contracting party, the constitution may also be seen as the first "international" agreement in Islamic history.

Subsequent treaties between Muslims and non-Muslims continued the precedent established in Medina of acknowledging a broad sphere of autonomy for the "people of the book": Jews, Christians, Sabeans, and (by extension) Zoroastrians, essentially all the religious communities believing in a scripture that were known to the Prophet. But subsequent agreements between the Muslims and other scriptuaries were not premised on the equality of the contracting parties. Instead, the Muslims were clearly the superior party and the agreement took the form of a concession granted by the Prophet to the religious community.

The Prophet's approach toward non-Muslim communities may be summarized as follows: First, in accordance with revelation, he considered religious affiliation to be the basis of political organization. Second, recipients of earlier revelations were acknowledged by the Islamic state to be autonomous religious communities, to be governed in their communal affairs according to their own laws. But, third, in their relations with Muslims and other non-Muslims living within the Islamic state, the scriptuaries were to be governed by Islamic law. In return, the Islamic state was to assure their security and autonomy; they were to be *ahl al-dhimma* (protected people). These broad principles of the Prophet's practice continued to be applied by the first four caliphs as the Islamic empire experienced explosive growth.

Some two to three centuries later, jurists rationalized these historical events as the Islamic ideal, making it the basis of Islamic international law. As we observed earlier, their foremost concern was to ensure the application and preservation of the shariʿa. Without divine law, society exists on the brink of anarchy in this world and perdition in the next. This understanding of the religious law led inevitably to the division of the world into two spheres: dar al-Islam, where the enforcement of shariʿa regulated and harmonized relations among its constituent elements, and dar al-harb, where the absence of shariʿa was presumed to foster lawlessness and insecurity.

Nevertheless, the theory did acknowledge the existence of a rudimentary "natural law" applying to relations between the two spheres. The idea of an international society was very much a part of Islamic international law, making possible diplomacy and treaties, travel and commerce, and rules of war. One of the most important aspects of siyar was the guarantee of free passage or security (*aman*) which any Muslim could give to a visitor from the dar al-harb. The converse of this provision was the obligation of Muslims traveling or residing in the dar al-harb to obey local laws, unless, of course, those laws contravened essential aspects of Islamic worship.

Natural law for the jurists was, however, clearly an insufficient basis for ordering international society. An emphasis on God's command as the ultimate source of legal validity led to a view of the dar al-Islam/dar al-harb relationship as one of active ideological contestation. The jurists' concern was to universalize application of the shari'a, their ultimate goal being to propagate the Islamic faith. If a non-Muslim government permitted the peaceful preaching of Islam within its domain, no ground for war emerged. Only if such preaching were foreclosed could the imam initiate war aimed at absorbing that territory into the dar al-Islam.

Jurists of the Shafi'i school interposed, between dar al-Islam and dar al-harb, a third category, *dar al-sulh* (or *dar al-'ahd*), the "abode of truce," comprising non-Muslim communities with which the Islamic state had treaty relations. According to al-Shafi'i, the truce could be contracted by the imam if necessity or the welfare of the Muslims required it. But the Shafi'i theory only suspended, not eliminated, the "contest." According to a precedent established by the Prophet's agreement with the pagan tribes of Mecca, the truce could not exceed ten years.

Muslim state practice never fully conformed to the theory, of course. As the dar al-Islam itself became factionalized, various Muslim rulers found support in the dar al-harb for their political ambitions. Yet the general outlines of the theory were never challenged or reformulated. The lingering influence of the medieval theory can be seen in nineteenth-century disputes among Indian 'ulama on whether British India was or was not part of dar al-Islam.

What is the status of the medieval theory today? If formal Muslim accession to the prevailing international legal regime were to determine the answer, then the medieval theory would have to be considered totally obsolete. All the Muslim-majority states are members of the United Nations. In fact, all (except the charter members) petitioned for membership within the first two years of independence. Moreover, the overwhelming majority of these states are signatories to the principal international treaties codifying international law and governing economic relations, environmental policy, and human rights. Nor does the evidence for the obsolescence of medieval theory end here. All the principles guiding relations among members of the OIC that are listed in its charter are derived from the UN Charter. These include the principles of sovereignty and equality of states, noninterference in domestic affairs, and prohibition of the use or the threat of force. Where, then, is the putative "Islamic revolt"?

The answer is not to be found in the militancy of radical Islam, which, despite its prominence in the international media, represents only a small part of Muslim opinion. Rather, it is to be found at the level of political discourse, which constrains policy options and pressures state elites to "Islamicize" their political programs. Today, every Muslim leader must make concessions to Islamic values. At the international level, such pressures were apparent when the OIC voted in 1980 to create an International Islamic Law Commission "to devise ways and means to secure representation in order to put forward the Islamic point of view before the International Court of Justice and such other institutions of the United Nations when a question requiring the projection of Islamic views arises therein."[16] This body has yet to convene, largely because the government elites who voted to form it realize that its findings may pose a challenge not only to the Western-originated international system, but to themselves as well.

I would suggest that although Muslim states have accommodated to the prevailing international norms, these norms have yet to be assimilated into Islamic political thought. These states have formally committed themselves to the principles of international law, but there has yet to occur a theoretical incorporation of these principles into a coherent, modern elaboration of Islamic international law. With or without the deliberations of the (still nonexistent) International Islamic Law Commission, Islamic discourse on international relations will remain for some time to come at the normative level, directed at what Islamic law *ought* to say on international issues. The medieval theory will continue to serve as a reference, even as modernists and fundamentalists redefine medieval views on dar al-Islam, dar al-harb, and jihad.

The modernist approach is characterized by the outright rejection of the medieval concepts or by a selective reinterpretation intended to assert the essentially nonbelligerent character of these concepts. Representative of the first approach is Mohammad Talaat al-Ghunaimi, who points out that the term *dar al-harb* is not mentioned in the Qur'an and therefore that the medieval categories have no Qur'anic basis. The theory, he concludes, is nothing more than a reflection of the historical circumstances of Abbasid jurists, and is not applicable to modern Islamic political life.[17] Marcel Boisard typifies the second approach, arguing that though the dar al-Islam/dar al-harb distinction is an intrinsic part of Islamic doctrine, it does not imply a permanent state of war between Muslims and non-Muslims. Dar al-harb is only that state where active oppression, corruption, and injustice are found, a state with which dar al-Islam obviously cannot coexist. If these conditions are present in a Muslim state, it "is identified with the 'world of war' even if its leaders claim to be Muslims."[18]

Boisard's reasoning is strikingly similar to that of the contemporary fundamentalists. Because the shari'a is today enforced in only a few Muslim states, the Muslim world cannot properly be said to constitute the dar al-Islam, except in the loose sense of a shared culture or heritage. It is, they argue, better called *dar al-nifaq*, the "abode of hypocrisy." The most radical fundamentalist groups push the argument even further. In the often-quoted manifesto of Sadat's assassins, entitled *Al-Farida al-gha'iba* (The Neglected Duty), 'Abd al-Salam Faraj charges unspecified Muslim "rulers of this age" with apostasy because "they were raised at the tables of imperialism."[19]

Faraj's argument is representative of the fundamentalists' view of the international order. Their focus is on Western imperialism, which, they believe, continues in an unceasing war to destroy Islam. Muslim rulers who have allied themselves with the West have, in effect, declared war upon Islam. Though employing the terminology of the medieval doctrine of dar al-Islam and dar al-harb, the fundamentalists have given new content to these expressions. They may be viewed as providing an Islamic version of the broader third-world critique of dependency. When a Muslim revolutionary like Ayatollah Khomeini characterizes international relations as the struggle between the *mustakbaran* (the powerful) versus the *mustad'afan* (the oppressed), he is employing in an Islamic context the same imagery used by many other third-world leaders. A third-world orientation is clearly evident in Khomeini's foreign policy. The Islamic Republic of Iran did not withdraw from the United Nations or renounce its commitment to the majority of international agreements ratified by the shah's regime. It did, however, promptly remove itself from the American-backed Central Treaty Organization. Like other third-world critics, the fundamentalists challenge not the constitutional order of international society, but rather the injustices of that order.

Justice

Justice may be seen without oversimplification to be the core value of Islamic ethics, for it runs like a binding thread throughout the Qur'an and the Prophetic traditions. The Qur'an's conception of justice is one of universally applicable principles, valid for all human beings, regardless of their status as Muslims: "O you who believe! Stand out firmly for justice, as witnesses to God, even as against yourselves, or your parents, or your kin, and whether it be against rich or poor" (4:135). "O you who believe! Be ever steadfast in your devotion to God, bearing witness to the truth in all equity, and never let hatred of anyone lead you into the sin of deviating from justice. Be just: this is closest to piety" (5:8).

Acting justly to "witness" God's truth is, the Qur'an indicates, an individual as well as collective obligation. The Muslim umma is termed the "median" community (2:143) and also the "best" community (3:110), because it "witnesses" God's command to "enjoin the right and forbid the wrong." Both characterizations should be seen as normative, not descriptive. The Muslim umma is exceptional to other human communities only so long as it fulfills its Qur'anic obligations (47:38).

The personal and collective struggle to realize justice upon earth is the essence of jihad. S. ʿAbdullah Schleifer has described jihad as "the instrument of sacralization of the social-political order in Islam,"[20] that is, as the duty to ensure that Muslim society and politics never become too divorced from Islamic ethics. Underlying the frequent use (and misuse) of this term in contemporary Muslim discourse is the widespread feeling that the realities of Muslim collective life have indeed strayed far from Islamic ideals. For the fundamentalists of the 1930s and 1940s, the Islamic movement's goal was social transformation through education and moral reform. For their less patient offspring of the 1980s and 1990s, the goal is revolutionary imposition of shariʿa by an Islamic state of their own creation. In short, the object of jihad today—whether defined by modernists or by fundamentalists—is to realize justice within the Muslim umma. One cannot hope to understand the Islamic revival, in its many and varied manifestations, unless one appreciates this fundamental fact.

The range of specific issues that are addressed in Muslim discussion of international justice is, of course, vast. Here I can only comment on three of the most salient: human rights, democracy, and distributive justice.

Human Rights

Is there a conception of human rights in Islam? Debate on this issue has become so acrimonious that it threatens to obscure the real issue: the systematic abuse of human beings by states that explicitly or tacitly define themselves as "Islamic." Much Muslim writing on this topic is hopelessly apologetic, struggling to prove that Islam introduced human rights into the human vocabulary roughly a millennium before Western theorists "discovered" or even "appropriated" the idea. Much Western writing, in turn, is highly contentious, suggesting that the language of human rights is fundamentally alien to "Islam," which is usually identified solely with Islamic law (the shari'a). Yet no adequate discussion of human rights in Islam—or any other topic—can begin without distinguishing Qur'anic ethics from its historical interpretation expressed as law.

Medieval jurists clearly recognized a sphere of individual autonomy and privacy to be protected from state intervention or other arbitrary intrusion. They gave moral and legal content to this protected sphere in the form of "duties" rather than "rights." Surmounting the mutual duties of human beings and the mutual duties of rulers and ruled were the duties of all people to God. From God's "rights" (*huquq Allah*) stemmed all human "rights," because God has commanded justice for all His creation. A number of Prophetic traditions elucidate this point, insisting that "no one truly believes until he wishes for his brother what he wishes for himself," and that "the whole of a Muslim for another Muslim is inviolable, his life, his property, and his honor."[21]

These traditions establish the mutual rights of Muslims. But what of non-Muslims? This is an area in which the shari'a, as it has come down to us, is often at odds with modern conceptions of human rights. The discriminatory provisions of the shari'a, while understandable in their historical context, are not justifiable, I would argue, given a *complete reading of Islamic ethics*. The Qur'anic verses quoted above (4:135 and 5:8) are in themselves entirely adequate to establish equity and reciprocity as the defining principles in an Islamic approach to universal human rights.

A problem even more important than religious discrimination is gender discrimination. This issue is extremely contentious because gender relations intrude upon so many "sacred" realms, including the regulation of sexuality and reproduction and the structure of family. The shari'a contains many provisions that are incompatible with international statements on the rights of women, including the woman's status as a legal person apart from her male guardian, her rights in inheritance, her rights in marriage, divorce, and custody of children, her right to work, live, and travel without a male guardian. Again, I can only repeat an argument I have made before: the discriminatory provisions of the shari'a are based upon specific verses that were held by jurists to be legal injunctions. These verses are part of a broader *ethical* position that the Qur'an develops regarding gender relations. The primary result of this ethical position is to affirm women's moral *as well as* legal rights. It is historically undeniable that the Qur'an's legal injunctions—despite their discriminatory aspects—represent a significant advance from the status of women in pre-Islamic Arabia. So for medieval jurists there was no tension between the specific legal injunctions revealed for Medinan society and the general ethical framework. This is no longer true, however. Modern Muslims must, therefore, return to the full ethical context of the Qur'an in order to derive new legal injunctions regarding the status of modern Muslim women. Once again, the full ethical context leads us to the principles of equity and reciprocity, the logical derivatives of faith in the equality of all persons as creations of God.[22]

Democracy

The abuse of human rights is directly related to the lack of democratic institutions in the vast majority of Muslim countries. It is quite telling that the worst human rights abusers are also those Muslim regimes that openly assert that representative government is inherently incompatible with Islam. It is disheartening that such disingenuousness is accepted uncritically by many in the West who ought to know better.

So is there an Islamic conception of democracy? Medieval political theory, as we have seen, left little scope for popular participation in politics. By virtue of their enforcement of the shari'a, the caliph and his ministers were owed obedience. They were not obliged in any way to consult "the people," and though they were supposed to rule justly, there was no mechanism to remove an unjust ruler short of his death. And though European imperialism disseminated democratic ideals to the Muslim world, it did little to implement them. It did succeed, however, in connecting concepts of participatory government with a foreign, hostile culture in the minds of many Muslim activists. The choice facing Muslim peoples today is therefore a bleak one: authoritarianism, either in the name of secular nationalism or in the name of Islam. The modernist advocacy of democracy has been squeezed virtually out of existence by the two.

Virtually, but not completely: Muslim societies are not immune to the slow but steady spread of democratic aspirations throughout the world, and organizations espousing democracy and human rights have in fact sprung up all over the Muslim world during the past decade. More often than not, demands for democracy are being made in the name of Islam.

The Qur'an provides little guidance regarding the form of government God ordains for man. Muslim advocates of democracy have latched on to one brief reference to the believers as those who "conduct their affairs by mutual consultation (*shura bainahum*)" (42:38). Because the Qur'an is not explicit on this issue, I believe that the soundest argument for representative government is to be found in Islamic ethics. If social justice is best realized within a democratic framework, as I believe human experience has shown, then this is the form of government that Islam requires.

Discussions of democracy in Islam also raise questions about the status of religious minorities. *Dhimmi* status often meant political discrimination against non-Muslims as well as discrimination in personal relations. Though most of the discriminatory practices found in the shari'a can be dealt with in the same way we dealt with human rights issues, the *jizya* (poll tax), which is explicitly mentioned in the Qur'an (9:29), remains a problematic issue within a democratic framework based upon the legal equality of citizens. Although jizya was treated by some medieval writers as a badge of the dhimmis' subordinate status within the Islamic state, that was not its legal rationale. Jizya was levied upon dhimmis in compensation for their exemption from military service in the Muslim forces. If dhimmis joined Muslims in their mutual defense against an outside aggressor, the jizya was not levied.[23] It can therefore be argued that in a modern Islamic state where all citizens bear equal responsibilities of citizenship, the jizya has become redundant.

Distributive Justice

The Muslim world today includes some of the world's most fabulously wealthy states at one end of the spectrum, and some of the most hopelessly impoverished at the other. There are few countries in the middle. Signs of discontent born of poverty and economic stagnation are legion. The Islamic movements gain their most ardent supporters from the ranks of unemployed or underemployed youth in the slums of every major Muslim city. Because the gap between rich and poor continues to grow, distributive justice may well prove the most explosive issue within the Muslim world of the coming century.

In recent years, distributive justice has emerged as an important topic in discussions among Muslim scholars of "Islamic economics." Underlying these discussions is the strong Islamic ethic of providing basic subsistence for the most disadvantaged members of society. This is both an individual obligation of personal piety as well as a state responsibility for social welfare. The ethical principle is formalized as one of the five "pillars of faith" in the form of a tax on surplus wealth (*zakat*), which is to be collected by the state and used to improve the conditions of the poorest members of society.

Unfortunately, discussions of distributive justice so far have remained at a highly theoretical level. They do little but reaffirm the obligations of "Islamic society" without specifying the identity of that society in modern terms.[24] If the society within which redistribution is to take place is the individual Muslim state, then the satisfaction of distributive justice claims will do little to improve the lives of the poorest Muslims. And if society is defined inclusively as the Muslim umma, as many modernists and fundamentalists would insist it should be, then the discussion must move on to consider how, practically speaking, wealth is to be redistributed from the wealthiest to the poorest Muslim countries. The principles guiding this discussion should, I believe, be cosmopolitan ones: the welfare of the individual Muslim, and not the economic condition of the country as a whole, should be paramount. To focus on countries or states will only exacerbate the existing disparities in income within each state.

Diversity

The Qur'an seems to give contradictory guidance on the issue of moral diversity. In the earlier Meccan verses, the question of faith is left to be decided by God in the next world. As for this life, the Meccan attitude is best captured in the closing line of Chapter 109: "To you your religion and to me mine." Muhammad is consoled after his initial failure to convert the pagan Meccans, as well as Jews and Christians, in the following verse: "If it had been your Lord's will, they would have all believed, all who are on earth. Will you then compel mankind against their will to believe?" (10:99).

This attitude of tolerance seems to shift in Medina, where the Qur'an becomes more aggressive and exclusivist in its polemic against not only the pagans but also Jews and Christians. The Qur'an warns Muslims in Medina not to take unbelievers (4:144) and Jews and Christians (5:51) as *awliya*, a broad term meaning "allies," "associates," or "protectors." Moreover, the Qur'an in Medina sanctions for the first time the use of force against the Muslims' enemies. Later Qur'anic verses, revealed after years of hostility between Muslims and the pagan Meccans, desert Arabs, and the Jewish tribes of Medina, suggest a belligerent, irreconcilable attitude toward non-Muslims:

> But when the forbidden months are past, then fight and slay the pagans wherever you find them, and seize them, beleaguer them, and lie in wait for them in every stratagem [of war]. (9:5)

> Fight against those who—despite having been given revelation before—
> do not believe in God nor the last day, and do not consider forbidden that
> which God and His Messenger have forbidden, and do not follow the re-
> ligion of truth, until they pay the *jizya* with willing hand, having been
> subdued. (9:29)

For medieval jurists attempting to rationalize the military conquests
of the early Muslim caliphs, these two verses were read as providing
legal injunctions regulating relations with non-Muslims. The problem,
however, was how to reconcile them with the other, more tolerant
verses, as well as important Prophetic precedents. To resolve this dilemma, many jurists argued that the earlier tolerant verses (which,
according to one jurist, number one hundred and fourteen verses
spread over fifty-six chapters!) were abrogated by the two later, more
intolerant ones.[25] Unless the non-Muslims willingly paid the jizya,
they were to be fought until they could be incorporated as dhimmis
within the Islamic state.

On closer inspection, however, the contradictory nature of the
Qurʾan's attitude toward moral diversity is more apparent than real.
Let us examine first the claim that the Qurʾan became progressively
more exclusivist and intolerant over time. This argument cannot be
sustained by even a superficial examination of the chronology of revelation. As Fazlur Rahman has argued, the Qurʾan's attitude toward
its rejecters was developed during the Meccan period and remained
fairly consistent into the Medinan period. The view that pagan Meccans, Jews, and Christians are groups distinct from the Muslims is
already beginning to be articulated in the later Meccan period. This
view was, of course, elaborated and developed according to the
changed social and political conditions of Medina. Yet the argument
of some orientalists that the Qurʾan begins to emphasize the separate
character of the Muslim community only when the Prophet had been
rejected by Jews and Christians in Medina is not borne out.[26] And
instead of steadily moving toward an attitude of war with other religious communities, the Medinan chapters contain many injunctions
on toleration, including the most significant verse on this topic: "Let
there be no compulsion in religion; truth stands out clear from error"
(2:256).

If we turn to the content of the Qurʾanic message itself, we find not
changes or "breaks" but a consistent theme being progressively elaborated. The Prophet believed, from the earliest stages of his teaching,
that he was bringing, not a new revelation to mankind, but the original guidance given to all the prophets acknowledged by the Jews and

Christians, as well as the pagan Arabs, who considered themselves descendants of Abraham and Ishmael. The fault that the Qurʾan repeatedly assigns to these people is innovation in religion, resulting ineluctably in sectarian strife. The Jews and Christians bear a particular obligation in this matter, because as self-professed believers in the one God, they are capable of discerning the essential truth of Islam *as well as each other's faith.*

> The Jews say, "The Christians have nothing to stand on," and the Christians say, "The Jews have nothing to stand on," while both recite the same book. (2:113)[27]

The Qurʾan thus presents Islam as the affirmation and the summation, not the denial, of earlier religions. Muslims have no monopoly on divine grace, either in this or in the next world (2:62; 5:69). The Qurʾan invites Jews and Christians to join Muslims in emphasizing the essential similarities in their beliefs (3:64). And if we read in their full context the verses used by medieval jurists to rationalize discrimination against non-Muslims, we find again the Qurʾan's overriding concern with justice:

> God does not forbid you, with regard to those who do not fight you because of your faith, nor drive you out of your homes, from dealing kindly and justly with them, for God loves those who are just. (60:8)

But the Qurʾan does not stop with the mere toleration of diversity, which is unavoidable, given man's unique capacity for moral choice. Instead, it transforms this inevitable diversity into an opportunity to promote its own moral vision for human life on earth:

> To each among you have We prescribed a law and a way. If God had so willed, He would have made you a single people, but His plan is to test you in what He has given you: So strive as in a race in all the virtues. The goal of you all is to God; it is He who will show you the truth of the matters in which you differ. (5:48)

Conclusion

In the final years of the twentieth century, a time that some have suggested would be the end of ideology or of history itself, the oldest kind of ideology has resumed its role in fashioning history. The "return of religion" has left many people bewildered, frustrated, fearful. Indeed, human beings have amply demonstrated their capacity to make out of religion a divisive, exclusivist, often destructive force.

This face of religion, whether it calls itself Islamic, Jewish, Christian, Hindu, or Sikh, is very much in view today all over the world.

For many Westerners observing the turbulence of Muslim politics, Islam appears adversarial, militant, even inimical to Western values and to the international society they support. Certainly there are many Muslims who share the belief that the civilizations of Islam and the West are fated to clash. Yet, as I have tried to show in this chapter, the contemporary Islamic revolt is as much against internal demons as it is against the "Great Satan." The Muslim focus today is essentially introspective. Given the widespread perception among Muslim activists, across a wide ideological spectrum, that Muslim politics do not reflect Islamic ethics, calls for reform are aimed primarily at the Muslim states themselves and their relations with one another, not at the international system as a whole. The international system as a whole figures in Muslim discourse only to the extent that it impinges upon the development of the ideal Muslim subsystem.

The Islamic challenges to the broader international society concern not its structure or even its emerging norms of human rights, religious tolerance, and democracy. For many Muslims today, the notion of an international society founded on these principles is seriously threatened not by cultural pluralism or religious diversity, but by the equivocation shown by Western powers in enforcing them. International law is called into question by the uneven application of its principles by the very Western states who advocate it so ardently. International institutions, most importantly the United Nations, are suspect as having become absolutely subservient to Western interests. In the early part of this century, the Islamic revival was fueled in part by men who had returned from Europe thoroughly disillusioned with the moral crisis of Western society that took it headlong into two world wars. For many Muslim critics of international relations today, the twentieth century does indeed begin and end in Sarajevo.

There is another face of religion that social scientists often neglect, but that is crucial to the work of moral and political philosophers. This is the central role that religion has always played in defining the essential, timeless, and shared qualities of human life. Religion has always been the most powerful force for uniting human beings in moral community, for motivating them toward constructive and humane behavior, and for emphasizing the universalistic over the particularistic aspects of human existence. Religion can at times make international order difficult, but it can also contribute to the evolution of a truly universal, representative, and just international society. To grasp this potential of religion is the common challenge facing both believers and unbelievers.

Notes

1. Albert Hourani, *Islam in European Thought* (Cambridge: Cambridge University Press, 1991), 9.

2. Two of the most well-known and influential elaborations of this view are Bernard Lewis, "The Roots of Muslim Rage," *Atlantic Monthly* (September 1990): 47–60; and Samuel P. Huntington, "The Clash of Civilizations?" *Foreign Affairs* 72 (Summer 1993): 22–49.

3. Quoted in Richard Frank, "Moral Obligation in Classical Muslim Theology," *Journal of Religious Ethics* 11 (1983): 208.

4. George Hourani, *Reason and Tradition in Islamic Ethics* (Cambridge: Cambridge University Press, 1985), 47.

5. Hourani, *Reason and Tradition*, 47.

6. Fazlur Rahman, *Major Themes of the Qur'an* (Minneapolis: Bibliotheca Islamica, 1980), 47.

7. Sayyid Qutb, *Milestones* (Indianapolis: American Trust Publications, 1993), 30.

8. I am indebted to Hourani's study of this topic in *Reason and Tradition*, 23–48.

9. Hourani, *Reason and Tradition*, 45.

10. Quoted in Muhammad Haykal, *The Life of Muhammad*, trans. Isma'il al-Faruqi (Indianapolis: American Trust Publications, 1976), 487.

11. Abu al-Hasan 'Ali al-Mawardi, *Al-Ahkam al-sultaniyya*, trans. E. Fagnan, *Les statuts gouvernementaux* (Beirut: Editions de patrimonie Arabe et Islamique, 1982), 14.

12. Muhammad ibn Ibrahim ibn Jama'a, *Tahrir al-ahkam fi tadbir ahl al-Islam* (al-Dawha: Dar al-Thaqafa, 1988), 56–57.

13. Ibn Khaldun, *The Muqaddimah: An Introduction to History*, trans. Franz Rosenthal (New York: Pantheon, 1958), 1:392–94.

14. Muhammad Iqbal, *Reconstruction of Religious Thought in Islam* (Lahore: Institute of Islamic Culture, 1989), 126.

15. Quoted in Farhang Rajaee, *Islamic Values and World View: Khomeini on Man, the State, and International Politics* (Lanham, Md.: University Press of America, 1983), 77.

16. 'Abdallah al-Ahsan, *OIC: The Organization of the Islamic Conference* (Herndon, Va.: International Institute of Islamic Thought, 1988), 36.

17. Mohammad Talaat al-Ghunaimi, *The Muslim Conception of International Law and the Western Approach* (The Hague: Martinus Nijhoff, 1968), 104.

18. Marcel Boisard, *Humanism in Islam* (Indianapolis: American Trust Publications, 1988), 154.

19. Quoted in Johannes J. G. Jansen, *The Neglected Duty* (New York: Macmillan, 1986), 169.

20. S. 'Abdullah Schleifer, "Understanding Jihad: Definition and Methodology," *Islamic Quarterly* 27 (1983): 121.

21. Narrated by Muslim, *Sahih Muslim* (Cairo: Dar al-Ihya al-Kutub al-'Arabiyya, n.d.), vol. 1:67 and vol. 4:1986.

22. The religious equality of men and women is firmly established in the Qur'anic verse 33:35.

23. See Louay M. Safi, "War and Peace in Islam," *American Journal of Islamic Social Sciences* 5 (1988): 39.

24. See, for example, the proceedings of the International Institute of Islamic Economics in Munawar Iqbal, ed., *Distributive Justice and Need Fulfillment in an Islamic Economy* (Islamabad: International Institute of Islamic Economics, 1988).

25. Mohammed Arkoun, *Rethinking Islam* (Boulder, Colo.: Westview, 1994), 97.

26. Rahman, *Major Themes of the Qur'an*, 163–65.

27. As Fazlur Rahman comments with regard to the meaning of "book" in this context, it does not mean "any specific revealed book" but is used "as a generic term denoting the totality of divine revelations." Rahman, *Major Themes of the Qur'an*, 164.

Part IV

WAR AND PEACE

9

War and Peace in Islam

BASSAM TIBI

ISLAM IS A SYSTEM of moral obligations derived from divine revelation and based on the belief that human knowledge can never be adequate. It follows that believers must act on the basis of Allah's knowledge, which is the exclusive source of truth for Muslims. Ethics in Islam, though concerned with man's actions, always relates these actions to the word of God as revealed to the Prophet, Muhammad, and as collected in the Qur'an. This understanding of ethics is shared by all Muslims, Sunni or Shi'i, Arab or non-Arab.[1]

In this chapter, I first identify the Qur'anic conceptions of war and peace that are based on this ethical foundation. I then consider several Islamic traditions pertaining to the grounds for war, the conduct of war, and the proper relation of Islam to the modern international system. I conclude that the Islamic worldview is resistant to change and that there are many obstacles to the development of an ethic of war and peace compatible with the circumstances of the modern age.

The basic scriptures of Islam, the Qur'an and the *hadith*, are written in Arabic. My effort here to understand Islamic thinking on war and peace focuses on the Qur'an and on interpretations of Islamic tradition in contemporary Sunni Islam. Because the most important trends in Sunni Islam have been occurring in the Arab world (all Sunni Muslims are, for example, bound by the *fatwas* of the Islamic al-Azhar university in Cairo), my references to the Arabic Qur'an, to the teachings of al-Azhar, and to authoritative sources for Islamic fundamentalism reflect not Arab centrism but the realities of Islam.

Conceptions of War and Peace

The Qur'an chronicles the establishment of Islam in Arabia between the years 610 and 632 C.E. In early Meccan Islam, before the founding of the first Islamic state at Medina, in a Bedouin culture hostile to state structures, one fails to find Qur'anic precepts related to war and peace. Most Meccan verses focus on spiritual issues. Following their exodus (*hijra*) from Mecca in 622, the Prophet and his supporters established in Medina the first Islamic political community (*umma*). All Qur'anic verses revealed between 622 and the death of the Prophet in 632 relate to the establishment of Islam at Medina through violent struggle against the hostile tribes surrounding the city-state.

Most debate among Muslims about the Islamic ethics of war and peace is based on literal readings of the Qur'anic verses pertaining to early Medina. Muslims believe in the absolutely eternal validity of the Qur'an and the hadith (the sayings and deeds of the Prophet). Muslims believe that human beings must scrupulously obey the precepts of the Qur'an. In addition, Muslims are generally reluctant to take a historical view of their religion and culture. Quotations from the Qur'an serve as the point of departure for discussions of war and peace.[2]

Qur'anic traditions of war are based on verses related to particular events. At times, they contradict one another. It is not possible, therefore, to reconstruct from these verses a single Islamic ethic of war and peace.[3] Instead, there are a number of different traditions, each of which draws selectively on the Qur'an to establish legitimacy for its view of war and peace.

The common foundation for all Islamic concepts of war and peace is a worldview based on the distinction between the "abode of Islam" (*dar al-Islam*), the "home of peace" (*dar al-salam*) (Q. 10:25), and the non-Muslim world, the "house of war" (*dar al-harb*).[4] This distinction was the hallmark of the Islamic system before the globalization of European society and the rise of the modern international system.[5] In fact, however, the division of the world in early Islam into the abode of peace and the world of unbelievers clashed with reality long before the intrusion of Europe into the Muslim world. Bernard Lewis, for example, argues that by the Middle Ages, the dar al-Islam was dismembered into a "multiplicity of separate, often warring sovereignties." Lewis also holds that "in international . . . matters, a widening gap appeared between legal doctrine and political fact, which politicians ignored and jurists did their best to conceal."[6] As we shall see, this refusal to come to terms with reality remains a hallmark of Islamic thought today.

The establishment of the new Islamic polity at Medina and the spread of the new religion were accomplished by waging war. The sword became the symbolic image of Islam in the West.[7] In this formative period as well as during the period of classical Islam, Islamic militancy was reinforced by the superiority of Muslims over their enemies. Islamic jurists never dealt with relations with non-Muslims under conditions other than those of "the house of war," except for the temporary cessation of hostilities under a limited truce.

The military revolution that took place between the years 1500 and 1800 signaled the start of modern times and, ultimately, the rise of the West and the concomitant decline of the world of Islam. Since the beginning of the seventeenth century, Muslims have tried to establish armies on the European model to offset the increasing weakness of the "abode of Islam."[8] The rise of the West as a superior military power ultimately led to the globalization of the European model of the modern state. The changed historical balance presented Muslims with a major challenge, for the dichotomy between dar al-Islam and dar al-harb is incompatible with the reality of the world of nation-states. Each of these changes created pressure for Muslims to rethink their holistic worldview and their traditional ethics of war and peace. But despite its incompatibility with the current international system, there has yet to be an authoritative revision of this worldview.

At its core, Islam is a religious mission to all humanity. Muslims are religiously obliged to disseminate the Islamic faith throughout the world: "We have sent you forth to all mankind" (Q. 34:28). If non-Muslims submit to conversion or subjugation, this call (da'wa) can be pursued peacefully. If they do not, Muslims are obliged to wage war against them. In Islam, peace requires that non-Muslims submit to the call of Islam, either by converting or by accepting the status of a religious minority (dhimmi) and paying the imposed poll tax, jizya. World peace, the final stage of the da'wa, is reached only with the conversion or submission of all mankind to Islam.

It is important to note that the expression dar al-harb (house of war) is not Qur'anic; it was coined in the age of Islamic military expansion. It is, however, in line with the Qur'anic revelation dividing the world into a peaceful part (the Islamic community) and a hostile part (unbelievers who are expected to convert to Islam, if not freely then through the instrument of war). In this sense, Muslims believe that expansion through war is not aggression but a fulfillment of the Qur'anic command to spread Islam as a way to peace. The resort to force to disseminate Islam is not war (harb), a word that is used only to describe the use of force by non-Muslims. Islamic wars are not hurub (the plural of harb) but rather futuhat, acts of "opening"the world to Islam and expressing Islamic jihad.

Relations between dar al-Islam, the home of peace, and dar al-harb, the world of unbelievers, nevertheless take place in a state of war, according to the Qur'an and to the authoritative commentaries of Islamic jurists. Unbelievers who stand in the way, creating obstacles for the da'wa, are blamed for this state of war, for the da'wa can be pursued peacefully if others submit to it. In other words, those who resist Islam cause wars and are responsible for them. Only when Muslim power is weak is "temporary peace" (*hudna*) allowed (Islamic jurists differ on the definition of "temporary"). The notion of temporary peace introduces a third realm: territories under temporary treaties with Muslim powers (*dar al-sulh* or, at times, *dar al-'ahd*).[9]

The attitude of Muslims toward war and nonviolence can be summed up briefly: there is no Islamic tradition of nonviolence and no presumption against war. But war is never glorified and is viewed simply as the last resort in responding to the da'wa to disseminate Islam, made necessary by the refusal of unbelievers to submit to Islamic rule. In other words, there is no such thing as Islamic pacifism.

The Grounds for War

The Western distinction between just and unjust wars linked to specific grounds for war is unknown in Islam. Any war against unbelievers, whatever its immediate ground, is morally justified. Only in this sense can one distinguish just and unjust wars in Islamic tradition. When Muslims wage war for the dissemination of Islam, it is a just war (futuhat, literally "opening," in the sense of opening the world, through the use of force, to the call to Islam); when non-Muslims attack Muslims, it is an unjust war (*'idwan*).

The usual Western interpretation of jihad as a "just war" in the Western sense is, therefore, a misreading of this Islamic concept. I disagree, for example, with Khadduri's interpretation of the jihad as *bellum iustum*. As Khadduri himself observes:

> The universality of Islam provided a unifying element for all believers, within the world of Islam, and its defensive-offensive character produced a state of warfare permanently declared against the outside world, the world of war. Thus *jihad* may be regarded as Islam's instrument for carrying out its ultimate objective by turning all people into believers.[10]

According to the Western just war concept, just wars are limited to a single issue; they are not universal and permanent wars grounded on a religious worldview.

The classical religious doctrine of Islam understands war in two ways. The first is literal war, fighting or battle (*qital*), which in Islam is understood to be a last resort in following the Qur'anic precept to guarantee the spread of Islam, usually when non-Muslims hinder the effort to do so. The other understanding is metaphorical: war as a permanent condition between Muslims and nonbelievers. The Qur'an makes a distinction between fighting (qital) and aggression ('idwan) and asks Muslims not to be aggressors: "Fight for the sake of Allah

against those who fight against you but do not be violent because
Allah does not love aggressors" (2:190). The same Qur'anic passage
continues: "Kill them wherever you find them. Drive them out of
places from which they drove you. . . . Fight against them until idola-
try is no more and Allah's religion reigns supreme" (2:190–92). The
Qur'anic term for fighting is here *qital*, not *jihad*. The Qur'an prescribes fighting for the spread of Islam: "Fighting is obligatory for
you, much as you dislike it" (2:216). The qital of Muslims against
unbelievers is a religious obligation: "Fight for the cause of Allah . . .
how could you not fight for the cause of Allah? . . . True believers
fight for the cause of Allah, but the infidels fight for idols" (4:74–76).

As noted above, Muslims tend to quote the Qur'an selectively to
support their own ethical views. This practice has caused a loss of
specificity in the meaning of jihad, as Saddam Hussein's use of the
term during the Gulf War illustrates.[11] The current dissension about
the concept of jihad dates from the rise of political Islam and the
eruption of sectarian religious strife. Present-day Islamic fundamentalist groups—groups whose programs are based on the revival of
Islamic values—often invoke the idea of jihad to legitimize their political agendas. The reason for this misuse of the concept is simple: most
fundamentalists are lay people who lack intimate knowledge of Islamic sources and who politicize Islam to justify their activities. Before the Gulf War, for example, this occurred in Egypt, during the
Lebanon War, and in the civil war in Sudan.[12] Through such overuse
and misuse, the concept of jihad has become confused with the related Islamic concept of "armed fighting" (qital). Therefore, there is a
great need for a historical analysis of the place of scripture in Islamic
tradition. Although Islamic ethics of peace and war are indeed mostly
scriptural, scriptural references can be adequately interpreted only in
a historical context.

As we have seen, Islam understands itself as a mission of peace for
all humanity, although this call (da'wa) can sometimes be pursued by
war. In this sense, the da'wa is an invitation to jihad, which means
fundamentally "to exert one's self" and can involve either military or
nonmilitary effort.[13] Jihad can become a war (qital) against those who
oppose Islam, either by failing to submit to it peacefully or by creating obstacles to its spread. Although Islam glorifies neither war nor
violence, those Muslims who fight and die for the da'wa are considered blessed by Allah.

During the very beginnings of Islam (that is, before the establishment of the city-state at Medina in 622), the revealed text was essentially spiritual and contained no reference to war. In the Meccan chapter al-Kafirun ("the unbelievers"), the Qur'an asks supporters of the

new religion to respond to advocates for other faiths in this manner: "You have your religion and I have mine" (109:6). In another Meccan chapter, the Qur'an simply asks believers not to obey unbelievers. Qur'anic verses from this period use the term *jihad* to describe efforts to convert unbelievers, but not in connection with military action. There is no mention of qital in the Meccan Qur'an. The Muslims then were, in fact, a tiny minority and could not fight. The verse "Do not yield to the unbelievers and use the Qur'an for your jihad [effort] to carry through against them" (25:52) clearly illustrates this persuasive rather than military use of the word *jihad*: in Mecca, the only undertaking the Qur'an could ask of believers was the argument.

After the establishment of the Islamic state at Medina, however, the Qur'an comes gradually to offer precepts in which jihad can take the form of qital (fighting). Although the Qur'an teaches the protection of life as given by God and prohibits killing, this norm has an exception: "You shall not kill—for that is forbidden—except for a just cause" (6:151). But it is misleading to interpret this verse as a Qur'anic expression of just war because, as noted above, the distinction between just and unjust war is alien to Islam. Instead, the verse tells Muslims to remain faithful to morality during the qital.

The Conduct of War

When it comes to the conduct of war, one finds only small differences between Islam and other monotheistic religions or the international laws of war. Islam recognizes moral constraints on military conduct, even in wars against non-Muslims. As in other traditions, two categories of restrictions can be distinguished: restrictions on weapons and methods of war, and restrictions on permissible targets. And, just as other traditions sometimes permit these constraints to be set aside in extreme situations, in Islamic law (*shari'a*) we find the precept "Necessity overrides the forbidden" (*al-darura tubih al-mahzurat*). This precept allows moral constraints to be overridden in emergencies, though the criteria for determining whether an emergency exists are vague.

Islamic doctrine regarding the conduct of war developed in an age in which the destructive weapons of industrial warfare were not yet available. The Qur'anic doctrine on the conduct of war is also shaped by pre-Islamic tribal notions of honor. The Qur'an asks believers to honor their promises and agreements: "Keep faith with Allah, when you make a covenant. . . . Do not break your oaths" (16:19). And: "Those who keep faith with Allah do not break their pledge" (13:19). It also prescribes that the enemy be notified before an attack.

Regarding permissible targets of war, Qur'anic doctrine is in line with the pre-Islamic norm of "man's boldness" (*shahama*) in strictly prohibiting the targeting of children, women, and the elderly. Consistent with this prohibition, as well as with the pre-Islamic tribal belief that it is not a sign of honor for a man to demonstrate his power to someone who is weaker, is the precept that prisoners be fairly treated (76:8–9). And because the goal of war against unbelievers is to force them to submit to Islam, not to destroy them, the rules of war forbid plundering and destruction.

Islam in the Age of the Territorial State

Like any text, Islamic scripture permits divergent readings or interpretations (*ta'wil*). I wish to turn now to a discussion of three divergent patterns of Islamic thinking about war and peace, each characteristic of a different period in Islamic history: the conformism of the Islamic scholar Ahmad bin Khalid al-Nasiri; the more recent conformism of al-Azhar; and finally, the contemporary fundamentalist reinterpretation of the concepts of jihad and qital. Conformism seeks to perpetuate, in an altered world, the traditional ethics and the religious doctrine on which it rests, whereas fundamentalism insists on the absolute truth of the religious doctrine.

The pattern of conformism is illustrated in Moroccan thought. Unlike most Islamic states, Morocco has been independent for more than three centuries. Moroccan dynastic history is state history, and is thus a good example of Islamic conformism. Morocco was the only Arab country the Turks failed to subordinate. Political rule in Morocco was legitimized by Sunni Islam in the sultanate (*makhzan*), just as Ottoman rule was legitimized by Sunni Islam in the caliphate. Though nineteenth-century Muslim thinkers in general were confused by the changing global balance of power, those Muslim ʿulama who stood in the service of the Moroccan sultan were in a better position to face the new reality. Ahmad bin Khalid al-Nasiri (1835–97) was the first Muslim ʿalim (man of learning) of his age to acknowledge the lack of unity in the Islamic community (umma), as well as Islam's weakness in the face of its enemies.

Al-Nasiri provided the legitimizing device for the politics of his Moroccan sultan Hassan I, even though he was reluctant to legitimize the quasi-sovereign Moroccan state and to repudiate the duty of waging war against unbelievers. Conformism like that of al-Nasiri remains the typical pattern among Muslim statesmen and their advisors, many of whom do not even know of al-Nasiri. This pattern is characterized by submission to international standards of law and conduct and acceptance of peaceful relations with non-Islamic countries. But it retains the traditional Islamic belief in the superiority of Islam and the division of the world into Islamic and non-Islamic realms.[14] Al-Nasiri continually refers to the "abode of Islam" (dar al-Islam), even though he has only his own country, Morocco, in mind.

Al-Nasiri based his case on two arguments, one scriptural and one expediential. He selectively and repeatedly refers to the Qur'anic verse "If they incline to peace, then make peace with them" (8:61), which becomes the normative basis for the peace established between Morocco and Europe. Al-Nasiri's expediential argument pertains to the conditions of the Islamic community (umma):

> No one today can overlook the power and the superiority of Christians. Muslims . . . are in a condition of weakness and disintegration. . . . Given these circumstances, how can we maintain the opinion and the politics that the weak should confront the strong? How could the unarmed fight against the heavily armed power?[15]

Despite these insights, al-Nasiri maintains that Islam is equally a "shari'a of war" and a "shari'a of peace." He argues that the Qur'anic verse "If they incline to peace, then make peace with them" rests on the notion of "Islamic interest" (al-maslaha). Under contemporary conditions, in al-Nasiri's view, the interest of Islam forbids Muslims to wage war against unbelievers:

> The matter depends on the Imam who is in a position to see the interest of Islam and its people in regard to war and peace. There is no determination that they must fight forever or accept peace forever. . . . The authority that cannot be contested is the opinion of the Imam [Sultan Hassan I]. . . . Allah has assigned him to fix our destiny and authorized him to decide for us.[16]

The neo-Islamic notion of maslaha is strongly reminiscent of the Western idea of the "national interest" of the modern state.

This pragmatic but submissive fatwa by a leading 'alim is reflected in the position of most contemporary 'ulama regarding war and peace. Their ethic of peace is implicitly determined by their view that non-Muslims are enemies with whom Muslims can, at best, negotiate an armistice (muhadana). The belief that true peace is only possible among Muslims persists, even though it runs counter to the idea of a pluralist, secular international society.

Today there are two contrary positions on the ethics of war and peace in Islam. The Sunni Islamic establishment, as reflected in the scholarship produced at al-Azhar university, continues the tradition of Islamic conformism, reinterpreting the Islamic notion of jihad to discourage the use of force. In contrast to this peaceful interpretation of Islamic ethics, contemporary Islamic fundamentalists have emphasized the warlike aspect of jihad, while also emphasizing the dichotomy between the dar al-Islam and the dar al-harb.

The authoritative textbooks of al-Azhar contain an ethic of war and peace characterized both by selective use of the sacred text and by free interpretation. Al-Azhar does not offer either a redefinition or a rethinking of the traditional ethics of war and peace in Islam; it simply offers one variety of Islamic conformism.

In the most authoritative textbook of this school, Shaykh Mahmud Shaltut asserts that Islam is a religion for all mankind, but acknowledges that it is open to pluralism.[17] Shaltut quotes the Qur'anic verse "We have created you as peoples and tribes to make you know one another" (49:13) to support the legitimacy of interpreting scripture at the service of pluralism. He also rejects the notion that Islam must resort to war to spread its beliefs, again quoting the Qur'an: "Had Allah wanted, all people of the earth would have believed in Him, would you then dare force faith upon them?" (10:99). War, he argues, is not a proper instrument for pursuing the call to Islam (da'wa). Because "war is an immoral situation," Muslims must live in peace with non-Muslims. Shaltut takes pride in the fact that centuries ago Islam laid the foundations for a peaceful order of relations among nations, whereas

> the states of the present [that is, Western] civilization deceive the people with the so-called public international law. . . . Look at the human massacres which those people commit all over the world while they talk about peace and human rights!

Peaceful coexistence should be sanctioned by treaties that "do not impinge on the essential laws of Islam."[18]

A two-volume textbook edited by the former shaykh of al-Azhar, Jad al-Haqq 'Ali Jad al-Haqq, continues the effort to establish the centrality of peace in Islamic ethics and offers a significant reinterpretation of the concept of jihad.[19] But, in line with Islamic tradition, there is no mention of states: at issue is the Islamic community (umma) as a whole on the one hand, and the rest of the world on the other.

In a chapter on jihad in the first volume of his textbook, Jad al-Haqq emphasizes that jihad in itself does not mean war. If we want to talk about war, he argues, we must say "armed jihad" (al-musallah), to distinguish between this jihad and the everyday "jihad against ignorance, jihad against poverty, jihad against illness and disease. . . . The search for knowledge is the highest level of *jihad*." Having made this distinction, the Azhar textbook downgrades the importance of armed jihad, since the daʿwa can be pursued without fighting:

> In earlier ages the sword was necessary for securing the path of the *daʿwa*. In our age, however, the sword has lost its importance, although the resort to it is still important for the case of defense against those who wish to do evil to Islam and its people. However, for the dissemination of the *daʿwa* there are now a variety of ways. . . . Those who focus on arms in our times are preoccupied with weak instruments.[20]

Jad al-Haqq also avoids interpreting the daʿwa as requiring the imposition of Islam on others: "The *daʿwa* is an offer to join in, not an imposition. . . . Belief is not for imposition with force." Earlier Meccan verses are quoted again and again in an effort to separate the daʿwa from any notion of qital or armed jihad. "Islam was not disseminated with the power of the sword. The *qital* (fighting) was an exception only for securing and also for the defense of the *daʿwa* (call) to Islam." Despite this substantial reinterpretation, however, the textbook insists on the traditional view of Islam as a mission for all of humanity, quoting the Qurʾan: "We have sent you forth as a blessing to mankind" (21:107).[21]

Al-Azhar believes that in the modern age, communication networks offer a much better medium than armed conflict for the pursuit of the daʿwa. Jad al-Haqq does not work out the details, however. He does not resolve the question of treaties between Muslims and non-Muslims, nor does he mention territorial states. Jad al-Haqq quotes the classical al-Qurtubi commentary on the Qurʾan.[22] According to this commentary, treaties creating an armistice (hudna) between Muslims and non-Muslims can be valid for a period of no more than ten years. The model here is the treaty of Hudaybiyya, negotiated by the Prophet with the Quraysh in a state of war: it was a limited truce. If the Muslims are powerful, they may not hold an armistice for more than one year; if they are militarily inferior, an armistice of ten years is allowed. There is no discussion of what occurs after that time, which implies that it is seen as heretical to revise classical doctrine and that there is no desire to review this doctrine in the light of changed international circumstances. The result is conformity or acquiescence to the new international system, but no effort to alter the classic categories.

Unlike al-Azhar conformists, who seek to read scripture in the light of present realities, Islamic fundamentalists are inclined to reverse the procedure: a true Muslim has to view reality in the light of the text. Islamic fundamentalism as a mass movement dates back to the 1970s, though its intellectual and organizational roots can be traced to 1928, when the Muslim Brotherhood (al-Ikhwan al-Muslimun) was created in Egypt.[23] The leading authorities on the political thought of Islamic fundamentalism are Hasan al-Banna, the founder of this movement, and Sayyid Qutb, its foremost ideologue. But they speak only for fundamentalism, which, because it is a recent trend within Islam, cannot be seen as representative of Islam as a whole—a mistake often made in the Western media.

In his treatise on jihad, Hasan al-Banna makes literal use of the Qur'an and hadith to support conclusions opposed to those of the Islamic conformists quoted above. According to al-Banna, the jihad is an "obligation of every Muslim" (*farida*).[24] *Jihad* and *qital* are used interchangeably to mean "the use of force," whether in the pursuit of resistance against existing regimes or in waging war against unbelievers. Fundamentalists follow the Islamic tradition of not considering states in the context of war and peace; the term "war" is used here to mean fighting among loose parties of believers and unbelievers, no matter how they are organized politically. And in contrast to traditionalists, who distinguish between the use of force to further Islam and wars of aggression ('idwan), fundamentalists apply the word *jihad* indiscriminately to any use of force, whether against unbelievers or against fellow believers whom they suspect of being merely nominal Muslims.

Al-Banna begins his treatise by quoting the al-Baqara verse referred to above: "Fighting is obligatory for you, much as you dislike it" (2:216). He continues with another quotation from the Qur'an: "If you should die or be slain in the cause of Allah, his mercy will surely be better than all the riches you amass" (3:158). And, "We shall richly reward them whether they die or conquer" (4:74). These and similar quotations serve as the basis for al-Banna's glorification of fighting and death in "the cause of Allah."

But al-Banna does not cite the tolerant Qur'anic verse from al-Kafirun, "You have your religion and I have mine," preferring instead to extend the obligation of the qital even against the "people of the book" (*ahl al-kitab*)—Christians and Jews—with the verse "Fight against those who neither believe in Allah nor in the Last Day . . . until they pay tribute out of hand and are utterly subdued" (9:29). Allah, he concludes, "has obliged Muslims to fight . . . to secure the pursuit of *al-da'wa* and thus of peace, while disseminating the great mission which God entrusted to them."[25]

With a few exceptions, the al-Azhar textbook does not treat the armed jihad (*jihad al-musallah*) as a duty for Muslims in the modern age. It downgrades the status of fighting (qital) while it upgrades the nonmilitary jihad against such evils as ignorance, poverty, and disease. In contrast, al-Banna draws a distinction between "low jihad" (al-jihad al-asghar) and "high jihad" (al-jihad al-akbar), ridiculing those Muslims who consider the qital to be a "low jihad." He considers this denigration of qital to be a misunderstanding of qital as the true essence of jihad: "The great reward for Muslims who fight is to kill or be killed for the sake of Allah." Al-Banna's treatise is in fact permeated with rhetoric glorifying death, which seems to legitimize the suicidal terrorist acts often committed by Islamic fundamentalists:

> Allah rewards the umma which masters the art of death and which acknowledges the necessity of death in dignity. . . . Be sure, death is inevitable. . . . If you do this for the path of Allah, you will be rewarded.[26]

It is clear that for al-Banna, peace is possible only under the banner of Islam. Non-Muslims should be permitted to live only as members of protected minorities under Islamic rule. In all other cases, war against unbelievers is a religious duty of Muslims.

The other leading fundamentalist authority, Sayyid Qutb, has revived the dichotomous Islamic division of the world into "the house of peace" (dar al-Islam) and "the house of war" (dar al-harb). He employs this dichotomy to establish that war against "unbelievers" is a religious duty for Muslims. Giving the old dichotomy a new twist, he coins the expressions "the world of believers" and "the world of neo-jahiliyya" (jahiliyya is the Islamic term for the pre-Islamic age of ignorance). For Qutb, modernity is nothing more than a new form of jahiliyya. Qutb claims that "the battle lying ahead is one between the believers and their enemies. . . . Its substance is the question kufr aw iman? (unbelief or belief?), jahiliyya aw Islam? (ignorance or Islam?)."[27] The confrontation, then, is "between Islam and the international society of ignorance"[28] —a confrontation in which victory is reserved for Islam.[29]

The large number of pamphlets industriously produced by Islamic fundamentalists during the past two decades seldom go beyond quoting passages from al-Banna and Qutb. Contemporary fundamentalists often cite passages like this from Qutb:

> The dynamic spread of Islam assumes the form of jihad by the sword . . . not as a defensive movement, as those Muslim defeatists imagine, who subjugate to the offensive pressure of Western orientalists. . . . Islam is meant for the entire globe.[30]

Qutb's repudiation of the mainstream conformist view that Islam resorts to war only for the defense of Muslim lands is central to fundamentalist thinking.

Qutb's influence is illustrated in Muhammad Na'im Yasin's 1990 book on jihad. The book develops an understanding of war between believers and unbelievers as a gradual process in which, in the last stage, "regardless of an attack of the Muslim lands by unbelievers, . . . fighting of Muslims against them ought to take place." Yasin then quotes the Qur'anic verse "Fight against the unbelievers in their entirety as they fight against you in your entirety" (9:36), commenting on the verse as follows: "The duty of *jihad* in Islam results in the necessity of *qital* against everyone who neither agrees to convert to Islam nor to submit himself to Islamic rule." He concludes that the ultimate "return to Allah cannot be pursued through wishful thinking but only through the means of *jihad*."[31] According to Colonel Ahmad al-Mu'mini, an officer in the Jordanian army, this offensive view of jihad must determine the military policies of all Islamic states.[32] Al-Mu'mini's views have been widely circulated.

As we have seen, some Muslims have made the effort to adapt Islamic doctrine to the modern international system, but many go only so far as to make pragmatic adjustments to the doctrine that mankind must either accept Islam or submit to Muslim rule. It is true that Islamic states subordinate themselves to international law by virtue of their membership in the United Nations. But although international law prohibits war, Islamic law (the shari'a) prescribes war against unbelievers.[33] Does the recognition of international law by Islamic states really indicate a revision of Islamic ethics regarding war and peace? Or does this recognition indicate no more than outward conformity of the Muslim world to international society?

Most Western authors on war and peace in Islam overlook the fact that there is no concept of the territorial state in Islam.[34] Therefore, Islamic thinkers view war as a struggle, not between states, but between Muslims as a community (umma) and the rest of the world inhabited by unbelievers (dar al-harb). In contrast, the classic treatise on Islamic "international law" by the Muslim legal scholar Najib Armanazi acknowledges that the international order established by the treaty of Westphalia—in which relations among states are organized on the basis of the mutual recognition of each other's sovereignty—is contradicted by the intention of the Arab conquerors to impose their rule everywhere. But despite this contradiction, Armanazi argues, Muslims do in practice recognize the sovereignty of states with whom they conduct relations on the basis of "the *aman*, customary law or the rule of honoring agreements ('ahd, 'uhud)." Nevertheless, "for Muslims war is the basic rule and peace is understood only as a temporary armistice. . . . Only if Muslims are weak [are their adversaries] entitled to reconciliation." And, he continues, "for Muslim jurists peace only matters when it is in line with the *maslaha* (interest) of Muslims."[35] Between Muslim and non-Muslim, peace is only a temporary armistice and war remains the rule.

In short, Muslim states adhere to public international law but make no effort to accommodate the outmoded Islamic ethics of war and peace to the current international order. Thus, their conduct is based on outward conformity, not on a deeper "cultural accommodation"— that is, a rethinking of Islamic tradition that would make it possible for them to accept a more universal law regulating war and peace in place of Islamic doctrine. Such a "cultural accommodation" of the religious doctrine to the changed social and historical realities would mean a reform of the role of the religious doctrine itself as the cultural underpinning of Islamic ethics of war and peace.[36] If this is correct, then Mayer's conclusion that "Islamic and international legal traditions, long separated by different perspectives, are now starting to converge in areas of common concern"[37] is far too optimistic. The convergence is limited to practical matters and does not reach to basic conceptions of war and peace.[38]

On the contrary, what we have seen, instead of convergence with Western ideas, is a revival of the classical doctrine of the dichotomy between dar al-Islam and dar al-harb. Muslim writers today commonly describe all the wars involving Muslim lands since 1798 (when Napoleon invaded Egypt) down to the Arab-Israeli wars and the Gulf War as "unjust wars" undertaken by the "crusaders" against the world of Islam.[39]

For Muslims, the modern age is marked by a deep tension between Islam and the territorial state.[40] In fact, there is no generally accepted concept of the state in Islam; the "community of believers" (umma), not the state, has always been the focus of Islamic doctrine. With a few exceptions, Islamic jurists do not deal with the notion of the state (*dawla*). As the Moroccan scholar ʿAbd al-Latif Husni writes in his study of Islam and international relations, recent defenders of the classical Islamic division of the world

> confine themselves to quoting classical Islamic jurists. In their writings we do not even find the term "state." This deliberate disregard indicates their intention to ignore the character of the modern system of international relations. They refuse to acknowledge the multiplicity of states which are sovereign and equal in maintaining the notions of *dar al-Islam* and *dar al-harb*.[41]

Though the Islamic world has made many adjustments to the modern international system,[42] there has been no cultural accommodation, no rigorously critical rethinking of Islamic tradition.[43]

Conclusion

In discussing the basic concepts of the Islamic tradition of war and peace, and their understanding by Muslims at the present, my focus has been on Muslim attitudes toward war. The ground for war is always the dissemination of Islam throughout the world. And in conducting war, Muslims are to avoid destruction and to deal fairly with the weak. Muslims do not view the use of force to propagate Islam as an act of war, given their understanding of the daʿwa as an effort to abolish war by bringing the entire world into the "house of Islam," which is the house of peace. For this reason, as we have seen, Islamic conquests are described by Islamic historians not as wars (hurub) but as "openings" (futuhat) of the world to Islam.

Despite the universal religious mission of Islam, the world of Islam was a regional, not a global, system.[44] The only global system in the history of mankind is our present international system, which is the result of the expansion of the European model. As we have seen, this modern international system has placed strain on the ethics of war and peace in Islam, generating the divergent responses of conformism and fundamentalism.

Islamic war/peace ethics is scriptural and premodern. It does not take into account the reality of our times, which is that international morality is based on relations among sovereign states, not on the religions of the people living therein. Though the Islamic states acknowledge the authority of international law regulating relations among states, Islamic doctrine governing war and peace continues to be based on a division of the world into dar al-Islam and dar al-harb. The divine law of Islam, which defines a partial community in international society, still ranks above the laws upon which modern international society rests.

The confrontation between Islam and the West will continue, and it will assume a most dramatic form.[45] Its outcome will depend on two factors: first, the ability of Muslims to undertake a "cultural accommodation" of Islamic religious concepts and their ethical underpinnings to the changed international environment; and second, their ability to accept equality and mutual respect between themselves and those who do not share their beliefs.

Notes

1. George Makdisi, "Ethics in Islamic and Rationalist Doctrine," in Richard G. Hovannisian, ed., *Ethics in Islam* (Malibu, Cal.: Undena Publications, 1985),

47. On the concept of knowledge in Islam, see Bassam Tibi, *Islamischer Funda-mentalismus, moderne Wissenschaft und Technologie* (Frankfurt am Main: Suhr-kamp Verlag, 1992), 80–93; and Tibi, "Culture and Knowledge," *Theory, Culture, and Society* 12 (1995), 1–24.

2. Representative of this method, and equally authoritative, is a book by the former shaykh of al-Azhar, ʿAbd al-Halim Mahmud, *Al-Jihad wa al-nasr* (Cairo: Dar al-Katib al-ʿArabi, 1968). This work is the point of departure for the other books published in Arabic that are cited here.

3. On this point, I disagree with Muhammad Shadid, *Al-Jihad fi al-Islam*, 7th ed. (Cairo: Dar al-Tawziʿ al-Islamiyya, 1989), the most widely known and au-thoritative study in Arabic on this topic, and with Majid Khadduri, *War and Peace in the Law of Islam* (Baltimore: The Johns Hopkins University Press, 1955). Both authors suggest, though from different points of view, that a con-sistent concept of jihad can be found in the Qurʾan. My reading of the Qurʾan does not support this contention.

4. Qurʾanic references are to the Arabic text in the undated Tunis edition published by Muʾassasat ʿAbd al-Karim b. ʿAbdallah. I have checked my translations against the standard German translation of Rudi Paret (Stuttgart: Kohlhammer Verlag, 1979), the new German translation by Adel Th. Khoury (Gütersloh: Gerd Mohn Verlag, 1987), and the often inadequate English trans-lation by N. J. Dawood, 4th ed. (London and New York: Penguin, 1974).

5. See Bernard Lewis, "Politics and War," in Joseph Schacht and C. E. Bos-worth, eds., *The Legacy of Islam*, 2d ed. (Oxford: Clarendon Press, 1974); Mar-shall G. S. Hodgson, *The Venture of Islam*, 3 vols. (Chicago: University of Chi-cago Press, 1974); Adam Watson, *The Evolution of International Society* (London: Routledge, 1992), 113ff.; and Hedley Bull, "The Revolt against the West," in Hedley Bull and Adam Watson, eds., *The Expansion of International Society* (Oxford: Clarendon Press, 1984), 217–28.

6. Lewis, "Politics and War," 173, 176.

7. See, for example, Beate Kuckertz, ed., *Das Grüne Schwert: Weltmacht Islam* (Munich: Heyne Verlag, 1992).

8. See David B. Ralston, *Importing the European Army: The Introduction of European Military Techniques and Institutions into the Extra-European World, 1600–1914* (Chicago: University of Chicago Press, 1990), esp. chs. 3 and 4.

9. See Sabir Tuʿayma, *Al-Shariʿa al-Islamiyya fi ʿasr al-ʿilm* (Beirut: Dar al-Jil, 1979), 217, 223ff.

10. Khadduri, *War and Peace*, 63–64. Khadduri concludes, I think prema-turely, that "at the present it is not possible to revive the traditional religious approach to foreign affairs. . . . The jihad has become an obsolete weapon" (p. 295). See the more recent survey by John Kelsay, *Islam and War: A Study in Comparative Ethics* (Louisville, Ky.: Westminster/John Knox Press, 1993).

11. See the Arabic text of the first call by Saddam Hussein to jihad in *Al-Muntada* (Amman) 5 (Sept. 1990), 21–22. The concept of jihad is considered by Kenneth L. Vaux, *Ethics and the Gulf War: Religion, Rhetoric, and Righteousness* (Boulder, Colo.: Westview Press, 1992), 63–86. See also James Piscatori, ed., *Islamic Fundamentalisms and the Gulf Crisis* (Chicago: American Academy of

Arts and Sciences, 1991), esp. the entry for jihad in the index (p. 259). Earlier, Islamic jihad had been interpreted in Western terms as a war of liberation grounded in the right of self-determination against colonial rule. On this topic, see Rudolph Peters, *Islam and Colonialism: The Doctrine of Jihad in Modern History* (The Hague: Mouton, 1979); Bassam Tibi, "Politische Ideen in der 'Dritten Welt' während der Dekolonisation," in Iring Fetscher and Herfried Münkler, eds., *Pipers Handbuch der politischen Ideen*, vol. 5 (Munich: Pipers Handbuch, 1987), 363–402; and Jean-Paul Charnay, *L'Islam et la guerre: De la guerre juste à la revolution sainte* (Paris: Fayard, 1986).

12. On Egypt, see Nabil ʿAbd al-Fattah, *Al-Mashaf wa al-saif* (Cairo: Madbuli, 1984), and Naʿmat-Allah Janina, *Tanzim al-jihad* (Cairo: Dar al-Huriyya, 1988); on Lebanon, see Martin Kramer, "Hizbullah: The Calculus of Jihad," in Martin Marty and Scott Appleby, eds., *Fundamentalisms and the State* (Chicago: University of Chicago Press, 1993); and on Sudan, see Bassam Tibi, *Die Verschwörung: Das Trauma arabischer Politik* (Hamburg: Hoffmann and Campe, 1993), 191–208.

13. See Shadid, *Al-Jihad fi al-Islam*.

14. The work of al-Nasiri has been republished in nine volumes: Ahmad bin Khalid al-Nasiri, *Al-Istiqsaʾ fi akhbar al-Maghrib al-aqsa* (Casablanca: Dar al-Kitab, 1955). I am relying on the comprehensive study by ʿAbd al-Latif Husni, *Al-Islam wa al-ʿalaqat al-duwaliyya: Namudhaj Ahmad bin Khalid al-Nasiri* (Casablanca: Afriqya al-Sharq, 1991), which examines al-Nasiri's work in its entirety. See also Kenneth Brown, "Profile of a Nineteenth-Century Moroccan Scholar," in Nikki Keddie, ed., *Scholars, Saints, and Sufis: Muslim Religious Institutions in the Middle East since 1500* (Berkeley and Los Angeles: University of California Press,1972), 127–48.

15. Quoted in Husni, *Al-Islam*, 141.

16. Quoted ibid., 149, 150.

17. Mahmud Shaltut, *Al-Islam ʿaqida wa shariʿa*, 10th ed. (Cairo: Dar al-Shuruq, 1980).

18. Shaltut, *Al-Islam*, 404, 409, 406.

19. Jad al-Haqq ʿAli Jad al-Haqq, for al-Azhar, *Bayan ila al-nas*, 2 vols. (Cairo: al-Azhar, 1984–88).

20. Ibid., 1: 277, 278–79.

21. Ibid., 1: 281; 2: 268; 1: 280.

22. Ibid., 2: 371.

23. See Richard Mitchell, *The Society of Muslim Brothers* (Oxford: Oxford University Press, 1969).

24. Hasan al-Banna, *Majmuʿat rasaʾil al-imam al-shahid Hasan al-Banna*, new legal ed. (Cairo: Dar al-Daʿwa, 1990), 275.

25. Al-Banna, *Majmuʿat rasaʾil*, 275, 287.

26. Ibid., 289, 291.

27. See Sayyid Qutb, *Maʿalim fi al-tariq*, 13th legal ed. (Cairo: Dar al-Shuruq, 1989); the quotation is from p. 201. For a commentary on Qutb's view, see Tibi, *Islamischer Fundamentalismus*.

28. Sayyid Qutb, *Al-Islam wa mushiklat al-hadarah*, 9th legal ed. (Cairo: Dar

al-Shuruq, 1988), 195. See also his *Al-Salam al-'alami wa al-Islam*, 10th legal ed. (Cairo: Dar al-Shuruq, 1992).

29. Sayyid Qutb, *Al-Mustaqbal li hadha al-din* (Cairo: Dar al-Shuruq, 1981).

30. Sayyid Qutb, *Ma'alim fi al-tariq*, 72.

31. Muhammad N. Yasin, *Al-Jihad: Mayadinahu wa asalibahu* (Algiers: Dar al-Irshad, 1990), 76, 77, 81.

32. Colonel (al-Muqaddam) Ahmad al-Mu'mini, *Al-Tabi'a al-jihadiyya fi al-Islam* (Constantine, Algeria: Mu'assasat al-Isra', 1991).

33. For an interpretation of the shari'a, see Ann E. Mayer, "The Shari'a: A Methodology or a Body of Substantive Rules?" in Nicholas Heer, ed., *Islamic Law and Jurisprudence* (Seattle: University of Washington Press, 1990), 177–98; and Bassam Tibi, *Islam and the Cultural Accommodation of Social Change* (Boulder, Colo.: Westview Press, 1990), 59–75.

34. The concept of an "Islamic state" (*dawla islamiyya*) is not found in the classical sources; it is a new idea related to the concerns of Islamic fundamentalism. See, among others, Muhammad Hamidullah, *The Muslim Conduct of State* (Lahore: Sh. Muhammad Ashraf, 1977); Abdulrahman A. Kurdi, *The Islamic State* (London: Mansell Publishers, 1984); and Bassam Tibi, *Die fundamentalistische Herausforderung: Der Islam und die Weltpolitik* (Munich: C. H. Beck, 1992). A more detailed discussion of the confusion between the terms "community" (umma) and "nation" may be found in Tibi, "Islam and Arab Nationalism," in Barbara F. Stowasser, ed., *The Islamic Impulse* (Washington, D.C.: Center for Contemporary Arab Studies, 1987), 59–74.

35. Najib al-Armanazi, *Al-Shar' al-duwali fi al-Islam*, reprint of the 1930 edition (London: Riad El-Rayyes Books, 1990), 226, 157, 163.

36. See Tibi, *Islam and Cultural Accommodation*.

37. Ann E. Mayer, "War and Peace in the Islamic Tradition: International Law," mimeo, ref. no. 141 (Philadelphia: University of Pennsylvania, Wharton School, Department of Legal Studies, n.d.), 45.

38. Because the Islamic perception of non-Muslims either as *dhimmi* (Christians and Jews as protected minorities) or as *kafirun* (unbelievers) is untenable in the international system, there is an urgent need to revise the shari'a in the light of international law. See Abdullahi Ahmed an-Na'im, *Toward an Islamic Reformation: Civil Liberties, Human Rights and International Law* (Syracuse, N.Y.: Syracuse University Press, 1990). This Islamic view of non-Muslims is incompatible with the idea of human rights, as an-Na'im clearly shows; on this point, see Ann E. Mayer, *Islam and Human Rights: Tradition and Politics* (Boulder, Colo.: Westview Press, 1991); and Bassam Tibi, "Universality of Human Rights and Authenticity of Non-Western Cultures: Islam and the Western Concept of Human Rights" (review article), *Harvard Human Rights Journal* 5 (1992), 221–26.

39. See Bassam Tibi, *Conflict and War in the Middle East* (New York: St. Martin's Press, 1993); and *Die Verschwörung*, 273–326.

40. For a different view, see James Piscatori, *Islam in a World of Nation-States* (Cambridge: Cambridge University Press, 1986), 40ff. I discuss this view in the introductory chapter of *Arab Nationalism: A Critical Inquiry*, 2d ed. (London: Macmillan, 1990).

41. Husni, *Al-Islam*, 59.

42. See the discussion above of the conformism of al-Nasiri and al-Azhar.

43. Bassam Tibi, *The Crisis of Modern Islam: A Preindustrial Culture in the Scientific-Technological Age* (Salt Lake City: University of Utah Press, 1988); Fazlur Rahman, *Islam and Modernity* (Chicago: University of Chicago Press, 1982); and W. Montgomery Watt, *Islamic Fundamentalism and Modernity* (London: Routledge, 1988).

44. Watson, *Evolution of International Society*, 112–19 and 214–18.

45. See Samuel P. Huntington, "The Clash of Civilizations?" *Foreign Affairs* 72 (1993), 22–49; and Bassam Tibi, *Der Krieg der Zivilisationen* (Hamburg: Hoffmann and Campe, 1995), esp. ch. 4.

10

Interpreting the Islamic Ethics of War and Peace

SOHAIL H. HASHMI

IF THEIR DISCOURSE on the Persian Gulf War is any indication, Muslims are hopelessly divided on the Islamic ethics of war and peace. One graphic indication of this division is found in the deliberations of the People's Islamic Conference, a group of Muslim activists and scholars from several countries originally convened to find a resolution for the Iran-Iraq War. During January 1991, in the weeks immediately before the Gulf War air campaign against Iraq, the conference was meeting simultaneously in Baghdad and Mecca, with the Baghdad group demonstrating sympathy with the Iraqi position and the Meccans supporting the anti-Iraq coalition. In the end, both groups issued communiques declaring their side's cause to be a "just" war, that is, *jihad*.

Muslim writers of many intellectual persuasions have long argued that Westerners hold an inaccurate, even deliberately distorted, conception of jihad. In fact, however, the idea of jihad (and the ethics of war and peace generally) has been the subject of an intense and multifaceted debate among Muslims themselves. So diffusely defined and inconsistently applied has the idea become in Islamic discourse that a number of religious opposition groups have felt compelled to differentiate their cause from competing "false" causes by naming themselves, tautologically, "Islamic" jihad.

Nevertheless, when the contemporary Islamic discourse on war and peace is studied in the context of recent historical events, including decolonization and the many conflicts in which Muslims have been involved, one can discern an emerging consensus among Muslim intellectuals on the current meaning of jihad. This consensus is by no means universal, and given the diffuse nature of religious authority in the Islamic tradition, debate on the ethics of war and peace is likely to continue. But as I hope to demonstrate, the concept of jihad in contemporary Islam is one that is still adapting to the radical changes in international relations that have occurred since the medieval theory was first elaborated. We are witnessing a period of reinterpretation and redefinition, one characterized by controversy and confusion about how the concept should be applied to contemporary events, but also by movement toward wider agreement on the essential points of an Islamic ethics of war and peace.

This chapter, in contrast to Bassam Tibi's presentation of the "basic religious doctrine," seeks to place the traditional legal discussion of war and peace within a broader ethical context. I begin by considering the conceptions of war and peace outlined in the two essential sources for any Islamic ethics, the Qur'an and practice (*sunna*) of the prophet Muhammad. These sections are necessarily to some extent exegetical, for my main contention is that a comprehensive ethical framework for addressing the question of violence in human society is present in the Qur'an and elaborated by the traditions of the Prophet. In the remaining two sections, I consider issues relating to the grounds for war and the means of war as treated by the medieval Muslim jurists. But my main purpose in these sections is to consider how these two categories of moral evaluation of war are today being reinterpreted by Muslim thinkers representing a wide spectrum of cultural and ideological backgrounds. The proper conclusion, I believe, is that Islam has more in common with Western ethical traditions than Tibi allows. Regarding the issue of the relationship between the Islamic tradition of jihad and the Western tradition of just war, I shall suggest that there is a growing convergence in conceptions of jihad and just war that permits a cross-cultural dialogue on the ethics of war and peace.

Much of the controversy surrounding the concept of jihad among Muslims today emerges from the tension between its legal and ethical dimensions. This tension arises because it is the juristic, and not the philosophical or ethical, literature that has historically defined Muslim discourse on war and peace. With the rise of the legalistic tradition, ethical inquiry became a narrow and secondary concern of Islamic scholarship. What we find from the medieval period are legal treatises propounding the rules of jihad and discussing related issues, but few ethical works outlining a framework of principles derived from the Qur'an and sunna upon which these rules could be based. With increasing political instability in the central Islamic lands beginning in the twelfth century, even legal development became moribund. The results have been particularly deleterious in the political realm. As Fazlur Rahman has observed, the stagnation of formal legal theory resulted in the increasing "secularization" of Islamic administrative law. As the dictates of the medieval Islamic law (*shari'a*) became anachronistic according to the demands of various Muslim states, jurists increasingly appealed to the notions of *maslaha mursala* (general interest) and *darura* (necessity) as justifications for various state practices.[1] The result has been the continual erosion of the ability of Islamic law to address contemporary political concerns and the reduction of Islamic ethics to the ad hoc application of principles to specific situations in a chaotic and unsatisfactory manner. One of the central dimensions of the current controversy concerning the shariʿa that is raging in the Muslim world—although it is not often phrased in this manner—is the need for a comprehensive Qurʾanic ethics as a precursor to the reform of law.

Conceptions of War and Peace in the Qurʾan

Ibn Khaldun observes in the *Muqaddima*, his celebrated introduction to a history of the world composed at the end of the fourteenth century, that "wars and different kinds of fighting have always occurred in the world since God created it." War is endemic to human existence, he writes, "something natural among human beings. No nation and no race is free from it."[2] Ibn Khaldun's brief comment summarizes rather well the traditional Islamic understanding of war as a universal and inevitable aspect of human existence. It is a feature of human society sanctioned, if not willed, by God Himself. The issues of war and peace thus fall within the purview of divine legislation for humanity. Islam, Muslims like to say, is a complete code of life, and given the centrality of war to human existence, the moral evaluation of war holds a significant place in Muslim ethical/legal discussion. The Islamic ethics of war and peace is therefore derived from the same general sources upon which Islamic law is based.

The first of these sources, of course, is the Qurʾan, which is held by Muslims to be God's final and definitive revelation to humanity. The Qurʾanic text, like other revealed scriptures, is not a systematic treatise on ethics or law. It is a discursive commentary on the actions and experiences of the prophet Muhammad, his followers, and his opponents over the course of twenty-three years. But as the Qurʾan itself argues in several verses, God's message is not limited to the time and place of its revelation; it is, rather, "a message to all the worlds" (81:27) propounding a moral code with universal applicability (39:41). From this commentary emerge broadly defined ethical principles that have been elaborated throughout Islamic history into what may be termed an Islamic conception of divine creation and man's place in it. In other words, although the Qurʾan does not present a systematic ethical argument, it is possible to derive a consistent ethical system from it.[3]

Why is humanity prone to war? The Qurʾanic answer unfolds in the course of several verses revealed at various times, the essential points of which may be summarized as follows:

First, man's fundamental nature (*fitra*) is one of moral innocence, that is, freedom from sin. In other words, there is no Islamic equivalent to the notion of "original sin." Moreover, each individual is born with a knowledge of God's commandments, that is, with the essential aspects of righteous behavior. But this moral awareness is eroded as each individual encounters the corrupting influences of human society (30:30).

Second, man's nature is to live on the earth in a state of harmony and peace with other living things. This is the ultimate import of the responsibility assigned by God to man as His vicegerent (*khalifa*) on this planet (2:30). True peace (*salam*) is therefore not merely an absence of war; it is the elimination of the grounds for strife or conflict, and the resulting waste and corruption (*fasad*) they create. Peace, not war or violence, is God's true purpose for humanity (2:208).

Third, given man's capacity for wrongdoing, there will always be some who *choose* to violate their nature and transgress against God's commandments. Adam becomes fully human only when he chooses to heed Iblis's (Satan's) temptation and disobeys God. As a result of this initial act of disobedience, human beings are expelled from the Garden to dwell on earth as "enemies to each other" (2:36, 7:24). Thus, wars and the evils that stem from them, the Qur'an suggests, are the inevitable consequences of the uniquely human capacity for moral choice.

The Qur'an does not present the fall of man as irrevocable, however, for God quickly returns to Adam to support and guide him (2:37). This, according to Islamic belief, is the beginning of continuous divine revelation to humanity through a series of prophets ending with Muhammad. God's reminders of the laws imprinted upon each human consciousness through His prophets are a manifestation of His endless mercy to His creation, because all human beings are potential victims of Iblis's guile, that is, potential evildoers, and most human beings are actually quite far from God's laws (36:45–46). When people form social units, they become all the more prone to disobey God's laws through the obstinate persistence in wrongdoing caused by custom and social pressures (2:13–14, 37:69, 43:22). In this way, the individual drive for power, wealth, prestige, and all the other innumerable human goals becomes amplified. Violence is the inevitable result of the human desire for self-aggrandizement.

Fourth, each prophet encounters opposition from those (always a majority) who persist in their rebellion against God, justifying their actions through various self-delusions. One of the principal characteristics of rejection of God (*kufr*) is the inclination toward violence and oppression, encapsulated by the broad concept *zulm*. When individuals choose to reject divine guidance, either by transgressing against specific divine injunctions or by losing faith altogether, they violate (commit zulm against) their own nature (fitra). When Adam and Eve disobey the divine command in the Garden, the Qur'an relates that they cry out in their despair not that they have sinned against God, but that they have transgressed against their own souls (7:23).

When an entire society rejects God, oppression and violence become the norm throughout the society and in relations with other societies as well. The moral anarchy that prevails when human beings abandon the higher moral code derived from faith in a supreme and just Creator, the Qur'an suggests, is fraught with potential and actual violence (2:11–12, 27, 204–5; chapter 7, *al-A'raf*, deals with this theme at length).

Fifth, peace (salam) is attainable only when human beings surrender to God's will and live according to God's laws. This is the condition of *islam*, the conscious decision to acknowledge in faith and conduct the presence and power of God. Because human nature is not sufficiently strong to resist the temptation to evil, it is necessary for man to establish a human agency, that is, a state, to mitigate the effects of anarchy and enforce divine law.

Sixth, because it is unlikely that individuals or societies will ever conform fully to the precepts of islam, Muslims must always be prepared to fight to preserve the Muslim faith and Muslim principles (8:60, 73).

The use of force by the Muslim community is, therefore, sanctioned by God as a necessary response to the existence of evil in the world. As the Qur'an elaborates in an early revelation, the believers are those "who, whenever tyranny afflicts them, defend themselves" (42:39). This theme of the just, God-ordained use of force for legitimate purposes is continued in several other verses. In the first verse that explicitly permits the Muslim community to use armed force against its enemies, the Qur'an makes clear that fighting is a burden imposed upon all believers (not only Muslims) as a result of the enmity harbored by the unbelievers:

> Permission [to fight] is given to those against whom war is being wrongfully waged, and verily, God has indeed the power to succor them: those who have been driven from their homelands against all right for no other reason than their saying: "Our Sustainer is God!"
>
> For, if God had not enabled people to defend themselves against one another, monasteries and churches and synagogues and mosques—in all

of which God's name is abundantly extolled—would surely have been destroyed. (22:39–40)

A subsequent verse converts this permission to fight into an injunction. The rationale given for using armed force is quite explicit: "Tumult and oppression (*fitna*) is worse than killing" (2:191).

These two verses clearly undermine the possibility of an Islamic pacifism. One verse in particular offers an implicit challenge to an ethical position based on the renunciation of all violence: "Fighting is prescribed for you, even though it be hateful to you; but it may well be that you hate something that is in fact good for you, and that you love a thing that is in fact bad for you: and God knows, whereas you do not" (2:216). There is, thus, no equivalent in the Islamic tradition of the continuing debate within Christianity of the possibility of just war. There is no analogue in Islamic texts to Aquinas's Question 40: "Are some wars permissible?" The Islamic discourse on war and peace begins from the a priori assumption that some types of war are permissible—indeed, required by God—and that all other forms of violence are, therefore, forbidden.

In short, the Qur'an's attitude toward war and peace may be described as an idealistic realism. Human existence is characterized neither by incessant warfare nor by real peace, but by a continuous tension between the two. Societies exist forever in a precarious balance between them. The unending human challenge is *jihad fi sabil Allah* (struggle in the way of God) to mitigate the possibility of war and to strengthen the grounds for peace. The resulting human condition may bear out the truth of the angels' initial protest to God that his decision to create man will only lead to corruption and bloodshed in the world. But the Qur'anic message is, if anything, continually optimistic about the human capacity to triumph over evil (5:56; 58:19, 22). God silences the angels, after all, not by denying their prognostication, but by holding out the possibility of unforeseen potential: "I know what you know not" (2:30).

Conceptions of War and Peace in the Sunna

The second source for the Islamic ethics of war and peace is the practice (sunna) of the prophet Muhammad. It is impossible to comprehend the Qur'an without understanding the life of the Prophet and impossible to comprehend the life of the Prophet without understanding the Qur'an. As the Prophet's wife, 'Aisha bint Abi Bakr, is reported to have said: "His character (*khuluqhu*) was the Qur'an."[4]

Muhammad was born into a milieu characterized by internecine skirmishes (*ghazwa*) among rival tribes. These were seldom more than raids undertaken for petty plunder of a neighboring tribe's flocks. If the conflict had any "higher" purpose, it was usually collective reprisal for an injury or affront suffered by a single member of the tribe according to the prevailing *lex talionis*. Larger confrontations for higher stakes, such as the actual conquest of territory, were rare, although not unknown. The Qur'an itself alludes in the 105th chapter to a full-scale invasion of the Hijaz by an Abyssinian army a few months prior to the birth of the Prophet in 570 C.E.

Naturally, tribal loyalty was the cornerstone of this society's ethos, and virtue was often equated with martial valor. It would, however, be incorrect to view pre-Islamic Arab culture as glorifying war. Imru'l-Qays, the renowned poet of the pre-Islamic period known as the *jahiliyya*, compares war before it is started to a young and alluring girl. But once a war begins, it quickly becomes like an old woman, hideous in appearance, unable to find any young suitor to embrace her.[5] Moreover, as Fred Donner points out, the ghazwa was often viewed by its participants as a sort of ongoing game, a struggle to outwit the opponent with a minimum of bloodshed. The aim was not to vanquish the foe but to demonstrate the qualities of courage, loyalty, and magnanimity—all components of masculine nobility included in the term *muruwwa*. Implicit in the Arab martial code were "rules of the game" that prohibited, among other things, fighting during certain months, the killing of noncombatants, and unnecessary spoliation.[6]

The conceptions of warfare existing in the jahiliyya undoubtedly influenced the Prophet's approach to the subject. In particular, many of the qualities of muruwwa were incorporated into Islam within a new ethical context, and the Prophet became the new exemplar of Arab chivalry.[7] But it would be false to suggest, as have some Western writers, that the Prophet's approach to war was largely an extension of the pre-Islamic Arab approach to the ghazwa.[8] Such a contention is not borne out by either the Prophet's practice or his (and the Qur'an's) self-image as a reformer of pagan Arab values.

We can construct an outline of the Prophet's approach to the ethics of war and peace not only by referring to the Qur'an, but also by making use of the large body of literature comprising the Prophet's sayings and actions (*hadith*) and biography (*sira*) compiled between the second and fourth Islamic centuries. It is clear from these records that from an early age, Muhammad was averse to many aspects of the tribal culture in which he was born. In particular, there is no indication that he ever showed any interest in affairs of tribal honor, particularly in the ghazwa. Throughout the Meccan period of his prophetic mission (610–22 C.E.), he showed no inclination toward the use of force in any form, even for self-defense. On the contrary, his policy can only be described as nonviolent resistance. This policy was maintained in spite of escalating physical attacks directed at his followers and at him personally. And it was maintained in spite of growing pressure from within the Muslim ranks to respond in kind, particularly after the conversion of two men widely considered to embody traditional Arab virtues, the Prophet's uncle Hamza and 'Umar ibn al-Khattab. Some Qur'anic verses reflect the growing tension among the Meccan Muslims over the use of force (16:125–28, 46:35). Nevertheless, the Prophet insisted throughout this period on the virtues of patience and steadfastness in the face of their opponents' attacks. When the persecution of the most vulnerable Muslims (former slaves and members of Mecca's poorer families) became intense, he directed them to seek refuge in the realm of a Christian king, Abyssinia.

The Prophet's rejection of armed struggle during the Meccan period was more than mere prudence based on the Muslims' military weakness. It was, rather, derived from the Qur'an's still unfolding conception that the use of force should be avoided unless it is, in just war parlance, a "last resort." This ethical perspective is clearly outlined in the continuation of a verse (42:39) cited earlier, which defines the believers as those who defend themselves when oppressed:

> The requital of evil is an evil similar to it: hence, whoever pardons [his enemy] and makes peace, his reward rests with God—for, verily, He does not love evildoers.
>
> Yet indeed, as for any who defend themselves after having been wronged— no blame whatever attaches to them: blame attaches but to those who oppress [other] people and behave outrageously on earth, offending against all right: for them is grievous suffering in store!
>
> But if one is patient in adversity and forgives, this is indeed the best resolution of affairs. (42:40–43)

The main result of these early verses is not to reaffirm the pre-Islamic custom of lex talionis but the exact opposite: to establish the moral superiority of forgiveness over revenge. The permission of self-defense is not a call to arms; military force is not mentioned, although neither is it proscribed. Instead, it should be seen as a rejection of quietism, of abnegation of moral responsibility in the face of oppression. Active nonviolent resistance and open defiance of pagan persecution is the proper Muslim response, according to these verses, and was, in fact, the Prophet's own practice during this period. Because the Meccan period of the Prophet's mission lasted almost thirteen years, three years longer than the Medinan period, it is absolutely fundamental in the construction of an Islamic ethical system. Clearly, jihad in this extended period of the Prophet's life meant nonviolent resistance. For potential Muslim nonviolent activists, there are many lessons to be learned from the Prophet's decisions during these years. But, regrettably, the Meccan period has received scant attention, either from Muslim activists or from jurists, historians, and moralists.[9]

The period that has been the traditional focus of Muslim and non-Muslim concern in discussing the Islamic approach to war and peace is the decade during which the Prophet lived in Medina (622–32 C.E.). It was in Medina that the Muslims became a coherent community, and it was here that jihad acquired its military component.

According to the early Muslim historians, the Prophet enacted a new policy toward the Quraysh, the ruling tribe of Mecca, within a year of settling in Medina: war aimed at redressing Muslim grievances. He authorized small raids against specific pagan targets, in particular caravans proceeding along the trade route to Syria. These raids, according to many orientalist accounts, were intended specifically to be a means of collecting booty in order to alleviate the financial distress of the immigrants to Medina as well as to provide an added incentive for potential converts. The raids, it is suggested, signaled a fundamental shift in the Prophet's approach to an emphasis upon violent struggle, a shift sanctioned by increasingly belligerent Qur'anic verses of the Medinan period.

Both the early historians' accounts and the subsequent orientalist speculations have been challenged by contemporary Muslim biographers of the Prophet. Muhammad Haykal, for example, argues that the early forays were not military expeditions but only small raids intended to harass the Meccans, impress upon them the new power of the Muslims, and demonstrate the necessity for a peaceful accommodation with the Muslims.[10]

Both positions in the debate are obviously speculative. The uncertainty regarding any shift in the Prophet's attitude toward the employment of violence is compounded by the uncertainty regarding the actual date of the Qur'anic revelation permitting fighting (22:39). Haykal himself implies that the Qur'anic permission to fight had already been revealed before these expeditions: "This peaceful show of strength by Islam does not at all mean that Islam, at that time, forbade fighting in defense of personal life and religion, or to put a stop to persecution. . . . What it did really mean at that time, as it does today or will ever do, was to condemn any war of aggression."[11]

Thus the Prophet's first year in Medina may rightly be characterized as a transition period in the evolution of his new policy toward the Meccans. The event that signals a clear break with pre-Islamic custom was the outcome of the third expedition, led by 'Abdallah ibn Jahsh during the prohibited month of Rajab in the second year A.H. (after *hijra*, the Prophet's flight to Medina in 622 C.E.). According to the Prophet's instructions to 'Abdallah, he and his companions were simply to reconnoiter Qurayshi positions outside Mecca. But when they came upon a Meccan caravan, the temptation to attack it overcame them. In the process they killed one man, took two others captive, and returned to Medina with the booty. Realizing that 'Abdallah had violated his instructions as well as the prohibition against fighting in that month, the Prophet rebuked 'Abdallah and refused to take any share of the booty. The incident also touched off an anti-Muslim propaganda campaign led by the Quraysh, making 'Abdallah and his compatriots even more unpopular with their fellow Muslims. It was upon this occasion that the following Qur'anic verse was revealed:

> They ask you concerning fighting in the prohibited months. Answer them:
> "To fight therein is a grave misdeed. But to impede men from following the
> cause of God, to deny God, to violate the sanctity of the holy mosque, to
> expel its people from its precincts is with God a greater wrong than fight-
> ing in the prohibited month. Tumult and oppression are worse than slaugh-
> ter." (2:217)

This verse is indicative of the continuing Qur'anic exposition of the Islamic ethics of war and its "appropriation" of certain pre-Islamic Arab values, now, in the context of the Medinan city-state, placed within an altered, more coherent moral framework. Fighting continues to be viewed as undesirable, and in some months is to be avoided altogether. In extremis, however, it is a legitimate response to injury and aggression already received at the hands of oppressors of religion. Even at this point it remains the less desirable choice and is to be exercised, the Qur'an repeatedly urges, with restraint and brevity (2:190, 193, 194; 8:61). Subsequent verses subject other pre-Islamic customs, including the ban on fighting near the Ka'ba, to the same moral evaluation (2:191).

Open warfare between the Muslims and the Quraysh was begun with the battle of Badr, fought in the month of Ramadan in 2 A.H. In the eight years following, the Prophet personally led or authorized over seventy military encounters, ranging in intensity from pitched battles in defense of Medina, to sieges, raids, and skirmishes against enemy targets. Such an astounding number of military engagements could only have had profound implications for the Prophet personally as well as for the nascent Muslim community. The preaching of

Islam and the conducting of the community's day-to-day activities had to occur within a milieu characterized by outright warfare against a range of enemies: Quraysh, bedouin tribes, the Jewish tribes of Medina, and the Byzantine empire. The Muslims of this period, according to one report, "did not sleep or wake except with their weapons."[12] Qur'anic verses of the period exhorting the Prophet and his followers to fight suggest the strain that the constant threat of war must have imposed upon the community (8:24, 65).

The battle of Badr was fought when the Prophet was fifty-four years old. And although it is clear that he personally conducted several key campaigns afterward, the combined evidence of the sources indicates that he remained a reluctant warrior. On several occasions he urged the use of nonviolent means or sought an early termination of hostilities, often in the face of stiff opposition from his companions. At the same time, consonant with Qur'anic revelation, he seems to have accepted as unavoidable fighting in defense of what he perceived to be Muslim interests. The essence of his approach to war is crystallized in the following words ascribed to him: "O people! Do not wish to meet the enemy, and ask God for safety, but when you face the enemy, be patient, and remember that Paradise is under the shade of swords."[13]

The Grounds for War

Ibn Khaldun continues his discussion of war in the *Muqaddima* by distinguishing four types of war. One arises from petty squabbles among rival families or neighboring tribes, another from the desire for plunder found among "savage peoples." These two types he labels "illegitimate wars." Then, reflecting the prevailing medieval approach, he divides legitimate wars into two types: jihad and wars to suppress internal rebellion.[14] This latter division of legitimate wars is the logical outgrowth of the medieval juristic bifurcation of the world into two spheres, *dar al-Islam* (the realm where Islamic law applied) and *dar al-harb* (the realm of war). According to the Sunni legal schools, jihad properly speaking was war waged against unbelievers. Because all Muslims were understood to constitute a single community of believers, wars between Muslim parties were usually classed in a separate category, *fitna* (literally, a "trial" or "test"). Like Plato, who has Socrates declare that Greeks do not make war on one another,[15] the Muslim jurists viewed intra-Muslim disputes as internal strife that should be resolved quickly by the ruling authorities. This approach to war among Muslims, important in medieval theory, has assumed greater significance in modern controversies about the definition of jihad.

The descriptions of jihad in the medieval texts reflect the historical context in which legal theory was elaborated. Because the medieval juristic conception of jihad provided legal justification for the rapid expansion of the Islamic empire that occurred in the decades following the Prophet's death, its connotations are offensive rather than defensive. Relatively little consideration was given to jihad defined as "defensive struggle," that is, war undertaken strictly to safeguard Muslim lives and property from external aggression. It was considered obvious that Muslims may wage war in self-defense, according to the Qur'anic verses cited earlier. This defensive war was *fard 'ayn*, a moral duty of each able-bodied Muslim, male or female.

More detailed discussion of jihad comes in the context of offensive struggles aimed at expansion of Islamic hegemony, an expansion aimed ultimately at the universal propagation of Islam. In the twelfth century, Ibn Rushd (Averroes) wrote a legal treatise that deals at some length with the conditions of jihad.[16] His treatise is representative of the medieval theory for two reasons. First, as one of the later medieval writers, he incorporates into his work the views of earlier scholars. Second, his treatise is typical of the methodology applied by earlier jurists in reconciling apparently conflicting verses of the Qur'an or actions of the Prophet.

Because the ultimate end of jihad is the propagation of the Islamic faith, not material gain or territorial conquest, Ibn Rushd, like other medieval writers, implicitly, if not always explicitly, separates the grounds for jihad from the grounds for war (harb or qital). Because Islam is viewed as a universal mission to all humanity, jihad is the perpetual condition that prevails between dar al-Islam and dar al-harb. Participation in the jihad to overcome dar al-harb was a *fard kifaya*, a moral obligation only for those capable of assuming it, namely able-bodied and financially secure adult males. Actual warfare, qital, arose only as the final step in a "ladder of escalation." The first step in any contact between the Muslim state and a foreign power was an invitation to allow the peaceful preaching of Islam. This was consonant with the practice of the Prophet, who allegedly had sent letters to the rulers of Byzantium, Iran, and Egypt for precisely this purpose. If a foreign ruler refused this invitation, he was to be offered the incorporation of his people into the Islamic realm as a protected non-Muslim community governed by its own religious laws, but obliged to pay a tax, the *jizya*, in lieu of performing military service. Only if the non-Muslims refused these conditions were there grounds for active hostilities. At this point, the Muslim ruler was not only permitted but required to wage war against them.

According to Ibn Rushd, the medieval jurists disagreed most on the question of when it was permissible to suspend jihad. The basis of the controversy was the apparent discrepancy between the Qur'an's "verses of peace" and "verses of the sword." In the eighth chapter, for example, is the following verse: "If they incline toward peace, incline you toward it, and trust in God: verily, He alone is all-hearing, all-knowing" (8:61). In the ninth chapter, however, we encounter the following commands: "And so, when the sacred months are over, slay the polytheists wherever you find them, and take them captive, and besiege them, and lie in wait for them at every conceivable place" (9:5); and

> Fight against those who—despite having been given revelation before—do not believe in God nor in the last day, and do not consider forbidden that which God and His Messenger have forbidden, and do not follow the religion of truth, until they pay the *jizya* with willing hand, having been subdued. (9:29)

As Ibn Rushd observes, some jurists held the opinion that the sword verses must be read in context with the peace verses, and that the ruler (*imam*) was therefore entitled to suspend jihad whenever he deemed it appropriate. Others read the sword verses as requiring continual warfare against unbelievers (both polytheists and the recognized "people of the book," that is, Jews, Christians, Sabaeans, and, by assimilation, Zoroastrians and others) until they had been incorporated within dar al-Islam. They invoked the interpretive principle of "abrogation" (*naskh*) to support their conclusion: because the sword verses had been revealed *after* the peace verses, the command to wage jihad against non-Muslims supersedes the permission to engage in peaceful relations.[17]

Thus, as Ibn Rushd's discussion makes apparent, the medieval juristic literature is characterized by fundamental disagreements on the grounds for war. But most of the legal scholars agree that the object of jihad is not the forcible conversion of unbelievers to the Islamic faith. This object would contradict several clear Qur'anic statements enjoining freedom of worship, including "Let there be no compulsion in religion; the truth stands out clearly from error" (2:256), and "If your Lord had so willed, all those who are on earth would have believed; will you then compel mankind, against their will, to believe?" (10:99). With regard to verse 9:5 (quoted above), which seems to sanction a war of mass conversion of all polytheists to Islam, most acknowledge

that the full context in which the verse occurs limits its application to
the pagan Arabs who were so implacably opposed to the earliest
Muslim community at Medina. The object of jihad is generally held
by these writers to be the subjugation of hostile powers who refuse to
permit the preaching of Islam, not forcible conversion. Once under
Muslim rule, they reason, non-Muslims will be free to consider the
merits of Islam.

The medieval theory of an ongoing jihad, and the bifurcation of the
world into dar al-Islam and dar al-harb upon which it was predicated, became a fiction soon after it was elaborated by medieval
writers. The "house of Islam" disintegrated into a number of rival
states, some of whom found themselves allied with states belonging
to the "house of war" in fighting their co-religionists. Nevertheless,
the idea that "Islam" and the "West" represented monolithic and mutually antagonistic civilizations underlay much Muslim and European
writing, particularly during the heyday of European imperialism in
the eighteenth and nineteenth centuries. Shades of this viewpoint are
very much apparent in our own day.

In his discussion of recent Muslim thinking on the grounds for
jihad, Bassam Tibi outlines two contending approaches, the "conformist" and the "fundamentalist." He suggests that the reinterpretation of
the medieval theory of jihad by modernists (as the conformists are
more commonly known) is half-hearted and that, in the end, it is the
fundamentalists' resurrection of the medieval dar al-harb/dar al-
Islam distinction that best characterizes the current Muslim view of
international relations generally and issues of war and peace in particular. His presentation, I think, does not adequately acknowledge
the significance of modernist challenges to the medieval theory or real
differences in how fundamentalists employ medieval terms like dar
al-harb.

It is important to recognize that modernists as well as fundamentalists believe that Islamic thought must be revived by returning to the
"true sources," that is, the Qur'an and sunna. This approach leads the
modernists to challenge many aspects of medieval legal doctrine regarding war and peace, beginning with the division of the world into
separate spheres. As they point out, this rigid bifurcation is nowhere
to be found in the Qur'an or the traditions of the Prophet. Although
the Qur'an's division of mankind into believers and unbelievers lends
support for such a view, modernist writers argue that the Qur'anic
verses cannot be interpreted to suggest a perpetual state of war between the two, nor any territoriality to the "house of Islam," when
these verses are taken in the full context of the Qur'anic message. In
one of the leading modernist expositions of Islamic international law,

Mohammad Talaat al-Ghunaimi, dismisses the dar al-Islam/dar al-harb distinction as an idea introduced by certain medieval legal thinkers in response to their own historical circumstances, but having no basis in Islamic ethics.[18]

Having undermined the medieval dichotomy, the modernists proceed to challenge the medieval conception of "aggressive jihad." Again, their method is to return to the "sources." When the Qur'anic verses and the Prophet's traditions on warfare are studied in their full context, they argue, jihad can only be a war of self-defense. As the influential Egyptian scholar Muhammad Abu Zahra writes, "War is not justified . . . to impose Islam as a religion on unbelievers or to support a particular social regime. The Prophet Muhammad fought only to repulse aggression."[19]

Turning to the fundamentalists, we do find a much more assertive, militant, violent interpretation of jihad. This is not surprising, given that most of the writers labeled "fundamentalist" are involved in revolutionary movements seeking to overthrow entrenched and militarily superior nationalist regimes. Yet if we probe even superficially beneath the rhetoric of the fundamentalists' polemics, we find real differences between their ideas and those of medieval legal theory, and real similarities uniting them with the modernists. It is true that there remains a large gap between the modernists and the most militant fundamentalist groups operating in the Muslim world today, but these groups, despite the media attention they receive, represent only the fringes of Islamic activism.

First, with respect to the fundamentalists' use of the expressions *dar al-Islam* and *dar al-harb*, there is a substantial difference between the use of these terms and others, such as *jahiliyya*, by writers like Hasan al-Banna and Sayyid Qutb, and their medieval connotations. Jahiliyya is used by the fundamentalists as a sweeping condemnation of cultural norms and political corruption that has only the vaguest connection with medieval ideas. Fundamentalist writers do argue that the origin of this anti-Islamic culture is Western, but their polemics are equally, if not mainly, focused on allegedly hypocritical Muslim rulers and other "Westernized" elites who actively propagate *jahili* culture in their own societies. Thus, the fundamentalist attack on Western values is not a resurrection of the medieval dichotomy between Islam and the rest of humanity. It is, I believe, the Muslim version of the attack on "neoimperialism" that characterizes many Third World polemics against the current international order. The dar al-Islam/dar al-harb dichotomy developed by medieval jurists was predicated on the moral and military superiority of Islamic civilization. When twentieth-century writers such as al-Banna, Qutb, Mawdudi, and Kho-

WAR AND PEACE   209

meini depict international politics as a struggle between Islam and the West, they are governed more by their understanding of the history of European colonialism and American policies in the Muslim world than by medieval notions of dar al-harb. They are motivated by faith in the moral superiority of Islam, but also by a painful awareness of the technological and military weakness of the Muslim world compared to the West.

Second, regarding the use of *jihad* by fundamentalist writers, there is again a substantial difference between recent and medieval works. The thrust of the medieval jihad is outward into the dar al-harb. Central to medieval theory is the issue of right authority. A war is jihad, that is, lawful, only when it is declared by a legitimate ruler, the imam, who bears responsibility for assessing the war's right intent and right conduct. Sunni writers discuss at considerable length the characteristics of a legitimate ruler, but devote almost no attention to illegitimate rulers. The medieval political theory favors acquiescing to any ruler who can maintain order and enforce the law, regardless of the means he has used to assume power. Thus, on the topic of political rebellion, the medieval theorists are generally quite conservative. Rebellion threatened the established order of dar al-Islam and the resulting anarchy undermined the religious life of the community. As a result, there is a strong bias against any right of rebellion and an emphasis on the need to speedily reincorporate rebels into the body politic.

With the emergence of postcolonial Muslim states, political legitimacy and the rights of the people in the face of oppressive regimes have emerged as central issues in Islamic discourse. These issues figure prominently, of course, in all fundamentalist literature.

Fundamentalists view themselves as a vanguard of the righteous, preparing the way for the elimination of jahili values from their societies and the establishment of a just "Islamic" order. The details of this order remain vague in the fundamentalist tracts. What is clear from these works is the view, supported by experience, that the secular, nationalist regimes ruling most Muslim countries today, backed by their Western supporters, will not willingly cede power, even if the majority of the population does not support them. They will maintain power by any means, including the violent repression of dissent. In other words, it is argued that these regimes have declared war on Islam within their countries, and that it is incumbent upon all true believers to respond by whatever means are necessary, including violence, to overthrow them. The fundamentalist writings are therefore focused on combating the social ills and international oppression that they believe face the Muslim community (*umma*) everywhere. Jihad is

for the fundamentalists an instrument for the realization of political
and social justice in their own societies, a powerful tool for internal
reform and one required by the Qur'an's command that Muslims "enjoin the right and forbid the wrong" (3:104). The thrust of the modern
jihad is thus very much inward. Warfare on the international level is
considered only to the extent that Western governments are viewed
as archenemies who impose corrupt and authoritarian regimes upon
Muslims. Jihad as an instrument for the imposition of Islamic rule in
non-Muslim states today hardly figures in fundamentalist works.
That goal has been postponed indefinitely, given the fundamentalist
position, which they share with many other Muslim writers, that
most of the Muslim countries themselves do not at present have Islamic governments.

One area in which modernists and fundamentalists are tending to
converge is upon the argument that jihad is an instrument for enforcing human rights. For example, the Iranian revolutionary leader Ayatollah Murtaza Mutahhari argues that "the most sacred form of jihad
and war is that which is fought in defense of humanity and of human
rights."[20] Similarly, the Indian/Pakistani scholar Maulana Abu al-A'la
Mawdudi writes that jihad is obligatory for Muslims when hostile
forces threaten their human rights, which in his analysis includes
forcibly evicting them from their homes, tampering with their social
order, and obstructing religious life.[21]

To some extent these arguments are a response to Western writings
on the international protection of human rights. But it is interesting to
note that whereas there is continuing debate in the West on the legal-
ity of humanitarian intervention against sovereign states, continuing
ambivalence toward the territorial state in Islamic thought lends
weight to the argument in favor of such intervention among a broad
range of Muslim writers.[22]

The Conduct of War

Because the goal of jihad is the call to Islam, not territorial conquest
or plunder, the right conduct of Muslim armies has traditionally been
an important concern within Islam. The Qur'an provides the basis for
ius in bello considerations: "And fight in God's cause against those
who wage war against you, but do not transgress limits, for God
loves not the transgressors" (2:190). The "limits" are enumerated in
the practice of the Prophet and the first four caliphs. According to
authoritative traditions, whenever the Prophet sent out a military

force, he would instruct its commander to adhere to certain restraints. The Prophet's immediate successors continued this practice, as is indicated by the "ten commands" of the first caliph, Abu Bakr:

> Do not act treacherously; do not act disloyally; do not act neglectfully. Do not mutilate; do not kill little children or old men, or women; do not cut off the heads of the palm-trees or burn them; do not cut down the fruit trees; do not slaughter a sheep or a cow or a camel, except for food. You will pass by people who devote their lives in cloisters; leave them and their devotions alone. You will come upon people who bring you platters in which are various sorts of food; if you eat any of it, mention the name of God over it.[23]

Thus, the Qur'an and the actions of the Prophet and his successors established the principles of discrimination and proportionality of means. But as Ibn Rushd's treatise makes clear, the elaboration of these broad principles created serious divisions among medieval jurists.

The legal treatises generally focus on a number of issues raised by the Qur'an itself: the treatment of prisoners, both combatants and noncombatants (47:4, 8:67); the granting of quarter or safe passage (*aman*) to residents of dar al-harb (9:6); and the division of booty (8:41). In addition, the jurists also dealt with the traditional concerns of ius in bello: the definition and protection of noncombatants and restrictions on certain types of weapon.

The legal discussions address three issues: Who is subject to damage in war? What types of damage may be inflicted upon persons? What types of damage may be inflicted upon their property? Underlying the differing opinions on these issues once again are the apparent contradictions between the peace verses and the sword verses. The jurists who contend that the sword verses provide a general rule superseding earlier revelation argue that belief is the decisive factor in establishing immunity from attack. Since verse 9:5, in their view, commands Muslims to fight all polytheists, only women and children (who were specifically designated by the Prophet as immune) are prohibited targets. All able-bodied polytheist males, whether actually fighting or not, may be killed.

Other jurists, who do not consider the peace verses to have been abrogated, maintain that capacity to fight is the only appropriate consideration, and therefore include old men, women, children, peasants, slaves, and hermits among prohibited targets.[24] The prohibition against direct attack, however, does not establish the absolute immunity of noncombatants, because, according to most jurists, all of these persons (except for hermits) are subject to the laws pertaining to prisoners of war. They may be enslaved or ransomed by the Muslim forces.

During the fighting, Muslims are permitted to inflict damage on the property of their enemies to the extent necessary to overcome them. Most jurists do not permit the unnecessary slaughter of animals, the destruction of homes, the cutting down of fruit trees, or the use of fire.[25] However, the eighth-century jurist Shaybani reports that Abu Hanifa, the founder of one of the four Sunni legal schools, allowed these tactics as well as the use of catapults and flooding to defeat the enemy. These methods may be employed against an enemy target even when women, children, and old men will be killed. If the enemy uses Muslims as shields, even then the Muslim forces may attack them. The reason given by Abu Hanifa is that if Muslims stopped attacking their enemies for fear of killing noncombatants, they would not be able to fight at all, "for there is no city in the territory of war in which there is no one at all of these . . . mentioned."[26]

Abu Hanifa's justification summarizes the medieval approach to noncombatant immunity. Muslim forces should exercise discrimination in war, but if "collateral damage" is inflicted, then the blame lies with the enemy, who made protection of noncombatants impossible. In general, the medieval theory views damage to the enemy as self-incurred harm. If Muslim forces violate the normal restrictions on conduct, it is because of provocation by the enemy. Yet strict reciprocity has never been established as a principle of the Islamic ethics of war: wanton disregard for humane treatment of combatants and noncombatants by the enemy does not permit Muslim armies to respond in kind.

In current Muslim discourse on war and peace, ius in bello issues receive very little attention. This is true despite the vast changes that have occurred in both the international law and the technology of warfare. The discussion that does occur is usually undertaken by modernists seeking to reinterpret the Qur'an and sunna so that Islamic injunctions correspond to current international practice.[27] Invariably these works concentrate on demonstrating the obsolescence of various aspects of medieval theory, such as the killing or enslavement of prisoners or the distribution of enemy property. More contemporary issues, such as the definition of noncombatant immunity and the use of terrorist methods by some Islamic groups, have yet to be treated systematically.

Far more relevant and interesting discussion of right conduct in war occurs in the context of specific conflicts. During the "war of the cities" toward the end of the Iran-Iraq War, for example, Mehdi

Bazargan and the Liberation Movement of Iran (LMI) repeatedly pro-
tested that Khomeini was violating Islamic prohibitions against targeting civilians when he authorized missile strikes against Baghdad
in retaliation for Iraq's Scud missile attacks against Teheran. In one
"open letter" to Khomeini, the LMI wrote:

> According to Islam, it is justifiable retribution only if we, with our own
> missiles, hit the commanders or senders of the Iraqi missiles rather than
> hitting civilian areas and killing innocent people and turning their homes
> and communities into ghost towns and hills of rubble, all in the name of
> striking military targets.[28]

But the LMI never developed its argument. Issues raised by its criticism, such as "double effect," "reciprocity," and "proportionality of
means," were never fully addressed.

More systematic discussion of just means occurred during the Persian Gulf War. In fact, ius in bello rather than ius ad bellum concerns
dominated Muslim debates on the ethics of the conflict. Among the
points raised by opponents of the anti-Iraq coalition's policies was
that the conflict should be treated as fitna, that is, a dispute among
Muslims. The rules concerning fitna developed by medieval jurists do
not permit Muslims to ally themselves with non-Muslims, particularly when military decision-making is in non-Muslim hands. The
prohibition was based on the belief that unbelievers would not apply
the stricter code of conduct incumbent upon Muslims when fighting
other Muslims. Critics of the Gulf War have argued that the conduct
of the war by the coalition validates the medieval jurists' concerns.
The massive air bombardment of Iraq's governmental and industrial
facilities, they charge, was disproportionate to the Iraqi provocation
and insufficiently discriminated between military and civilian targets.
Moreover, the slaughter of Iraqi troops fleeing Kuwait City on the
"highway of death" directly contravened one of the central points of
Islamic law, namely that the goal of all military campaigns against
other Muslims should be to rehabilitate and not to annihilate the
transgressing party.

The most glaring area of neglect in contemporary Islamic analyses
of ius in bello concerns weapons of mass destruction. So far, no systematic work has been done by Muslim scholars on how nuclear,
chemical, and biological weapons relate to the Islamic ethics of war.
This is an astonishing fact in light of the development of nuclear technology by several Muslim countries and the repeated use of chemical
weapons by Iraq. In discussing the issue with several leading Muslim
specialists in international law, I have found a great deal of ambivalence on the subject. Most scholars cite the Qur'anic verse "Hence,

make ready against them whatever force and war mounts you are able to muster, so that you might deter thereby the enemies of God" (8:60) as justification for developing nuclear weaponry. Muslims must acquire nuclear weapons, I have been repeatedly told, because their enemies have introduced such weapons into their arsenals. There is unanimous agreement that Muslims should think of nuclear weapons only as a deterrent and that they should be used only as a second-strike weapon. But Islamic discussion of this topic remains at a very superficial level. There is little appreciation of the logistics of nuclear deterrence and of the moral difficulties to which a deterrence strategy gives rise.

Conclusion

Is the Islamic jihad the same as the Western just war? The answer, of course, depends upon who is defining the concepts. But after this brief survey of the debates that have historically surrounded the Islamic approach to war and peace and the controversies that are continuing to this day, I think it is safe to conclude that even though jihad may not be identical to the just war as it has evolved in the West, the similarities between Western and Islamic thinking on war and peace are far more numerous than the differences.

Jihad, like just war, was conceived by its early theorists basically as a means to circumscribe the legitimate reasons for war to so few that peace is inevitably enhanced. Jihad, like just war, is grounded in the belief that intersocietal relations should be peaceful, not marred by constant and destructive warfare. The surest way for human beings to realize this peace is for them to obey the divine law that is imprinted on the human conscience and therefore accessible to everyone, believers and unbelievers. According to the medieval view, Muslims are obliged to propagate this divine law, through peaceful means if possible, through violent means if necessary. No war was jihad unless it was undertaken with right intent and as a last resort, and declared by right authority. Most Muslims today disavow the duty to propagate Islam by force and limit jihad to self-defense. And finally, jihad, like just war, places strict limitations on legitimate targets during war and demands that belligerents use the least amount of force necessary to achieve the swift cessation of hostilities.

Both jihad and just war are dynamic concepts, still evolving and adapting to changing international realities. As Muslims continue to interpret the Islamic ethics of war and peace, their debates on jihad will, I believe, increasingly parallel the Western debates on just war.

And as Muslims and non-Muslims continue their recently begun dialogue on the just international order, they may well find a level of agreement on the ethics of war and peace that will ultimately be reflected in a revised and more universal law of war and peace.

Notes

1. Fazlur Rahman, "Law and Ethics in Islam," in Richard G. Hovannisian, ed., *Ethics in Islam: Ninth Giorgio Levi Della Vida Biennial Conference* (Malibu, Cal.: Undena Publications, 1985), 9.

2. Ibn Khaldun, *The Muqaddimah: An Introduction to History*, trans. Franz Rosenthal (Princeton: Princeton University Press, 1967), 2:73.

3. The Qur'an argues in several places for the inner consistency of the moral code elaborated within it. See 4:82, 25:32, and 39:23. These verses are part of an extended debate contained in the Qur'an against the Meccan polytheists as well as Christians and Jews who argued that the Qur'an was Muhammad's own agglomeration of disparate scriptures and moral codes.

4. Ahmad b. ʿAbdallah Abu Nuʿaim al-Isfahani, *Dalaʾil al-nubuwwa* (Hyderabad: Daʾirat al-Maʿarif al-ʿUthmaniyya, 1977), 139.

5. Cited in M. Abu Laylah, *In Pursuit of Virtue: The Moral Theology and Psychology of Ibn Hazm al-Andalusi* (London: Ta-Ha Publishers, 1990), 51.

6. Fred Donner, "Sources of Islamic Conceptions of War," in John Kelsay and James Turner Johnson, eds., *Just War and Jihad: Historical and Theoretical Perspectives on War and Peace in Western and Islamic Traditions* (New York: Greenwood Press, 1991), 34.

7. See the valuable study by Toshihiko Izutsu, *Ethico-Religious Concepts in the Qurʾan* (Montreal: McGill University Press, 1966), 74–104.

8. Montgomery Watt, for example, writes: "It was essentially from the light-hearted razzia [the corrupted form of ghazwa] that the Islamic idea and practice of the jihad or holy war developed." W. Montgomery Watt, "Islamic Conceptions of the Holy War," in Thomas Murphy, ed., *The Holy War* (Columbus: Ohio State University Press, 1976), 142.

9. There are, however, some significant modern examples of Muslim advocacy and practice of nonviolent resistance. See Ralph E. Crow, Philip Grant, and Saad E. Ibrahim, eds., *Arab Nonviolent Political Struggle in the Middle East* (Boulder, Colo.: Lynne Rienner Publishers, 1990).

10. Muhammad Husayn Haykal, *The Life of Muhammad*, trans. Ismaʿil Ragi al-Faruqi (Indianapolis: North American Trust, 1976), 204.

11. Haykal, *Life of Muhammad*, 208.

12. Jalal al-Din al-Suyuti, *Asbab al-nuzul* (Cairo: Dar al-Tahrir liʾl-Tabʿ waʾl-Nashr, 1963), 128.

13. Imam Bukhari, *Sahih al-Bukhari*, trans. Muhammad Muhsin Khan (Beirut: Dar al-Arabia, 1985), 4: 165.

14. Ibn Khaldun, *Muqaddimah*, 224.

15. Plato, *The Republic*, trans. Allan Bloom (New York: Basic Books, 1968), 150.

16. Ibn Rushd, *Bidayat al-mujtahid*, in Rudolph Peters, ed. and trans., *Jihad in Medieval and Modern Islam* (Leiden: E. J. Brill, 1977), 9–25.

17. Ibn Rushd, *Bidayat al-mujtahid*, 22–23.

18. Mohammad Talaat al-Ghunaimi, *The Muslim Conception of International Law and the Western Approach* (The Hague: Martinus Nijhoff, 1968), 184.

19. Muhammad Abu Zahra, *Concept of War in Islam*, trans. Muhammad al-Hady and Taha Omar (Cairo: Ministry of Waqf, 1961), 18.

20. Ayatollah Murtaza Mutahhari, "Defense: The Essence of *Jihad*," in Mehdi Abedi and Gary Legenhausen, eds., *Jihad and Shahadat: Struggle and Martyrdom in Islam* (Houston: Institute for Research and Islamic Studies, 1986), 105.

21. Abu al-A'la Mawdudi, *Al-Jihad fi'l-Islam* (Lahore: Idara Tarjuman al-Qur'an, 1988), 55–56.

22. For a more detailed discussion of this issue, see Sohail H. Hashmi, "Is There an Islamic Ethic of Humanitarian Intervention?" *Ethics and International Affairs* 7 (1993), 55–73.

23. Quoted in John Alden Williams, ed., *Themes of Islamic Civilization* (Berkeley and Los Angeles: University of California Press, 1972), 262.

24. Ibn Rushd, *Bidayat al-mujtahid*, 16–17.

25. The prohibition against using fire in warfare was based on a tradition of the Prophet: "No one is free to punish by means of fire, save the Lord of the Fire"—that is, God. Ibn Rushd, *Bidayat al-mujtahid*, 18.

26. Muhammad ibn al-Hasan al-Shaybani, *Kitab al-siyar al-kabir*, trans. Majid Khadduri, *The Islamic Law of Nations* (Baltimore: The Johns Hopkins University Press, 1966), 101–2.

27. Two important modernist discussions of the means of war are Abu Zahra, *Concept of War in Islam*, 44–68, and Muhammad Hamidullah, *The Muslim Conduct of State*, 7th ed. (Lahore: Sh. Muhammad Ashraf, 1977), 202–54.

28. Liberation Movement of Iran, "A Warning Concerning the Continuation of the Destructive War" (Houston, Tex.: Maktab, 1988), 14.

Glossary

adab — morals or polite behavior

ahadith — see *hadith*

ahl al-hall wa'l-ʿaqd — "people who loosen and bind," the leaders of a community

ahl al-kitab — "people of the book," Christians, Jews, and Sabeans

akhlaq — ethics

ʿalim (pl. *ʿulama*) — scholar trained in the religious sciences

aman — security; safe passage for a non-Muslim traveling or residing in Islamic territory

awqaf — see *waqf*

dar al-harb — "territory of war," area where Islamic law is not applied

dar al-Islam — "territory of Islam," area where Islamic law is applied

dar al-sulh — "territory of truce," area with which Muslims have a treaty of nonbelligerency

darura — necessity, a state in which certain religious requirements may be temporarily suspended

dawla — state or government

dhimmi — "protected" non-Muslim living permanently within the Islamic state

fard (pl. *furud*) *ʿayn* — religio-moral obligation incumbent upon the individual

fard kifaya — religio-moral obligation incumbent upon the community, the performance of which by some excuses the individual

fatwa — nonbinding legal opinion rendered by a religious scholar, the *mufti*

fiqh — corpus of jurisprudence produced by classical scholars

fitna — trial or testing; often used in reference to civil strife among Muslims

furud — see *fard*

hadith (pl. *ahadith*) — authoritative report of a saying or action of the prophet Muhammad

hijra — the migration of the Prophet and his followers from Mecca to Medina in 622 C.E.

hisba — regulation or censorship of public morals, particularly fair dealing in the marketplace, performed by the *muhtasib*

ijmaʿ — consensus of the Muslim community or of the religious scholars

ijtihad — independent reasoning to deduce a point of law, performed by a qualified jurist, the *mujtahid*

imam — in general, any leader of a Muslim community; used by Sunnis to refer to the caliph; used by Shiʿis to refer to leaders of the community from the family of the Prophet

iman — faith in God

jahiliyya — the period of "ignorance" in Arab history before the advent of Islam *jihad* — virtuous struggle; used by classical scholars to refer to the struggle (by war if necessary) to expand the area in which Islamic law prevailed

jizya — a poll tax on non-Muslims residing within the Islamic state; often interpreted by Muslim jurists as symbolic of the non-Muslims' inferior status, but in practical terms it was compensation for their exemption from military service

kafir (pl. *kafirun*) — one who denies faith in God; an ingrate

kalam — theology

khalifa (pl. *khulafa*) — caliph; the successor to the Prophet as leader of the community, according to Sunnis

kufr — denial of faith in God

maslaha — general welfare of society

mazalim — court of complaints, where petitioners could appeal grievances directly to the ruler or his agent

mufti — see *fatwa*

muhtasib — see *hisba*

mujtahid — see *ijtihad*

naskh — abrogation or qualification of one Qur'anic verse by another

shari'a — divine law or moral code, derived from the Qur'an and *sunna*, as interpreted by classical jurists; some modernists limit *shari'a* to Qur'an and *sunna*, preferring to call classical legal rulings *fiqh*

shura — consultation

sunna — in general, custom or usage; most often refers to the moral example set by the prophet Muhammad, as reported in *hadith*

'ulama — see *'alim*

umma (pl. *umam*) — religious community; used frequently to refer to the community of Muslims worldwide

waqf (pl. *awqaf*) — property set aside as religious endowment or trust

zakat — a tax on surplus wealth assessed on Muslims as one of the five essential obligations of faith

Contributors

DALE F. EICKELMAN is Lazarus professor of anthropology and human relations at Dartmouth College and a former president of the Middle East Studies Association of North America. His books include *Moroccan Islam; The Middle East and Central Asia: An Anthropological Approach; Knowledge and Power in Morocco*; and *Muslim Politics* (with James Piscatori).

HASAN HANAFI is professor of philosophy at Cairo University. He has served as secretary-general of the Egyptian Philosophical Society as well as vice president of the Arab Philosophical Society. His publications include more than fourteen books, three critical editions, and four translations. His most recent books are *Islam in the Modern World* (2 vols.) and *The Anguish of the Scholar and the Citizen* (2 vols.).

SOHAIL H. HASHMI is Alumnae Foundation associate professor of international relations at Mount Holyoke College. He has published numerous works on Islamic ethics and political theory, specifically relating to international relations. He is currently coediting, with Steven Lee, a book on ethics and weapons of mass destruction.

FARHAD KAZEMI is professor of politics and Middle Eastern studies and the vice provost of New York University. His most recent publications include *Peasants and Politics in the Contemporary Middle East* (edited with John Waterbury), *Civil Society in Iran* (two special issues of *Iran Nameh*), and articles on the politics of reform in the Middle East in professional journals and edited volumes.

JOHN KELSAY is Richard L. Rubinstein professor of religion at Florida State University. His publications include *Islam and War: A Study in Comparative Religious Ethics* and (as coeditor with James Turner Johnson) *Cross, Crescent, and Sword* and *Just War and Jihad*.

MUHAMMAD KHALID MASUD is academic director of the International Institute for the Study of Islam in the Modern World (ISIM) in Leiden. His special interest is Islamic law and jurisprudence. He is the author of works on the legal philosophy of Abu Ishaq al-Shatibi, and editor (with Brinkley Messick and David Powers) of *Islamic Legal Interpretation: Muftis and their Fatwas*.

JACK MILES is senior advisor to the president at the J. Paul Getty Trust. His work has appeared in numerous national publications, including the *Atlan-*

tic Monthly, the *New York Times*, the *Boston Globe*, the *Washington Post*, and the *Los Angeles Times*, where he served for ten years as literary editor and as a member of the newspaper's editorial board. He is the author of *God: A Biography*, which won the Pulitzer Prize in 1996, and *Christ: A Crisis in the Life of God*.

SULAYMAN NYANG is professor of African studies at Howard University. He is a specialist in Islamic studies and the sociology of religion in Africa. His publications include *Religious Plurality in Africa and Islam* and *Islam, Christianity, and African Identity*. A former diplomat, he served as Gambia's deputy ambassador to Saudi Arabia and several other Middle Eastern and northwest African states.

BASSAM TIBI is professor of international relations at the Georg-August University in Göttingen, where he also heads the Center for International Relations. His books include *Arab Nationalism: A Critical Inquiry*, *Islam and the Cultural Accommodation of Social Change*, and *The Crisis of Modern Islam*.

M. RAQUIBUZ ZAMAN is the Charles A. Dana professor and chair of the Department of Finance and International Business at Ithaca College. He has authored and edited four books and contributed articles to numerous books and scholarly journals. He has also served as director of publications for the Association of Muslim Social Scientists, consultant to the World Bank, and consultant to the Food and Agricultural Organization of the United Nations.

Index

'Abd al-Hakim, Khalifa, 106
'Abd al-Raziq, 'Ali, 12–13
'Abdallah ibn Jahsh, 203
'Abduh, Muhammad, 89, 124, 152
Abou El Fadl, Khaled, 28
Abu al-Qasim al-Ansari, 151
Abu Bakr, 34n8, 88, 211
Abu Hanifa, 93, 212
Abu Sulayman, 'Abdulhamid, 93–94
Abu Ya'la, 88
Abu Yusuf, 88, 94
Abu Zahra, Muhammad, 208
Abu Zaid, Nasr Hamid, 73
Adelkhah, Fariba, 128–29
al-Afghani, Jamal al-Din, 89, 124
Afghanistan, x, 57
ahl al-kitab (people of the book), 44, 59,
    91, 109–10, 159, 185, 206. *See also* ethi-
    cal pluralism, groups, religious
    minorities
Ahmad Khan, Sayyid, 89, 152
'Aisha bint Abi Bakr, 199
Akbar, 119–20, 135, 141
Algeria, 29
'Ali ibn Abi Talib, 27, 34n8, 156
'Ali, Muhammad, 103, 105
Armanazi, Najib, 187–88
Ash'arites, 109, 139, 150–52
assassination, 28–29
Ataturk, Mustafa Kemal, 89
authoritarianism: based on religious le-
    gitimation, 65; in the Islamic world,
    42–44, 129, 165; pluralist challenge to,
    116; theocratic, 70
awqaf (religious endowments), 60–61
al-Azhar university, 175, 182–86

al-Baghdadi, 88
Baha'is, 49
al-Banna, Hasan, 185–86, 208
bay'a (allegiance to the ruler), 48
Bazargan, Mehdi, 212–13
Bellah, Robert, 117
Bin Laden, Osama, vii, xi, 116
Binsaid, Said, 127

bioethics, 142–44
Boisard, Marcel, 161–62
*The Book and the Qur'an: A Contemporary
    Interpretation* (Shahrur), 127
boundaries: in the civil society/govern-
    ment relationship, 14–17; *dar al-Islam*
    and *dar al-harb*, 107, 154–55, 159–62,
    176–77, 186, 188, 204–5, 207–9; defin-
    ing, 80–81; international relations (*see*
    international relations); land, establish-
    ing ownership of, 81–85; mental and
    physical, 107–11; national, 87–88, 96–
    98; religion as a maintainer of, 106–11;
    religion as a source of, 102–6; *umma*,
    unity of (*see* umma). *See also* property
Bousquet, Georges-Henri, 140
Bukhari, Imam, 104
Bush, George W., vii
al-Buti, Said Ramadan, 124

Cairo Declaration on Human Rights in
    Islam, 50
caliphate: ideals of and reality of kingly
    power, 156–57; rebellion, response to
    legitimate, 25–28; support of to main-
    tain unity of the *umma*, 88; traditional
    authority of, 165; *'ulama*, relationship
    with, 12–15, 17, 20 (*see also* comple-
    mentarity thesis)
citizenship: *bay'a* (allegiance to the ruler),
    48; fundamentalist view of and reli-
    gious minorities, 48–50; Islamic con-
    ception of, 24–25, 41; legally
    differentiated rights under Islamic law,
    44–45; as part of the social imaginary,
    129
civil society: conceptions of, 3–4, 39–40,
    56–57; family life in the sphere of, 22–
    23; ingredients of an Islamic, 58–61; in
    Islamic society, 4, 38–39, 53 (*see also*
    complementarity thesis); prospects for,
    72–74; religion and politics, relation-
    ship of (*see* complementarity thesis);
    responsibilities, fulfillment in, 68–69;
    risks of imbalance in, 69–70; state-